Black Workers' Struggle for Equality in Birmingham

The Working Class in American History

Editorial Advisors
James R. Barrett
Alice Kessler-Harris
Nelson Lichtenstein
David Montgomery

A list of books in the series appears at the end of this book.

Black Workers' Struggle for Equality in Birmingham

Edited by

Horace Huntley

and

David Montgomery

Afterword by Odessa Woolfolk

University of Illinois Press

Urbana and Chicago

First Illinois paperback, 2007

Manufactured in the United States of America

∞ This book is printed on acid-free paper.

The Library of Congress cataloged the cloth
edition as follows:
Black workers' struggle for equality in Birmingham /
edited by Horace Huntley and David Montgomery ;
afterword by Odessa Woolfolk.
p. cm. — (The working class in American history)
Includes bibliographical references and index.
ISBN 0-252-02952-6 (cloth : alk. paper)
1. African American labor union members—Alabama—
Birmingham—Interviews. 2. African Americans—
Employment—Alabama—Birmingham—History.
3. African Americans—Civil rights—Alabama—
Birmingham—History. I. Huntley, Horace, 1942–
II. Montgomery, David, 1927– III. Series.
HD6490.R22U63 2004
331.88'092'3960730761781—dc22 2004007253

PAPERBACK ISBN 978-0-252-07493-6

Contents

Preface: The Birmingham Civil Rights Institute's Oral History Project

Horace Huntley

The Oral History Project of the Birmingham Civil Rights Institute (BCRI) began in December 1994.[1] Among the first persons interviewed was Colonel Stone Johnson. The Colonel, as he is affectionately called, was born in Lowndes County, Alabama, in 1919, and like most other interviewees, he's from the Black Belt of Alabama.[2] The Oral History Collection consists of more than three hundred interviews to date. These are housed in the archives of the BCRI and are open to the public. The concept of the Oral History Project emerged during the institute's developmental stages. The founders felt strongly about the need to gather personal accounts of the "foot soldiers" in the civil rights movement.

Initially, a BCRI advisory committee was established to identify potential interviewees. In addition, the institute requested that all visitors sign a log, and a registry for "Unsung Heroes of the Civil Rights Movement—1956–1965" was also displayed where every visitor could register. The Civil Rights Registry requested name, address, and level of participation. The respondent could check if he or she marched, served as a security guard, was arrested, worked as a committee or board member, served meals, sang in the choir, worked voter registration, or participated in other activities. Advertisements were also placed in the local media requesting that persons interested in being interviewed for the project contact the institute. Many who responded became part of the BCRI Oral History Project. The project is ongoing, and there are obviously many more persons to be interviewed.

It is imperative to continue to document on tape the stories of those who participated in the movement. Who is more qualified to tell the story than the participants? We must not allow more of the story to be lost to the passage of time. The project has investigated and will attempt to make sense of a period in history when the status quo came under attack from the black community and progressives in the white community. These interviews document the civil rights struggles of the 1950s and 1960s and add to the understanding of the psychology and anatomy of Birmingham and the South. It is important to learn how different segments of society looked at the family, occupations, education, criminal justice, politics, and economics. Through discussions of these and related topics, one will be able to discern how Birmingham and its people matured to the stage of confronting themselves about injustice.

In addition to recording noted leaders, it is imperative to preserve the histories of the unsung participants in the grassroots movement. Industrial workers, pool-hall attendees, health-care workers, children, law enforcement personnel, and domestics, in addition to educators, ministers, business owners, civic leaders, attorneys, and other professionals and nonprofessionals, have been consulted. The interviews include the old and young and blacks and whites.

Approximately ninety interviews were conducted at Miles College.[3] Most of the others took place at the institute. We collected background information for those interviewed so we would know where they were from and, if they were not from Birmingham, why and how they came to the city. We wanted to know about their family, education, work, and their perspectives on and experiences in the area of race relations.

The original interviews are on audio and video tape. They have been transcribed, cataloged, indexed, and are available in hard copy. They vary in length from thirty minutes to eight hours. The versions that appear in this volume have been edited and abridged. We tried to retain, as much as possible, the original flavor of the interviews by keeping the actual words of the interviewee. We rearranged portions of some interviews to clarify and provide more continuity. As an interviewer, I have had the privilege of sitting with, talking and listening to, and absorbing the information from these reservoirs of knowledge. I apologize in advance, because the text that you read here cannot capture the spirit, animation, and power of the actual interviews. These people have known Birmingham and the South intimately, and they have worked to change it for the better.

Birmingham has been called the Johannesburg of the South because of its history of racist domination. The city lived up to its name and reputation through the sixth decade of the twentieth century. It has also been called Bombingham, the Tragic City, and the Magic City. In the 1950s and 1960s, black residents read the letters "MUN" on the licenses plates of municipal cars, particularly police cars, as "Murder-U-Niggers." Black people generally perceived the municipal authorities and the Ku Klux Klan in the same light. Birmingham has gone from a Klan stronghold in the 1920s to being designated an "All-American City" in 1970 by the National Civic League. There was a war between the Confederate and American concepts of peoplehood represented by the two flags. The Confederate flag represented the Ku Klux Klan and backwardness, and the American flag represented the quest for equality and betterment. The All-American City designation was perceived by blacks as furthering the quest for equality. The question, then, is how does a city go from one extreme to the other? The answer lies in the relationship that its people, black and white, have had with each other in this journey from backwardness to betterment.

A glimpse at the city's history is instructive. Birmingham was developed in the latter part of the nineteenth century as a mecca for industrial development because of its vast mineral resources. It is the only place in the world that possesses all the necessary ingredients for the manufacture of iron and steel within a six-mile radius. All of the necessary resources were found in and around Jones Valley, an untapped reservoir waiting to yield the essence of productivity and progress to this part of the world. Black and white workers came in record numbers to the area because work was plentiful.

Birmingham is a post–Civil War city and has no antebellum past. It came into being during the Jim Crow era and matured along with the "separate but equal" doctrine that ensued from the United States Supreme Court decision in the *Plessy v. Ferguson* case of 1896. In the 1890s there was interracial cooperation among workers in the locals of the United Mine Workers of America and the Western Federation of Miners. If these labor organizations could have retained their thrust of equitable racial associations, the city possibly would not have degenerated to the abyss of the racial divide.

Birmingham's civil rights and labor histories have always been closely connected and have called up many of the same demons: divisiveness, fear, manipulation, terror, intimidation, illogic, and greed. In addition, class divisions, the fear of job loss and bodily harm, white manipulation of traditional black leadership, the ability of the police and the Klan to terrorize and intimidate, and the illogic of turning away half of one's clientele because they were black have set the tone for the city's history. When all else fails, racial divisiveness has always stifled social, political, and economic progress in Birmingham. The emotionalism that race brought to the labor and civil rights struggles created a disadvantage that was difficult to overcome. The disadvantage was not seen as simply black and white, but also as "red," or a Communist conspiracy. As Robin D. G. Kelley has written, "The popular perception of Communists as 'foreigners' and 'nigger lovers' whose sole purpose was to wage a race war in the South created a huge barrier between these Northern white idealists and Alabama's white working-class communities. No matter how many white

Southerners agreed with the Party's program, the Reds were still outsiders who had no roots among white Alabamians."[4]

This volume is the first of several publications of selected interviews in various categories, including foot soldiers, students, professionals, whites, and ministers. Each will be introduced by a noted academic or activist. This volume on labor and the civil rights movement features an introduction by David Montgomery. He allows the interviewees to tell their own stories of migration, discrimination at the workplace, "breaking down barriers," and police brutality in their own words. He uses the interviews to tie work and unionism to workers' involvement in the movement, skillfully giving the reader a glimpse into working-class history in the first half of the twentieth century.

Notes

1. See Horace Huntley, "The Birmingham Civil Rights Institute, a Memorial to the Civil Rights Struggle," *Black Collegian* 31.3 (Apr. 2001): 100–101.

2. The strip of land in the middle of the state of Alabama that extends from Georgia on the east to Mississippi on the west, including counties from Russell to Greene. The rich black soil and the many black people that inhabited that area characterize the land.

3. A Colored Methodist Episcopal (CME) school located in the industrial city of Fairfield, a western suburb of Birmingham.

4. Robin D. G. Kelley, *Hammer and Hoe: Alabama Communists during the Great Depression* (Chapel Hill: University of North Carolina Press, 1990), 30.

Acknowledgments

This project would not have been possible without the able assistance of many who gave unselfishly of their time and talents. Lola Hendricks set up all of the interviews and collected invaluable information from each interviewee to help prepare the interviewers for their task. Interviewers included Binnie Myles and Bette Hanson, who were indispensable in the first phase. The first ninety interviews were conducted at Miles College with the aid of Ricky Lee. The transcribers were Yvonne Agee, Eleanor Caver, Corrie May, Kimberly Falkner, Carrie Weeks, Tanyika Blevins, and Liz Draper. Kimberly Falkner also served as a proofreader, along with Eric Watson, Kecia Lightner, Eleanor Caver, and Beth Campbell. Kimberly Falkner and Tiwania Glover are responsible for cataloging the index for the Oral History Project. Ahmad Ward and especially Kimberly Falkner were indispensable with their computer skills and advice. Bringing the interviews from a spoken to a written version was greatly assisted by Braden Phillips-Welborn, Laura Williams, Desiree Fisher, James Jones, and Nakeshia Jackson Leverette. A special thanks to Michelle Craig, who made herself consistently available on a voluntary basis. She edited, abridged, read, and reread transcriptions, helped to develop the biographies, and was a tremendous assistance in organizing the final manuscript. Odessa Woolfolk, the president emeritus of the BCRI board of directors; Wayne Coleman, the archivist; and Braden Phillips-Welborn greatly assisted in categorizing the interviews. Laurel Anderson assisted in the development of the biographies and proofreading. The executive director, Lawrence Pijeaux, and the board of directors of the BCRI assisted financially and were encouraging throughout the entire process.

Black Workers' Struggle for Equality in Birmingham

Introduction: Union Activists in Industry and in the Community

David Montgomery

"Birmingham wasn't nothing but a smoke stack" when Mattie Collins Haywood arrived there in 1939. She had moved there from the countryside, as had many thousands of other people, because the Birmingham-Bessemer region had a voracious appetite for workers. Steel mills and pipe foundries dominated the horizon, while hillsides in the vicinity were pocked with coal and iron mines. But that was not all. As Reuben Davis remembers the Collegeville neighborhood, "in the mornings about 6:30 you could see men going to work in different directions. L&N was to the east, U.S. Pipe and ACIPCO was to the west, Sayreton Mines was to the north, and then you see ladies going to Norwood, which was where the ladies worked as maids and cooks. . . . They would put [baskets of clothes] on their head and walk to Norwood to their jobs."[1]

It was in these mines, mills, and neighborhoods that black working people struggled individually and collectively to improve their conditions of life. Even under the harsh oppression of legal segregation they organized into labor unions of many different types, and they discretely formed study groups and networks of known and trusted activists, which linked together members of different unions. Their unions were theaters of conflict and of mobilization against racial discrimination every bit as significant as were churches, schools, and public spaces. Networks of union activists proved to be of decisive importance in creating, sustaining, and protecting the organizations of the civil rights movement that historians have made better known, especially the Alabama Christian Movement for Human Rights (ACMHR), led by the Reverend Fred Shuttlesworth. Organized black workers gave the civil rights movement in industrial Birmingham its distinctive character and tenacity. Those qualities enabled African American workers, together with students, clergy, professionals, and white allies, to win their historic victories over segregation between 1961 and 1963. But as these recollections also make clear, the struggles of Birmingham's black working people for equality and justice had begun many decades before the 1960s, and they have continued to the present day.

Off the Land

Most of the African Americans whose recollections appear in these interviews had come to Birmingham from the farmland of Alabama's Black Belt and from as far off as Mississippi (while other migrants came from even farther afield). They hoped to earn a better living than farm work allowed and to escape abusive landlords. Even Jimmie Louis Warren, who gave everyone the benefit of the doubt and initially described farm life in benign terms, saw his father swindled of his share of the crop and later had to hustle a friend off to safety in the North when that friend seized a wrench with which the landlord was threatening to beat him. The women among the interviewees were especially likely to stress the brutality of rural life, as did Rosa P. Washington and Ludie Mae Martin, though Mattie Collins Haywood also remembers with nostalgia the pleasure of producing her own pork, milk, and butter and the sense of sharing that pervaded life on the farm. But she adds that, looking back, "I hated working for nothing"—getting paid only when the crop was in, if then. She first drew regular wages when she filled in on the job of her sick sister in Forestdale. All those in search of income learned, as Colonel Stone Johnson puts it, that "the closer you get to Birmingham, the more money you can make."

Johnson also remembers, however, that white workers arrived "by the truckload . . . from Cullman or Huntsville, somewhere up in North Alabama," during World War II. In fact, the proportion of Jefferson County's steel workers and miners who were white grew steadily from 46 percent in 1930 to 67 percent in 1970, with important consequences for the nature and outcome of civil rights struggles.[2] At the turn of the century, however, 10 to 15 percent of the white population had been born in the North, and a quarter of the adult white males were of immigrant stock. Even though many of the European immigrants quickly turned around and left the region, almost half of the white iron and steel workers at that time were of foreign birth or parentage (in the nineteenth century predominantly British and Irish, but increasingly from southern and eastern Europe).[3] Many of these oral histories note the importance of Italian neighbors in everyday encounters and in the city's political life.

All the interviewees agree that the jobs open to African American men in the Birmingham region's mines, mills, railroad yards, and construction sites were confined to heavy and often dangerous manual labor, while black women earned money through scrubbing clothes or floors or by caring for white households. While black workers found their earnings in Birmingham more promising than the living they could eke out of the land, the city's industrial development had been based from the start on wage scales well below those paid by northern factories. During the late 1930s and the 1940s, when thousands of black workers built unions to improve their earnings, New Deal legislation on wages, hours, education, and social security, augmented by huge wartime procurement orders, also raised local industrial standards. Moreover, new technology sharply reduced the steel industry's need for unskilled labor. In Alabama, as elsewhere in the South, industrial firms found many applicants for most jobs, so they could be highly selective. They hired white workers in ever larger numbers, just as Colonel Stone Johnson observed. The production force in new southern auto and aircraft factories that sprang up during the 1940s and 1950s was almost entirely white, just as had been the case in both old and new textile mills. In South Carolina, whites were hired for more than 90 percent of the newly created manufacturing jobs. Even in Jefferson County's steel and coal production, whites had become a majority of the workers by 1950. By the 1950s, therefore, workplace struggles of African Americans focused not only on improving wages and working conditions but especially on breaking down the racial barriers to promotion into the more skilled categories of labor.[4] These interviews richly document that aspect of the struggle for civil rights, which has been overshadowed by the battle to desegregate public accommodations in most historians' accounts.

Starting in the 1920s and increasing during and after World War II, most dramatically in the 1950s and early 1960s, when the region's iron mines had been closed down and its increasingly automated steel mills laid off thousands, many black and white residents sought to improve their fortunes in Detroit, Chicago, New York, Pittsburgh, or Cleveland (whose black inhabitants called it "Alabama North"). The total population of Birmingham declined by over twenty-one thousand between 1950 and 1960.[5] Ludie Mae Martin, David P. Earle, Rosa P. Washington, and Asbury Howard Jr. had been among those who ventured north, though they subsequently had reasons to return to Birmingham.

Reuben Davis comments on this transformation, observing that when he had come back from the navy at the end of 1945, "it was commmon that practically everyone who wanted a job could get a job." But, he adds, "the thing about it [was], all the jobs available were lower end and the most difficult of working." During the massive exodus from southern farmland brought about by the increasing mechanization of agriculture after the war, however, black newcomers to Birmingham found even the "lower end" of industrial jobs steadily harder to find. By the spring of 1963, when civil rights demonstrators clashed daily with Bull Connor's police, dogs, and fire hoses, Davis's description of abundant but low-paid jobs no longer fit Birmingham's industry. Modernization of sheet and tin mills, larger open hearths, and what the historian Judith Stein has called "a virtual revolution in the handling of material" had sharply reduced the need for unskilled laborers in steel. Machine mining and pit closings had cut the number of Alabama's coal miners in half between 1940 and 1960, while the 3,026 remaining black miners represented only 25 percent of the total force. Imported iron ore from Venezuela had enabled U.S. Steel and other companies to close the ore mines on Red Mountain. White workers then vastly outnumbered black workers among new hires in steel and pipe mills. Within the mills both the preservation of accumulated seniority rights and access to better jobs had become for African Americans a question not only of improvement but of survival. Birmingham had begun its transition from a city where black men sought industrial and construction work while black women toiled in white homes into a center of service and technical work, where the University of Alabama and its related health centers were soon to emerge as the largest employer.[6]

Elias Hendricks Sr. underscores the point that even when there had been work aplenty in Birmingham, the city "was nothing to write home about." He explains: "We were in an environment that just wasn't conducive to decent things for black folks. Everywhere, whether you were in the union or out of the union, you still was one of those people when it come around to it." As he goes on to explain: "The *Dred Scott* decision . . . [had] said that a black man had no rights that a white man have to respect, and those guys lived up to that kind of thinking, . . . and they were able to get away with it."

No single feature of neighborhood life appears more often in these interviews than the arbitrary rule and unrestrained brutality of the police. "When I first came to Birmingham," said Rev. Joseph Lewis Rogers, "you find a dead man on the street or on a railroad most any day." George Price recalls the dangers of walking home from his welder's job late at night, when "the police was on a rampage." Others shared Reuben Davis's youthful experience of running from patrol cars to escape having their heads trapped in the car window and clubbed by the police. Rosa P. Washington was sweeping a waiting room of the Greyhound terminal in 1961 when Police Commissioner Bull Connor brought his menacing "regiment of police" to the "loading zone where the buses came into the station" to provide a hostile reception to the Freedom Riders, whose bus had been burned near Anniston. Long before and long after the highly publicized police assaults on street demonstrators in April and May 1963, community life was marked by police terror. The historian Robin D. G. Kelley has pointed out that routine police repression actually increased after those events, along with popular defiance of the police, reaching "an all-time high between 1963 and the early 1970s, and, of course, black male youth from poor communities accounted for a majority of the incidents."[7]

Union Town

The ways in which the men and women whose interviews appear in this book became involved in civil rights struggles were all related to their activities at work. Labor unions provided an important vehicle for their involvement. The older generation came to the civil rights movement through their union activities. Younger workers, who came of age at the peak of the movement, carried the community-based struggle for equality and desegregation back onto the job and into their unions.

Ever since the 1870s, the Greenback-Labor party, the Knights of Labor, the United Mine Workers, the railroad brotherhoods, the craft unions of the American Federation of Labor (AFL), and the independent unions of African Americans had all left their marks on the region's history.[8] By the 1950s virtually every type of union could be found there. The unions of steel workers, iron miners, and coal miners were all biracial, though that did not necessarily mean that they were egalitarian. Craft unions in construction often had black members (more often than in most of the North) but maintained segregated locals and hiring lists. The prominence of Colonel Stone Johnson's father as financial secretary and later business agent for Local 62 of the Operative Plasterers and Cement Finishers illustrates the role African American officers played in construction locals.[9] Brotherhoods of railroad engineers, firemen, and conductors had enrolled only white employees, and since the early part of the twentieth century they had tried to drive black workers clear off the trains. As several of these interviews reveal, however, black activists in other railroad brotherhoods, like those of oilers and of clerks, provided crucial support to the ACMHR, in addition to waging important struggles in the railroad yards. Unions comprised entirely of black workers also had an important presence in the post office, where President Woodrow Wilson had segregated the civil service in 1913. Since 1921, the American Cast Iron Pipe Company (ACIPCO) had boasted an elaborate employee representation plan as a paternalistic alternative to trade unions. The interviews reveal clearly that all these institutions shaped networks of African American activists and framed the strategies of workplace and neighborhood struggles.[10]

At the dawn of the twentieth century, coal miners had been the driving force behind a general revival of trade unionism in northern Alabama, and the majority of coal miners at the time were African Americans. Alabama's District 20 of the United Mine Workers of America (UMWA) had capitalized on the momentum generated by their union's historic 1897 strike triumph in the Central Competitive Field (north of the Ohio River, between Pittsburgh and St. Louis) to bring Alabama's major coal companies under contract. The district expanded its membership to fourteen thousand by 1903 (more than half of them black workers), raised wages, and curbed company mistreatment of miners. During the same years more than ten thousand other workers had joined local unions and affiliated with the Birmingham Trades Council. Many of those local unions accepted only white members. In fact, white bricklayers, machinists, and telephone linemen sometimes struck to drive black workers out of their trades. At the same time, some two thousand black furnacemen, coke workers, and laborers in Birmingham and Bessemer affiliated with the Trades Council through racially separate locals. The unions of coal miners and iron miners, however, organized both the black majorities and the white minorities in their occupations into the same unions. Moreover, those unions strongly influenced the political lobbying of the State Federation of Labor, even after African Americans had been effectively disfranchised by the white primary and the state's 1901 constitution.[11]

This was also the age in which legal segregation was consolidated. It is hardly surprising, therefore, that the interracial unions provoked hostile commentary and violent attacks. Such unions carefully walked the tightrope of racial etiquette, disavowing "social equality" while stressing their members' common economic objectives and deliberately electing white presidents and black vice presidents at all levels of the union structures (including the State Federation of Labor until 1905). But they could not avoid rousing the fury of business leaders. Although Alabama's coal was excellent for industrial use, the state's iron ore was of poor quality, and the products of its steel mills had to compete for markets in other parts of the country, where the "Pittsburgh-plus" pricing system was rigged against them. Birmingham's industry therefore had only two assets: abundant coal and cheap labor. Nature had provided the first. Racial subjugation, both on the land and in industry, preserved what one Tennessee Coal and Iron (TCI) executive called the "greatest, best and cheapest labor market in the United States."[12]

The recessions of 1903 and 1907 allowed the companies to strike back at the unions. The coal mines owned by TCI and other steel companies (known as "captive mines") ended their contracts with the UMWA and decimated the union over the course of a two-year strike. In 1908 almost all the mines not owned by steel companies followed suit. The state government again used the National Guard to bring in strikebreakers and to disperse strikers' interracial tent colonies, union officers were lynched, and prominent Birmingham citizens threatened to unleash racial violence that would make the recent mob assault on the black community in Springfield, Illinois, "look like six cents" unless the union called off the strike. Governor Braxton Bragg Comer told union leaders that he and members of the legislature would not tolerate "idle blacks" in his state and were "outraged at the attempts to establish social equality between black and white miners."[13]

By 1909 the UMWA had fewer than three hundred members left in Alabama. The atmosphere of repression in company towns was reinforced by widespread employment of convict labor in the mines of TCI until 1911 (and at other mines until the state outlawed the practice in 1928), the use of company stores, debt enforcement, and vagrancy laws to keep miners tied to their jobs, and brutal "shack rousers" to turn them out to work each morning that the company had work for them. A vigorous revival of coal miners' unions during World War I was snuffed out by fierce governmental repression during the strike of 1920–21. By the end of the twenties, the UMWA had closed down the offices of District 20. Although the region's industrial labor force was still preponderantly African American, what remained of a trade-union movement in Birmingham was confined during the 1920s to a handful of craft unions on railroads, in construction, and in local trucking, virtually all of which either excluded black workers from membership or relegated them to auxiliary locals.[14] TCI had sought to supplant unions with company paternalism after 1908, and it expanded its carefully segregated welfare activities after 1921. Some of the oral histories in this collection reflect the positive side of the corporate initiatives. David P. Earle recalled that the company elementary schools, for which miners paid with a compulsory checkoff from their wages, were superior to the county's public schools and paid their black teachers better than the county did. Rosa P. Washington had the same high opinion of ACIPCO's company school, as did James Greene of TCI's elementary school.

The acquisition of TCI by the United States Steel Corporation in 1908 had secured northern corporate domination of the region's economy, while a political alliance between company executives (locally known as the "Big Mules") and Black Belt planters kept the state government hostile to unions and implacably committed to racial segregation. The coal baron Charles DeBardeleben, who personally directed his guards' machine-gun fire against a UMWA strikers' parade at his Amcar mine in 1935, boasted that he was "'one of the greatest believers of White Supremacy.'"[15]

Poll tax and literacy qualifications authorized by the state constitution of 1901 barred all but a handful of black adults and most propertyless whites from voting. In Jefferson County only 21 percent of the voting-age population was registered to vote in 1938 (a peak year for early efforts by labor to increase voter registration), and many of those who had registered actually could not vote because they had fallen behind in their poll taxes. The historian Robert Norrell has calculated that twenty thousand people out of a population of five hundred thousand could decide any election.[16]

The Great Depression introduced two new features into Birmingham life, both of which contributed to the resurgence of a strong union presence depicted in these oral histories. The first is the abrupt appearance of the Communist party in working-class neighborhoods. The Communists made a potent impression on black Birmingham through their militant campaign to free the nine young men convicted of rape in a sham trial at Scottsboro, the armed resistance of sharecroppers at Camp Hill, their incessant street demonstrations against evictions and for government aid to the unemployed (especially after the community chest had expunged destitute African Americans from its rolls), and public demonstrations of black women demanding to be registered as voters. The city quickly adopted an ordinance outlawing the party, but that did not stop its public activities. Although party membership was never large (the Communist leader Hosea Hudson in his narrative recalled a peak of "six or seven hundred members," while his biographer, Professor Nell Irvin Painter, estimated 250), neighborhoods like Collegeville had weekly meetings by 1932, and Communist leaflets were often distributed under cover of night. The members recruited by the Communist party in Birmingham were virtually all African Americans and workers, though employers routinely fired those discovered in their employ.[17]

In the second major effort of the Depression era, rebuilding the union movement, the Communists were by no means alone. The UMWA swept back into the region, and a strike of twenty-one thousand miners (not authorized by the UMWA) brought 90 percent of the state's miners substantial raises and union contracts by the end of 1934 and led even the nonunion Debardeleben mines to pay wages equal to union scale.[18] David P. Earle recalls how the all-black Local 109 of the Laundry Workers–AFL met in the Jehovah's Witness Hall while preparing for its long strike, which was supported by the white streetcar workers, who were notorious for their hostility to black passengers but who also demanded union labels on their laundered uniforms.[19] Eula McGill also remembers the wives of steel workers and coal miners descending on the stores of Bessemer to demand union labels on merchandise.

Black steel workers held ever larger Sunday meetings and marches in 1937, though the white workers who participated, Hosea Hudson observed, were "white coal miners . . . coming from the coal mine locals over to the steel plant workers and talking, in order to encourage the Negroes to stick to the union."[20]

The Mine, Mill, and Smelter Workers began years of doggedly persistent struggle for recognition, bringing mostly black but also many white ore miners to meetings in African American churches, which were defended against night riders by armed guards. The miners waged unsuccessful strikes in 1934 and 1936 before they finally won a contract with TCI in 1938.[21]

The unions affiliated with the Congress of Industrial Organizations (CIO) also sought to promote a more progressive political climate by encouraging white and black workers to register as voters. A local of the UMWA in Walker County set the pace for this activity by borrowing money from a local bank to pay the poll taxes of its members. It directed every white member to go to the court house and pay his own tax, then to accompany a black member and ensure his acceptance as well. Thanks to this strategy 218 white miners and 267 black miners qualified to vote in 1937 in a county where only two African Americans had voted previously. In Birmingham itself leaders of the Workers Alliance (a united front of organizations of the unemployed sponsored by various left-wing groups) and the CIO created a Right to Vote Club to encourage registration despite the city's hostile environment.[22] The leading black international organizer of the UMWA, Alabama-born Walter Jones, gained such stature among working people that his 1937 funeral in Birmingham was attended by twelve hundred mourners.[23]

The legacy of these efforts of 1937–38 is evident in several ways in the interviews. One is the prominence in subsequent efforts to register black voters of the city of Bessemer and of Asbury Howard and George Price of the Mine, Mill, and Smelter Workers, as well as of Asbury Howard Jr. Another is the legendary hue that surrounded the UMWA. Witness the nickname "John L. Lewis" assigned to Will Hall, the outspoken local UMWA officer who helped Colonel Stone Johnson guard Reverend Shuttlesworth's house and church against bombers after 1956. Witness also the fact that the partner of Jerome "Buddy" Cooper in the city's law firm that channeled union funds to bail out freedom marchers in 1963 was William Mitch Jr., the son of the coal miners' white district leader who had cultivated close ties between the union and the black community during the thirties.

By 1938, labor's political efforts had laid the foundations of a new political force that challenged the rule of the Big Mules. Alabama's Democratic party divided into two antagonistic camps, one supporting the business-planter alliance, and the other featuring personalities like Governor Bibb Graves and Senator Lister Hill, who were friendly to labor. Eula McGill, a white worker who was then active in the United Textile Workers in Prattsville, remembers joining the National Women's Trade Union League and driving up to Washington to meet with Eleanor Roosevelt. When news that McGill had been a guest at the White House reached local papers, she was fired from her job at Birmingham's Selma Manufacturing Company.[24]

Less than two years later, however, McGill and Roosevelt were both among the twelve hundred delegates who gathered in Birmingham's Municipal Auditorium to form the Southern Conference on Human Welfare (SCHW). One quarter of the delegates were African Americans, and by far the largest bloc of white and black delegates had been sent by unions. But academics, publishers, clergy, and public officials from all over the South were also there. Even Alabama's governor and two U.S. senators made appearances. By the end of the meeting, the wide range of political views represented had generated more bickering than agreements. Prominent white delegates treated the question of segregation obliquely, if at all. And the new police commissioner, Bull Connor, stormed into the auditorium with a contingent of police to compel the delegates to reorder their seating arrangements, which were in violation of city segregation ordinances. Nevertheless, despite their evident hesitation and uncertainty, conference leaders concluded that the dawn of social progress in the South had appeared.[25]

The state's conservative leaders struck back hard, trumpeting warnings against Communism and racial equality. The right-wing Constitutional Educational League had established its national headquarters in Birmingham in 1937. Hundreds of thousands of copies of the pamphlet *Join the C.I.O. and Help Build a Soviet America* by its leader, Joseph P. Kamp, circulated throughout the state and the rest of the country. Bull Connor vigorously enforced the state's new antipicketing law in Birmingham. After the AFL had expelled the CIO unions, the federation opposed all candidates endorsed by the CIO, while its local counsel, John W. Altman, warned: "Organized Labor in Alabama will not tolerate social equality between the whites and the blacks as advocated by the Communists." As a result of this intense pressure from the Right, observed Robert J. Norrell, the "political arena in Birmingham . . . abounded with men elected with labor support but who later forsook the workers."[26]

As the oral histories make clear, however, black workers, war veterans, and civil rights attorneys mounted an increasingly effective attack against discrimination and mistreatment on the job during and immediately after World War II. As black and white workers and their families inundated the centers of southern war industries, such public spaces as streetcars became arenas of almost daily confrontations. Federal legislation authorizing absentee soldiers to register and vote provoked many white Alabamans to share the anxiety of the one who wrote to his daughter: "'all white people in Alabama are buying pistols and other ammunition in preparation for the race war which is coming.'"[27]

Although unions enjoyed considerable success in improving wages for their members, they were swimming against the tide of anticommunism and racism. Returning black veterans were killed by white mobs and police across the South in 1946—five by Connor's police in the first six weeks of the year alone. When the national Democratic party renominated Harry S. Truman for president on a platform that included guarantees of civil rights, Alabama's Sidney Smyer, Frank Dixon, and Bull Connor mobilized a secession movement known as the Birmingham Plan. Under their leadership the Dixiecrats held a raucous convention in Birmingham's Municipal Auditorium and nominated Strom Thurmond for president on the State's Rights ticket. They saw to it that Truman's candidacy did not even appear on the ballot in Alabama. His Progressive party opponent, Henry Wallace, was prevented by Bull Connor and the Klan from holding a public meeting in Birmingham, while Wallace's running mate, Glenn Taylor, who came to the city to address the convention of the Southern Negro Youth Congress, was thrown in jail for entering the church by the wrong entrance. In this atmosphere the SCHW was denounced by the House Committee on Un-American Activities as a "most deviously camouflaged Communist-front organization"; it held its last meeting and dissolved.[28]

The cruelest blow of all to those who hoped to keep alive the progressive spirit embodied in the SCHW was that the CIO had joined the anticommunist crusade. When it launched Operation Dixie in 1946, it publicly repudiated the SCHW along with the Highlander Folk School, which had been important in training CIO activists during the 1930s (as it would be for civil rights activists two decades later). After the press had singled out Hosea Hudson, the president of Steelworkers Local 2815 at Jackson Foundry, as a Communist, the Birmingham Industrial Council expelled him, and the foundry fired him. An arbitrator upheld the dismissal on the grounds that the publicity had made Hudson a cause of "dissension" in the plant.[29] The atmosphere of fear and suspicion helps one understand Reuben Davis's wary visit to the FBI to discuss a message of support from New York, which he received after he had been fired by the L&N in 1950.[30]

In the wake of the 1948 presidential elections, the CIO raided its own affiliate on Red Mountain—the Mine, Mill, and Smelter Workers. Mine Mill had opposed Truman's cold war foreign policy, which the CIO had endorsed. In a National Labor Relations Board (NLRB) election in the spring of 1949, secessionists supported by the United Steelworkers-CIO narrowly defeated Mine Mill in TCI's mines. Not only did the election see black miners overwhelmingly supporting Mine Mill and the newer white members voting for the CIO, but the Ku Klux Klan had openly entered the battle on the CIO side, assaulting veteran white activists who remained loyal to Mine Mill and parading through Bessemer in cars and robes to proclaim its support of the CIO.[31] Anticommunism provided a banner under which the growing white membership of the CIO in Jefferson County could rally against the CIO's official commitment to racial equality and against those "quite a few whites" whom Asbury Howard Jr. remembered continuing into the late 1950s to support the Bessemer Voters' League, created by Mine Mill. Ever since the 1930s Birmingham's militants had looked to Washington and to national union headquarters for support in dealing with a fiercely hostile society. Now the federal government and those unions were demanding political conformity as the price of continued support and redefining the terms in which the union cause and African American liberation might receive a sympathetic hearing from those quarters.[32]

Washington and Birmingham

During the middle decades of the twentieth century, prospects for social reform in Alabama depended heavily on support from federal authorities and from the headquarters of the CIO, the NAACP, the National Negro Congress, and other national organizations. Historians have vigorously debated the question of whether New Deal legislation helped or hindered the self-organization of industrial workers and the efforts of black workers to win equal treatment on the job.[33] For Alabama the answer is clear. Such outside assistance as they could obtain proved decisive in making gains possible. The National Industrial Recovery Act of 1933 had mandated that collective bargaining be part of the codes of trade practices adopted by all industries. Although that requirement turned out to have little meaning for most southern textile workers, whose unions were stamped out while federal authorities watched uselessly, the outcome in Alabama was different. The national strike had been initiated by Alabama locals, and their indigenous leadership (like Eula McGill) largely survived the national disaster, while the state's governor had declined to follow the example of his counterparts in Georgia, North Carolina, and South Carolina and unleash the National Guard against the strikers. Consequently, by 1936 the 3,744 members of the United Textile Workers in Alabama outnumbered those in all other southern states taken together. The combined impact of local initiatives and federal labor agencies was even more evident in the case of unions like the UMWA and Mine Mill with long histories in their industries and widespread support among black workers, which effectively seized upon that provision to assist their resuscitation. In both cases, major strikes initiated by Alabama workers forced recalcitrant employers to sign on to National Recovery Administration (NRA) standards (and in the case of coal, to improve those standards). Over the course of the decade the intervention of federal agencies offset iron-mine owners' strategy of resisting the CIO by promoting company unions, such as the appropriately named Brotherhood of Captive Miners, by strictly enforcing segregation practices (which had previously been only loosely observed in iron-mining towns) and by violent repression.[34]

The famous 1937 agreement signed by U.S. Steel recognizing the Steel Workers Organizing Committee (CIO) as the bargaining agent for its members throughout the nation gave the union a strong enough foothold at TCI to survive the next three years, despite heavy layoffs and concerted counterattacks by a company union and by the AFL. The NLRB, created by the Wagner Act of 1935, forced TCI to reinstate 160 iron miners whom the corporation had discharged for union activity and to negotiate in 1938 its first contract with Mine Mill. After the NLRB held an election at TCI's steel mills and certified the United Steelworkers in 1942, white workers in the mills rushed to enroll in that union, whose members had previously been almost all black, just as white miners had flocked into Mine Mill after its contract victory in 1938.[35]

Moreover, two decisions by the U.S. Supreme Court during the early 1940s had opened opportunities for collective struggle, which workers interviewed for these oral histories quickly seized. Both of these decisions were made possible only by President Roosevelt's appointment of new justices in the aftermath of his 1937 "court packing" effort, among whom were Frank Murphy, William O. Douglas, and Alabama's own Hugo Black. The first decision was *Steele v. Louisville and Nashville Railroad Company* (1944). The case had been brought before the courts by Bester William Steele, who had been a locomotive fireman on the L&N since 1910. Steele was chairman of the International Association of Railway Employees, an organization formed by black railroad workers in 1934 with the aid of the eminent attorney Charles Hamilton Houston to seek legal action against the rigid barriers to promotion those workers had long faced. Although many African Americans were locomotive firemen in the South, none were allowed into the Brotherhood of Locomotive Firemen and Engineers (BLFE), and none could be promoted to the rank of engineer (that is, to the right side of the cab). As automatic coal feeders and diesel engines reduced job prospects for all firemen, the BLFE negotiated an agreement with the Southern Carriers Conference in 1941, specifying that no "nonpromotable" man could subsequently be employed as a fireman. Not only did this agreement bring new hiring of African Americans to a halt, it also prompted the downgrading or dismissal of many firemen with years of seniority. Steele was excluded first from passenger and then from freight runs and assigned finally to stoke the boilers of a yard switch engine.

When the attorneys Charles Hamilton Houston and Arthur D. Shores brought suit on Steele's behalf, Alabama courts promptly dismissed the case. But the new majority on the U.S. Supreme Court agreed to hear an appeal, and in December 1944 it issued what the historian Eric Arnesen in his magisterial study of black railroad workers has called "the single most significant decision [the Court] would ever issue on the question of race and railroad labor."[36]

Although the Court did not order the BLFE to admit African Americans to membership, it did assert that the privileges of bargaining over company rules accorded the union by the 1934 Railway Labor Act did not allow any union "to destroy or discriminate against the rights of those for whom it legislates." On the contrary, even a racially exclusive union was "also under an affirmative constitutional duty equally to protect those rights." Although the struggle over the rights and prospects of black firemen was to continue in a variety of different guises through the 1970s, African Americans who had long been excluded from railroad brotherhoods or assigned to auxiliary branches quickly learned to insist that the unions live up to what the Court had called the "duty of fair representation" under the Railway Labor Act.[37] As their interviews reveal, Colonel Stone Johnson, Reuben Davis, and their workmates in Birmingham's huge L&N yards wasted no time in figuring out ways to do so.

Reuben Davis's accomplishments had also been shaped by a second decision, which had been made by the Supreme Court some ten months before *Steele.* We must consider both of them together to appreciate his reminiscences. In April 1944 the Court had struck down a central pillar of the edifice of African American disfranchisement—the white primary. In the city of Birmingham only white citizens had been eligible to vote in Democratic primaries since 1888. Reversing the Court's own earlier position (that a political party was a private association and could admit or exclude whom it pleased), the justices ruled with only two dissenting votes that when the Democratic party conducted a primary election for candidates for government office, it acted as "an agency of the state, and may not, consistently with the Fifteenth Amendment, exclude Negroes from voting in primary elections by adopting a resolution restricting party membership to white citizens."[38]

The ruling had special resonance in Alabama, because the state legislature had recently adopted a wartime measure specifying that veterans of the armed forces were not required to pay the poll tax in order to vote. Reuben Davis was discharged from the navy in December 1945, and within days he had registered to vote. At that time, he recalled, out of some eight thousand African Americans living in the Collegeville area, only eleven were allowed to vote. Moreover, he joined the Progressive Democratic Council, made up largely of black professionals and businessmen, to mobilize what few black voters in the region were eligible behind the most promising white candidates in the Democratic primaries.[39] That was precisely what conservatives in the state legislature most feared, and, warning that sixteen thousand black veterans in Birmingham threatened to dominate the city's political life, the legislators proposed to the voters the Boswell Amendment to the state constitution, giving boards of registrars authority to test an applicant's knowledge of the U.S. Constitution. In November 1946 the amendment carried the state by a narrow margin, while heavy majorities supported the disfranchising measure not only in upper-class Mountain Brook but also in Acipco and other working-class constituencies, where the new registrars subsequently used the amendment also to block registration of white voters, warning that "mass registration . . . would result in social and economic calamity."[40] This was the test that Harvey Lee Henley Jr. failed in 1960 when he did not know the name of the mayor of his Mississippi birthplace, which he had left twenty-one years earlier at the age of three.

Bessemer and Red Mountain soon became the eye of the storm in the struggle for the vote. The Mine Mill union was the driving force behind the Bessemer Voters' League. Even after 1952, when raids by the United Steelworkers had virtually wiped out Mine Mill, its eastern vice president Asbury Howard and local officer George Price continued to head the Bessemer Voters' League and also to bring hundreds of their union's members into Bessemer's NAACP (to the dismay of its national office) until Alabama outlawed the association. Asbury Howard Jr. recalls that his father brought back from the 1959 Kansas City convention of his international union a cartoon of a handcuffed black man with hands clasped together in prayer and with a caption: "Hands that can still pray. Lord, help all Americans to see that you intended human beings everywhere to have the same rights." When police saw a local white artist preparing a version of the cartoon for a poster, they arrested Asbury Howard Sr. and the artist on charges of violating a city ordinance forbidding "any publication or handbill of an obscene . . . libelous or scurrilous nature . . . or any abusive or intemperate matter tending to provoke a breach of the peace." After the trial, in which Howard was found guilty and sentenced to six months in jail, he was assaulted and beaten by a white mob outside the court house, and his son was subsequently arrested for coming to his father's aid.[41]

During the immediate postwar years, returning African American war veterans not only reinvigorated the struggle for the right to vote, they also made use of even segregated unions and of the Supreme Court's 1944 *Steele* decision to win access to jobs that had previously been denied them. The recollections of Reuben Davis provide a case in point. As a youngster he had harbored the impossible dream of someday becoming a locomotive engineer. His father, who oiled bearing boxes in the L&N yard, wanted his son to take advantage of his good schooling at Parker High School to prepare himself at Tuskegee for a white-collar job, but he instead secured a laborer's job on the railroad through the intercession of a neighbor (who provided the necessary personal introduction to a hiring boss that appears in every recollection).[42] Soon drafted into the navy, he learned that the best position his education could secure him was that of a steward in the PT boat squadron of future President John F. Kennedy. But despite his frustration, Davis had also seen black seamen "operate cranes and drive trucks," and he returned to the L&N yards determined to use his GI Bill entitlements for mechanical training that would prepare him to qualify as a journeyman machinist (*not* a machinist's helper, as many black men in the roundhouses were categorized throughout their working lives).

Turned down by the master mechanic of the yards—only white youths could become apprentice machinists—Davis brought suit in district court under the *Steele* decision. But the judge ruled against him, after the roundhouse foreman had testified that Davis was "hotheaded." Davis's hopes of becoming a machinist repairing locomotives had proved as futile as his dreams of driving a locomotive. But his personal battle against job discrimination was only beginning, for he had been elected chairman of Local 1044 of the International Brotherhood of Firemen and Oilers, the AFL union to which the Railway Labor Board had long since awarded jurisdiction over roundhouse and shop laborers, as well as stationary firemen, oilers, and helpers (that is, most of the jobs held by black men in southern railroad yards).[43] The nationwide strike movement on the railroads in the spring of 1946 had reinvigorated many of the brotherhoods, and Local 1044 proved no exception. Keeping "a copy of the union contract and a New Testament [in his pocket] all the time," Davis not only enforced union work rules vigorously but also filed suit against the company (again using the *Steele* decision) to promote every single black laborer under his jurisdiction (including his father) to higher-rated jobs and succeeded in making some of them journeymen car repairmen by 1950.[44]

As Colonel Stone Johnson, then a truck driver for the Hormel Packing Company office in the L&N yards and a grievance man in the Brotherhood of Railway Clerks, recalls, the master mechanic sent out word: "I want Reuben Davis's job at all costs." After an apparent attempt to kill Davis by sabotaging his Fordson tractor failed, a foreman entrapped him into refusing a job assignment and got him fired. Although his union brought a grievance before the National Railway Labor Board and after three years of hearings won his reinstatement, Davis had by that time enrolled in a General Motors school in Flint,

Michigan, and then returned to teach auto mechanics at Dunbar High School in Bessemer. He quit the L&N after one summer's work in 1953.[45]

During that last summer at the railroad yard, Reuben Davis was also chairman of the pulpit committee of the Bethel Baptist church in Collegeville. He helped select a new pastor, Reverend Fred Shuttlesworth. Before three more years were out, he and his former trade union colleagues who were still at the L&N yards were to become key members of the Alabama Christian Movement for Human Rights. The Movement sought through nonviolent direct action and federal intervention to bring about the total eradication of legal segregation in Birmingham.[46]

Unions and Segregation

Although most of the black union activists interviewed in this collection became active in one way or another in the ACMHR, no local unions endorsed or officially engaged in the Movement's desegregation campaigns of 1956–63. In fact, the one local white member of the United Steelworkers who took part in desegregating a bus terminal waiting room, the Presbyterian lay minister Lamar Weaver, was mobbed and driven out of town in 1957.[47] As the union attorney Jerome "Buddy" Cooper reveals in his interview, however, the international unions of auto and steel workers did discreetly provide bail money for the 1963 student demonstrators, at the request of President John F. Kennedy. Later that same year the United Rubber Workers dispatched some visibly burly white members to Tuscaloosa to dissuade Klansmen from their own local from attacking black students, whom Governor Wallace blocked from entering the University of Alabama.[48]

More generally, as the United Packinghouse Workers leader Elias Hendricks Sr. observes in his interview, "the civil rights movement would have not been able to do a lot of the things that they were able to do had it not been for the labor movement, because they [unions] could get in some doors that black people just couldn't get in." The doors to which Hendricks refers hinged on the close ties of the AFL-CIO to the national and state Democratic party. As the historian Alan Draper has shown, the state labor councils of the South were the labor movement's primary political agencies. None of the councils' presidents came from interracial industrial unions, yet, Draper concluded, "with a few exceptions, these councils opposed segregationists, defended the national Democratic Party's record, and in some cases worked with black organizations in voter registration campaigns." In 1957 and 1958 the AFL-CIO's Committee on Political Education (COPE) quietly lent financial assistance to black voter-registration efforts in Birmingham and Montgomery, and after the enactment of the 1965 Voting Rights Act, registration campaigns became a major component of the union leadership's effort to counterbalance the stampede of white voters to the Republican column.[49]

In 1954 it had still been possible for a coalition of labor, liberal, and African American organizations to put James Folsom in the governor's office with the largest vote to that date in Alabama's history. But although Folsom vetoed a variety of bills designed to block school segregation and to institute vouchers for segregated private schools, by early 1956 the rising power of the Citizens' Councils had shattered his power and popular support. The state labor council focused its efforts on voter registration campaigns and on the struggle simply to keep public schools open, while leaving the word "integration" unspoken. Despite the union leaders' caution, local unions abandoned the state council in droves, so that by 1965 it represented less than half the local unions in the state and became heavily dependent on the national AFL-CIO for its own operational funds. The national federation itself turned in desperation to the Jewish Labor Committee and the Southern Regional Council to develop educational programs intended to hold its membership together around common economic interests. But in 1964 Barry Goldwater won 69 percent of Alabama's votes for president, and (as in 1948) the incumbent, now Lyndon B. Johnson, did not even appear on the state's ballot. COPE's southern regional director, Daniel Powell of Alabama, wrote its Washington headquarters: "I am afraid that a majority of our union membership in the South today is more aware of and in sympathy with the program and policies of the John Birch Society than they are with the program and policies of the AFL-CIO."[50]

Elias Hendricks Sr. was well aware that the unusual influence of black members and white leftists on the Chicago headquarters of the Packinghouse Workers had made his own organization, as he put it, "a very liberal union." He had been imprisoned at the employer's instigation for his effort to desegregate bathhouse facilities at the North Birmingham Armour packinghouse as early as the 1940s, in a preview of the more successful sit-ins staged by Harvey Lee Henley and his friends two decades later to integrate the lunch rooms at ACIPCO, just as other Movement activists were doing at downtown restaurants.

Elsewhere the story could be very different, even in biracial unions. Separate seniority lists prevailed in most union contracts, along with ceilings on promotions so solid that one black veteran of the Korean War in the Fairfield tin mill called them "the 38th parallel."[51] As the oral histories of Harvey Lee Henley Jr., James Greene, Luther McKinstry, Ludie Mae Martin, and Jimmie Louis Warren illustrate, workers used their unions (even hostile ones) and federal agencies (when they were willing to act) in persistent efforts to break through those ceilings from World War II onward. The resistance such efforts faced from employers, foremen, and many white fellow workers had always been intense, but that resistance gained extra strength and outside support in the aftermath of the Supreme Court's 1954 decision against school segregation.

Ludie Mae Martin discovered this in a very personal way when news of the Court's ruling came out: a white teacher at Wheeler Business College, where Martin worked as a maid, abruptly stopped letting her use the college's facilities in the evening to learn typing. Harvey Lee Henley Jr. recalled that after headlines about court orders to integrate the University of Alabama and the public schools appeared, the Klan staged processions of "a hundred cars, sometimes with a big cross on the truck and the white sheets and hoods on," to terrorize his hometown Johns, Alabama (a historic stronghold of black coal miners' unionism since the 1890s). Others remembered Klan literature on company bulletin boards and outspoken Klansmen elected to local union offices. Colonel Stone Johnson could easily identify the notorious Klan bomber J. B. Stoner riding around in a "Yellow Cab . . . all night, every night." The state legislature soon declared that it had nullified *Brown v. Board of Education,* and state courts outlawed the NAACP on the grounds that it was an unregistered "foreign corporation."[52]

The White Citizens' Councils, launched in Mississippi to defend segregation, were brought to Alabama by the initiative of the real estate magnate Sidney Smyer and other veterans of the Dixiecrat movement. Their influence spread quickly, along with that of revitalized (and sometimes competing) Klans, from Mountain Brook to Birmingham's mills and union locals, while George Wallace rose to power coupling his rhetorical identification with white steel workers against "pointy headed liberals" with the pledge of "segregation forever." Jimmie Louis Warren in the Iron Molders Union and Luther McKinstry in the Steelworkers recalled that they had confronted acknowledged Klansmen holding high offices in their locals. In 1961 the national NAACP representative Herbert Hill reported: "'the Ku Klux Klan and White Citizens' Council forces . . . have moved into many local unions and made them, in effect, virtual extensions of segregationist organizations.'"[53]

The overwhelmingly white workforce at the Hayes Aircraft Corporation went one step farther. Hayes Aircraft was the city's second largest employer (after TCI) and a major sponsor of right-wing activities. Like the huge Lockheed plant in Marietta, Georgia, the Hayes management judged only white workers to be qualified to fill its production jobs. Moreover, the company's founder, Lewis Jeffers, was a major figure in the Democratic party, and its chief of security was Art Hanes, the future mayoral candidate who was prominent in both Citizens' Councils and the John Birch Society. Urged on by those company executives the workers voted to leave the AFL-CIO and join the segregationist Southern Crafts, Inc. Although that union soon collapsed when the company refused to offer it a wage increase, the Citizens' Council remained strong among Hayes workers.[54] As the historian Alan Draper concluded, the majority of white union members in Alabama then wanted both the racist solidarity cultivated by the Citizens' Councils *and* the power of local and national AFL-CIO unions to win and preserve wages and working conditions.[55]

Because the Steelworkers were the largest and most influential union in Jefferson County, that union became a major theater for clashes between champions of segregation and black members demanding the right to advance in the mills in the context of declining levels of employment. Historians today disagree sharply in their evaluation of the union's response: Bruce Nelson and Robert J. Norrell have depicted the union as a bastion of white supremacy, despite its egalitarian rhetoric, while Judith Stein has vigorously defended the union's efforts and situated the conflict over job integration in the context of national economic policies that sacrificed the steel industry to the larger objective of winning the cold war.[56] Although the testimony provided by these oral histories is not enough to provide a definitive answer to this debate, it does provide some important insights.

None of the workers interviewed here support the contention of Robert J. Norrell that unionization had made job prospects worse for African Americans than they had been during the open-shop decades.[57] In the first place, as Hendricks so bluntly puts it, union jobs paid "fair wages," and those wages were "yours to keep," so that various people in authority could no longer decide on payday that "they want some of your money." Second, union contracts fixed pay scales for the job, ending the power of supervisors to pay each individual worker as they wished (usually with the admonition not to tell anyone else what they were getting). The fight for such gains usually allied white and black workers. In addition to negotiating an industry-wide pattern of job classifications soon after World War II, the Steelworkers had ended U.S. Steel's 17.5 cents per hour North-South wage differential by 1954.

These economic gains were evident to Deborah McDowell in the pride of the members of her mother's social club in Pipe Shop, who "bought U.S. Savings Bonds and made biweekly deposits to passbook accounts held at Birmingham Trust National Bank. Most were not extravagant, just comfortable, making sure that their husbands' salaries from Pyne Mine or TCI or Pullman Standard or U.S. Pipe and Foundry paid for modest homes—nothing fancy or palatial—but, as they were were to say with smugness, 'their own.'"[58] Or, as George Holloway, a long-time black leader of the United Auto Workers in

Memphis put it: "The CIO really contributed to the civil rights movement, I think. The CIO brought better wages, so parents got interested in schooling and began to send kids to college."[59] Many of the high school and college students arrested for demonstrating against segregation in Birmingham's streets early in the 1960s were daughters and sons of these union members.

Moreover, in response to black members' dissatisfaction with the district director, Reuben Farr (who had been a leader in the earlier raids against Mine Mill), the Steelworkers international union had appointed Howard Strevel from Tennessee to the district staff in 1951. Strevel signaled a new era by providing official support to a wildcat strike by black coke workers against unsafe conditions and setting up the first integrated picket lines in the history of the union. It was Strevel who completed the negotiations to merge lines of promotion for black and white workers in 1963 at the very moment that Bull Connor's dogs were attacking demonstrators on the street outside, as remembered by Jerome "Buddy" Cooper.[60]

Third, the interviewed black trade unionists ardently championed seniority as a basic principle of workplace justice, just as white union members did. They fought racist distortions of that principle. Luther McKinstry worked as a hooker (attaching materials to a crane's electromagnet) on a line of promotion that should have led directly to a crane operator's position, with first bid to go to the person longest on the job. But he found that, even after the 1962–63 agreements that Howard Strevel and Buddy Cooper had negotiated with TCI merging racially defined lines of promotion, his local, which had protested those agreements, still "circled" some skilled positions in such a way as to keep their occupants white. The crane operator's job was one of them, so that crane jobs went to white workers from other promotion lines. "Break that circle out of here," said McKinstry in his interview. "There is no come up here and then leap over here. You start here, you go straight up the line. Physical fit, seniority, and ability put you all the way to the top." What could be a more elementary union principle?

Even after the enactment of the equal employment provisions (Title VII) of the Civil Rights Act of 1964, a long struggle was needed to put that principle into practice. Judith Stein has written that Virgil Pearson, Thomas Johnson, Jimmie Lee Williams, McKinstry, and other black members of the Steelworkers organized a protest march through Fairfield to the steel works in June 1966, timed to coincide with similar marches on U.S. Steel mills in Pittsburgh and Los Angeles. McKinstry then enlisted the assistance of Richard A. Graham of the new federal Equal Employment Opportunities Commission (EEOC) and brought suit in 1972 against both U.S. Steel and the Steelworkers union. The outcome of the trial was a historic consent decree issued by Judge Samuel C.

Pointer, which laid the basis for uniform seniority systems throughout the steel industry nationwide.[61]

Looking back on that consent decree twenty years later, the white Birmingham Steelworkers leader E. B. Rich, who had himself been violently harassed when he had overruled local officers opposing the 1962–63 agreement merging lines of promotion, expressed a view remarkably similar to McKinstry's. As Rich told Judith Stein: "overall the Pointer decree strengthened the rights of our membership, white and black. We got more out of the consent decree than we would ever have gotten out of negotiations, a tough set of seniority rules."[62]

Finally and most important, these interviews reveal something that has received too little attention from historians of unions in Birmingham or elsewhere: the unions were crisscrossed with networks, caucuses, and study groups organized by black workers.[63] These informal organizations directly linked black union members to civil rights mobilizations based in churches and in community organizations. Often, as these recollections reveal, the networks based in union activity made the better known marches and court cases possible.

Jimmie Louis Warren was hardly twenty years old when he went to work for U.S. Pipe in 1962. In company with young friends he challenged segregation everywhere from a college ball game at Legion Field to his white-dominated local of the Molders Union. They went on to establish a committee that met each Sunday afternoon at the YMCA. "I, myself, the guys that work at U.S. Pipe that was on this committee we formed, and also ACIPCO Pipe Shop and U.S. Steel, and Stockham Valve, we had people from each plant," he recalls. "Then we filed so many complaints then that [the EEOC] had to put a branch here [in Birmingham]. That's how it came about."[64] Over at ACIPCO, which had kept out all unions, Harvey Lee Henley, having learned about President Kennedy's 1961 order against discrimination at companies with federal contracts, organized a Committee for Equal Job Opportunity and used his contacts with the Student Nonviolent Coordinating Committee for information and advice, while he also participated in three successive but unsuccessful campaigns to unionize the plant.[65]

Although these caucuses were formed by younger workers at the height of the civil rights struggle, Colonel Stone Johnson reveals how black members of several unions in the L&N yards under the mentorship of President Lewis Berry of the Firemen and Oilers and August U. Morris (Reverend Shuttlesworth's uncle), who was president of the black auxiliary of the racially exclusive Railway Clerks local, had met regularly more than fifteen years earlier. They would, in Johnson's words, "get together and have a little pow-wow away from the union hall." Among other things, they studied the complex company rule book. It was the company rule against "horseplay" on the job that Johnson used with consummate skill to stop white workers ("usually in supervisory positions") from routinely kicking black men. It was also through his "influence with the men out here in the union, and during the meeting nights" that Johnson organized volunteer watchmen (officially entitled "ushers") to protect Reverend Shuttlesworth's home and church after they had been bombed on Christmas night, 1956. He selected men to be ushers on the basis of their standing and known behavior in their unions.

These caucuses, study groups, and simple circles of acquaintances provided a sphere of self-organized workers' activity that has been largely ignored by writings on the civil rights movement. Their importance takes nothing away from the role of the ACMHR, whose officers were virtually all ministers. Even though only George Price, the welder and former Mine Mill leader who was a founder and board member of the ACMHR, was in the thick of the decisive 1963 street demonstrations, one worker after another testified that it was the weekly mass meetings of the Movement that kept them abreast of what was happening elsewhere in the world and revitalized their own strength and commitment. "One of my really top motivations was Fred Shuttlesworth," asserted Johnson. Nevertheless, all knew that to be arrested in the streets would mean certain dismissal from their jobs. Moreover, despite their respect for the nonviolent movement and their adherence to its philosophy when they were directly engaged in its activities, none of them personally believed in nonviolence. "I had to retaliate, whether it meant life or death," said Asbury Howard Jr.

Finally, all those who were asked agree that the movement is needed again today, but they add that ecomomic rights should be the focal point of its renewal. "I seen a whole lot of heartaches and pain," said Jimmie Louis Warren, "but it was worth that. I got able to move up." The unionized industrial economy in which he moved up, however, has been disappearing since the 1970s. New economic opportunities for many African Americans in the South have been accompanied by stagnant or even declining living standards for many others. By the 1980s, African American office holders occupied leading positions in the city and county governments—a remarkable tribute to the transformation of southern political life brought about by decades of struggle for the right to vote and ultimately by the Voting Rights Act of 1965. The current political issues stressed by the interviews, however, are jobs, health care, and poverty.

"The struggle is coming all over again," said Reuben Davis. "We are hurting now, far more than we were before the struggle." African American working people had won full access to public accommodations and to participation in the city's government just as most of Birmingham's industrial jobs disappeared. The department stores, where the Movement integrated service in defiance of fire hoses, beatings, and imprisonment, have all closed. As the white Birmingham native Paul Hemphill put it graphically, the dynamiting of homes and churches in Birmingham was replaced by the blasting of a highway route through Red Mountain so that white residents could move to new suburbs. White voters flocked to the Republican party, which promised solutions to all social problems in the free market.[66]

As he considers what lies ahead, Harvey Lee Henley Jr. observes: "we need to go back to what our foreparents did and see how they dealt with these situations. We got to get ourselves closer together because we are similar to the same problem now. I think we are going to reverse, or we are going to repeat what we went through."

Notes

I am indebted to Lisabeth Pimentel and Grace Palladino, for their assistance in the research for this essay, and to Glenda Gilmore, John Higginson, and Bruce Nelson, for their incisive comments on earlier drafts.

1. Quotations from the interviews that follow this introduction will not be cited individually here.

2. Robert J. Norrell, "Caste in Steel: Jim Crow Careers in Birmingham, Alabama," *Journal of American History* 73 (Dec. 1986): 676.

3. Paul Worthman, "Working Class Mobility in Birmingham, Alabama, 1880–1914," in *Anonymous Americans: Explorations in Nineteenth-Century Social History*, ed. Tamara K. Hareven (Englewood Cliffs, N.J.: Prentice-Hall, 1971), 175–80.

4. Norrell, "Caste in Steel," 676; Judith Stein, "Southern Workers in National Unions: Birmingham Steelworkers, 1936–1951," in *Organized Labor in the Twentieth-Century South*, ed. Robert H. Zieger (Knoxville: University of Tennessee Press, 1991), 183–222. The preference of southern employers for white workers after the New Deal improved economic standards is analyzed well in Gavin Wright, "The Civil Rights Revolution as Economic History," *Journal of Economic History* 59 (June 1999): 267–89 (on South Carolina, see 279).

5. Robin D. G. Kelley, *Race Rebels: Culture, Politics, and the Black Working Class* (New York: Free Press, 1994), 81. Between 1940 and 1970, the net migration of African Americans out of the South totalled 4,163,000 people, while white outmigration, heaviest in the 1940s, had already turned to net movement of 1,807,000 into the South during the 1960s and rose to 3,556,000 into the South during the 1970s, when African Americans also entered the South in greater num-

bers than they left, though not on such a scale as whites. Wright, "Civil Rights Revolution," 281.

6. Judith Stein, *Running Steel, Running America: Race, Economic Policy, and the Decline of Liberalism* (Chapel Hill: University of North Carolina Press, 1998), 41–50, 224–27 (quotation on 50); L. Edwin Brown and Colin Davis, eds., *It Is Union and Liberty: Alabama Coal Miners and the UMW* (Tuscaloosa: University of Alabama Press, 1999), 99, 113; Norrell, "Caste in Steel," 676; Kelley, *Race Rebels,* 77–100. Despite a resurgence of mine employment during the 1970s (producing primarily for electrical power plants), more than 80 percent of the state's miners were white by the time of the long coal strike of 1977–78. Robert H. Woodrum, "Wildcats, Caravans, and Dynamite: Alabama Miners and the 1977–1978 Coal Strike," in *It Is Union and Liberty,* ed. Brown and Davis, 111–29.

7. Kelley, *Race Rebels,* 90. Diane McWhorter, *Carry Me Home: Birmingham, Alabama; The Climactic Battle of the Civil Rights Revolution* (New York: Simon and Schuster, 2001), emphasizes the close relations and collaboration between the police, the Ku Klux Klan, and the business community, especially from the 1930s to the early 1960s.

8. See Herbert G. Gutman, "Black Coal Miners and the Greenback-Labor Party in Redeemer Alabama, 1878–1879: The Letters of Warren D. Kelley, Willis Johnson Thomas, 'Dawson,' and Others," *Labor History* 10 (Summer 1969): 506–35; Melton A. McLaurin, *Knights of Labor in the South* (Westport, Conn.: Greenwood Press, 1978); Paul Worthman, "Black Workers and Labor Unions in Birmingham, Alabama, 1897–1904," *Labor History* 10 (Summer 1969): 375–407; Daniel Letwin, *Challenge of Interracial Unionism: Alabama Coal Miners, 1878–1921* (Chapel Hill: University of North Carolina Press, 1998); Brian Kelly, *Race, Class, and Power in the Alabama Coalfields, 1908–21* (Urbana: University of Illinois Press, 2001); Karin A. Shapiro, *A New South Rebellion: The Battle against Convict Labor in the Tennessee Coalfields, 1871–1896* (Chapel Hill: University of North Carolina Press, 1998); Robert H. Zieger, ed., *Organized Labor in the Twentieth-Century South* (Knoxville: University of Tennessee Press, 1991); Philip Taft, *Organizing Dixie: Alabama Workers in the Industrial Era,* rev. and ed. Gary M. Fink (Westport, Conn.: Greenwood Press, 1981).

9. I am grateful to Grace Palladino of the Samuel Gompers Papers for this information about the elder Mr. Johnson.

10. On railroads, see Eric Arnesen, *Brotherhoods of Color: Black Railroad Workers and the Struggle for Equality* (Cambridge, Mass.: Harvard University Press, 2001). On the post office, see David Ziskind, *One Thousand Strikes of Government Employees* (New York: Columbia University Press, 1940), 121–24; Gary M. Fink, ed., *Labor Unions* (Westport, Conn.: Greenwood Press, 1977), 294–95. On ACIPCO, see *Pettway v. American Cast Iron Pipe Company,* 494 F. 2d 211; 1974 U.S. App. LEXIS 8928 at 67–71.

11. Paul B. Worthman, "Black Workers and Labor Unions in Birmingham, Alabama, 1897–1904," *Labor History* 10 (Summer 1969): 375–407; Letwin, *Challenge of Interracial Unionism,* 127–92.

12. George Gordon Crawford quoted in Kelly, *Race, Class, and Power,* 9. The code of conduct by which biracial unions sought to survive in a white supremacist enviromnent is vividly described by George Sinclair Mitchell, "The Negro in Southern Trade Unionism," *Southern Economic Journal* 2 (Oct. 1936): 26–33.

13. Quoted in Kelly, *Race, Class, and Power,* 23.

14. Kelly, *Race, Class, and Power,* 162–202 (on convict miners, see 54–57, 71–72, and 91–94). On District 20, see Peter Alexander, "Rising from the Ashes: Alabama Coal Miners, 1921–1941," in *It Is Union and Liberty,* ed. Brown and Davis, 70.

15. Quoted in McWhorter, *Carry Me Home,* 52; Alexander, "Rising from the Ashes," 77. On the development of the business-planter alliance, see Letwin, *Challenge of Interracial Unionism,* 15–30; Jonathan M. Wiener, *Social Origins of the New South: Alabama, 1860–1885* (Baton Rouge: Louisiana State University Press, 1978).

16. Alexander Keyssar, *The Right to Vote: The Contested History of Democracy in the United States* (New York: Basic Books, 2000), tables A.10 and A.11; J. Morgan Kousser, *The Shaping of Southern Politics: Suffrage Restriction and the Establishment of the One-Party South, 1880–1910* (New Haven, Conn.: Yale University Press, 1974); Robert J. Norrell, "Labor at the Ballot Box: Alabama Politics from the New Deal to the Dixiecrat Movement," *Journal of Southern History* 57 (May 1991): 207.

17. Nell Irvin Painter, *Narrative of Hosea Hudson: His Life as a Negro Communist in the South* (Cambridge, Mass.: Harvard University Press, 1979), 17–18, 112, 114; Robin D. G. Kelley, *Hammer and Hoe: Alabama Communists during the Great Depression* (Chapel Hill: University of North Carolina Press, 1990), 13–116. On Scottsboro, see Dan T. Carter, *Scottsboro: A Tragedy of the American South* (Baton Rouge: Louisiana State University Press, 1969); James A. Miller, Susan D. Pennybacker, and Eve Rosenhaft, "Mother Ada Wright and the International Campaign to Free the Scottsboro Boys, 1931–1934," *American Historical Review* 106 (April 2001): 387–430. On Camp Hill, see Theodore Rosengarten, *All God's Dangers: The Life of Nate Shaw* (New York: Alfred A. Knopf, 1974), 305–30.

18. Alexander, "Rising from the Ashes," 70–82.

19. On streetcar drivers and black passengers, see Kelley, *Race Rebels,* 57–58; Karen Ferguson, "The Politics of Exclusion: Wartime Industrialization, Civil Rights Mobilization, and Black Politics in Atlanta, 1942–1946," in *The Second Wave: Southern Industrialization from the 1940s to the 1970s,* ed. Philip Scranton (Athens: University of Georgia Press, 2001), 51–54.

20. Painter, *Narrative of Hosea Hudson,* 251. Judith Stein has argued that in TCI's rolling mills the local leadership was comprised of white rollers, an occupation that had traditionally been prominent in steel workers' unions. But the introduction of continuous strip mills late in the 1930s enabled the company to get rid of many of those highly skilled workers. Stein, "Southern Workers in National Unions," 190–91.

21. Horace Huntley, "Iron Ore Miners and Mine Mill in Alabama, 1933–1952" (Ph.D. dissertation, University of Pittsburgh, 1976), 53–95. For general estimates of union growth during the 1930s, see Taft, *Organizing Dixie,* 84, 91, 93, 110–16;

Norrell, "Labor at the Ballot Box," 203. The Communists had fiercely criticized the UMWA contract of 1934, and William Mitch in particular, and played a prominent role in the unofficial strike. See Kelley, *Hammer and Hoe,* 60–65.

22. Norrell, "Labor at the Ballot Box," 205–6. The black Walker County coal miner Leon Alexander provided a vivid account of the intervention of the UMWA and of William Mitch personally to enable him to vote during the Folsom administration. William H. Chafe, Raymond Gavins, and Robert Korstad, eds., *Remembering Jim Crow: African Americans Tell about Life in the Segregated South* (New York: New Press, 2001), 277–81.

23. Alexander, "Rising from the Ashes," 72.

24. Norrell, "Ballott Box," 211–15. For more on McGill, see Jacqueline Dowd Hall, James Leloudis, Robert Korstad, Mary Murphy, Lu Ann Jones, and Christopher Daly, *Like a Family: The Making of a Southern Cotton Mill World* (Chapel Hill: University of North Carolina Press, 1987), 318, 347–48.

25. John F. Egerton, *Speak Now against the Day: The Generation before the Civil Rights Movement in the South* (New York: Alfred A. Knopf, 1994), 185–97. See also Linda Reed, *Simple Decency and Common Sense: The Southern Conference Movement, 1938–1963* (Bloomington: Indiana University Press, 1991).

26. Norrell, "Labor at the Ballot Box," 211–24 (quotations on 213 and 223). Alabama's antipicketing law of 1923 was ruled an unconstitutional violation of freedom of speech by the Supreme Court in 1940, in a case involving the AFL. *Thornhill v. Alabama,* 310 U.S. 88; 60 Sup. Ct. 736.

27. Quoted in Keyssar, *Right to Vote,* 246.

28. Egerton, *Speak Now against the Day,* 361–68, 498–501; McWhorter, *Carry Me Home,* 62–78; Norrell, "Labor at the Ballot Box," 232–33. The legacy of the SCHW was carried on by the much smaller and more radical Southern Conference Educational Fund, formed in 1946. See also Richard M. Dalfiume, "The Forgotten Years of the Negro Revolution," *Journal of American History* 55 (Jan. 1968): 90–106.

29. Egerton, *Speak Now against the Day,* 446–48; Robert Korstad and Nelson Lichtenstein, "Opportunities Found and Lost: Labor, Radicals, and the Early Civil Rights Movement," *Journal of American History* 75 (Dec. 1988): 786–811; Painter, *Narrative of Hosea Hudson,* 353–62, 389; Barbara S. Griffith, *Crisis of American Labor: Operation Dixie and the Defeat of the CIO* (Philadelphia: Temple University Press, 1988).

30. Davis's response is similar to the evasive response of the prominent black unionist from Memphis, Earl Fisher, before Senator James O. Eastland's Senate Internal Security Subcommittee in 1951. See Michael Keith Honey, *Black Workers Remember: An Oral History of Segregation, Unionism, and the Freedom Struggle* (Berkeley: University of California Press, 1999), 213–36.

31. Huntley, "Iron Ore Miners and Mine Mill," 110–71 (for the parade, see 162). See also Horace Huntley, "The Rise and Fall of Mine Mill in Alabama: The Status Quo against Interracial Unionism, 1933–1949," in *The Journal of the Birmingham Historical Society: An Anthology Honoring Marvin Yeomans Whiting,* ed. James L.

Baggett (Birmingham, Ala.: Birmingham Historical Society, 2000), 197–208; "The Red Scare and Black Workers in Alabama: The International Union of Mine, Mill, and Smelter Workers, 1945–1953," in *Labor Divided: Race and Ethnicity in United States Labor Struggles, 1835–1960*, ed. Robert Asher and Charles Stephenson (Albany: State University of New York Press, 1990), 129–45.

32. For insightful discussions of how the cold war transformed claims for civil rights, see Penny M. Von Eschen, *Race against Empire: Black Americans and Anticolonialism, 1937–1957* (Ithaca, N.Y.: Cornell University Press, 1997); Mary L. Dudziak, *The Cold War and Civil Rights: Race and the Image of American Democracy* (Princeton, N.J.: Princeton University Press, 2000).

33. See, for example, Christopher L. Tomlins, *The State and the Unions: Labor Relations, Law, and the Organized Labor Movement in America, 1880–1960* (New York: Cambridge University Press, 1985), and Staughton Lynd, ed., *"We Are All Leaders": The Alternative Unionism of the Early 1930s* (Urbana: University of Illinois Press, 1996), and compare them with Melvyn Dubofsky, *State and Labor in Modern America* (Chapel Hill: University of North Carolina Press, 1994), and David Brody, *Workers in Industrial America: Essays on the Twentieth-Century Struggle* (New York: Oxford University Press, 1980).

34. Janet Irons, *Testing the New Deal: The General Strike of 1934 in the American South* (Urbana: University of Illinois Press, 2000); G. C. Waldrep III, *Southern Workers and the Search for Community: Spartanburg County, South Carolina* (Urbana: University of Illinois Press, 2000); Bryant Simon, *A Fabric of Defeat: The Politics of South Carolina Millhands, 1910–1948* (Chapel Hill: University of North Carolina Press, 1998), 109–36; Alexander, "Rising from the Ashes," 72–79; Huntley, "Iron Ore Miners and Mine Mill," 68–95; Alan Draper, "The New Southern Labor History Revisited: The Success of the Mine, Mill, and Smelter Workers Union in Birmingham, 1934–1938," *Journal of Southern History* 62 (Feb. 1996): 87–108. The figures in Alabama textile-union membership are from Irons, *Testing the New Deal,* 162.

35. Stein, "Southern Workers in National Unions," 187–94; Huntley, "Iron Ore Miners and Mine Mill," 68–95.

36. Arnesen, *Brotherhoods of Color,* 207. For more on Bester Steele, see the interview with David P. Earle in this volume.

37. Arnesen, *Brotherhoods of Color,* 181, 205–9 (quotations on 207). For the text of the decision, see *Steele v. Louisville and Nashville,* 323 U.S. 192; 65 Sup. Ct. 226 (1944).

38. *Smith v. Allwright,* 321 U.S. 649; 64 Sup. Ct. 757. For a discussion of the case, see Keyssar, *Right to Vote,* 245–49.

39. On the Progressive Democratic Council, see Glenn T. Eskew, *But for Birmingham: The Local and National Movements in the Civil Rights Struggle* (Chapel Hill: University of North Carolina Press, 1997), 350 n.33. Eskew calls it the "Progressive Democratic Association."

40. Norrell, "Labor at the Ballot Box," 228–29, 207 (the quotation from the Jefferson County registrar, H. A. "Gus" Thompson, is on 231).

41. For details of this incident, see the *Birmingham World,* Jan. 28, 31, and Feb. 4, 1959; Court of Appeals of Alabama, *Asbury Howard Sr. v. City of Bessemer,* 40 Ala. App. 317; 114 So. 2d 158.

42. An unusual feature of this introduction, however, is that the neighbor was Lewis Berry, the leader of the Firemen and Oiler's local union, who later was a central figure in the caucus of black activists from the various unions in the L&N yards. See Colonel Stone Johnson's interview in this volume.

43. Fink, *Labor Unions,* 105–6.

44. This remarkable accomplishment is recounted in somewhat different ways in both Reuben Davis's and Colonel Stone Johnson's interviews in this volume.

45. The eminent economic historian Gavin Wright argues that as late as the 1960s, despite the popularity of courses in auto mechanics in the South and the high demand of southern automobile plants for "qualified applicants," the Southern Regional Council reported that auto mechanics courses were "offered only at white high schools, not black." Wright, "Civil Rights Revolution," 280.

46. Andrew M. Manis, *A Fire You Can't Put Out: The Civil Rights Life of Birmingham's Reverend Fred Shuttlesworth* (Tuscaloosa: University of Alabama Press, 1999), 68–70, has an account of Shuttlesworth's appointment to Bethel that differs from Davis's. Manis also reveals that Davis protested vigorously when Shuttlesworth left Birmingham for Cincinnati in 1961 (282–83).

47. Eskew, *But for Birmingham,* 135.

48. The Tuscaloosa story is elaborated in McWhorter, *Carry Me Home,* 459, on the basis of her own interview with Cooper. To be sure, neither President Kennedy nor Governor Wallace wanted their elaborately staged confrontation to erupt in violence in the presence of television cameras. Both men were aware, however, that many white workers from the nearby Goodyear Rubber plant had participated in the 1956 riot at the University of Alabama protesting the admission of Autherine Lucy. James W. Vander Zanden, "The Southern White Resistance Movement to Integration," (Ph.D. dissertation, University of North Carolina, 1957), 160.

49. Alan Draper, *Conflict of Interests: Organized Labor and the Civil Rights Movement in the South, 1954–1968* (Ithaca, N.Y.: ILR Press, 1994), 86–106 (quotation on 90).

50. Vander Zanden, "Southern White Resistance Movement," 154–162; Draper, *Conflict of Interests,* 27–33, 113, 162 (quotation from Powell on 115).

51. Freddy Rogers quoted in Stein, *Running Steel,* 55.

52. McWhorter, *Carry Me Home,* 107–8.

53. Pete Daniel, *Lost Revolutions: The South in the 1950s* (Chapel Hill: University of North Carolina Press, 2000), 209–27; McWhorter, *Carry Me Home,* 98–114; Herbert Hill quoted in Bruce Nelson, "'CIO Meant One Thing for the Whites and Another Thing for Us': Steelworkers and Civil Rights, 1936–1974," in *Southern Labor in Transition, 1940–1995,* ed. Robert H. Zieger (Knoxville: University of Tennessee Press 1997), 131. On Wallace's appeal to steel workers, see Stein, *Running Steel,* 64–65.

54. McWhorter, *Carry Me Home,* 180–81; Eskew, *But for Birmingham,* 108. President Kennedy's 1961 order banning employment discrimination by companies with federal contracts opened the way to integration of southern aircraft factories, with the Lockheed Marietta works, which was owned by the government, declared a "pilot plant in the South" for the equal employment program three years before the passage of the 1964 Civil Rights Act. Richard S. Combes, "Aircraft Manufacturing in Georgia: A Case Study of Federal Industrial Investment," in *Second Wave,* ed. Philip Scranton, 36–37. A staff member of the United Auto Workers touring the South in 1956 found many white members furious at President Walter Reuther's support for civil rights and threatening to decertify their locals. In fact, very few locals followed the example of the Hayes workers and carried through that threat. Kevin Boyle, *The UAW and the Heyday of American Liberalism, 1945–1968* (Ithaca, N.Y.: Cornell University Press, 1995), 26.

55. Draper, *Conflict of Interests,* 26. Draper writes that the secession movement at Hayes never even got as far as an NLRB election (25–26).

56. Bruce Nelson, *Divided We Stand: American Workers and the Struggle for Black Equality* (Princeton, N.J.: Princeton University Press, 2001); Norrell "Caste in Steel"; Stein, *Running Steel.*

57. Norrell, "Caste in Steel." In an essay that is basically a tribute to the career of Herbert Hill of the NAACP, Bruce Nelson has highlighted the effort of thirteen African American members of the United Steelworkers Local 2401 in Atlanta, among them pioneer activists of the local, to decertify the union in 1962 in protest against the terms of an upgrading agreement it had negotiated with the Atlantic Steel Company. The NLRB rejected the petition, younger black members of the local benefited from the agreement and supported it, and the NAACP subsequently dropped the case in order to focus its efforts on decertifying an independent union in Houston, Texas, which had openly blocked the upgrading of black members. Nelson, "'CIO Meant One Thing,'" 113–45.

58. Deborah E. McDowell, *Leaving Pipe Shop: Memories of Kin* (New York: Scribner, 1996), 184.

59. Honey, *Black Workers Remember,* 170. See also the testimony of Matthew Davis on the link between union living standards and activist children (240–41).

60. Stein, *Running Steel,* 37, 43–59; Eskew, *But for Birmingham,* 366 n.26. Traditionally, in southern steel strikes white pickets had turned back other white workers, while black pickets confronted fellow black workers.

61. Stein, *Running Steel,* 101–10, 157–68.

62. Ibid., 167. Important groups fighting to expand rank-and-file democracy in the United Steelworkers of America strongly protested the nationwide imposition of the consent decree from above, while other workers resisted the upgrading of black workers it allowed in northern mills. See Nelson, *Divided We Stand,* 279–84. But see the experience of the black UMWA leader Earl Brown, who fought successful struggles to break job racial barriers in coal mines and won the warm support

of white miners during the 1960s while organizing in the Klan stronghold Tuscaloosa County. Chafe, Gavins, and Korstad, *Remembering Jim Crow,* 237–45.

63. Insightful discussions of black caucuses within unions can be found in Honey, *Black Workers Remember,* 265–66; Nelson, *Divided We Stand,* 115–25, 232, 246–50, 272–75; Ruth Needleman, "Black Caucuses in Steel," *New Labor Forum* 2 (Fall/Winter 1998): 41–56. I am grateful to Bruce Nelson for bringing these important initiatives to my attention. Unlike the networks discussed here, however, these important caucuses were formed by black members of the same local or international union.

64. Warren also commented that even his Molders local, against which he filed complaints with the EEOC, kept the company from firing him when he raised one upgrading grievance after another on the job.

65. In his biography of Arthur Goldberg, who was Kennedy's secretary of labor, David L. Stebenne notes that groups of black workers brought "several hundred" more cases to Kennedy's Committee on Equal Employment Opportunities than two previous federal committees had heard in six years, but the committee had little success in actually overcoming discrimination. David L. Stebenne, *Arthur J. Goldberg: New Deal Liberal* (New York: Oxford University Press, 1996), 244–45.

66. Paul Hemphill, *Leaving Birmingham: Notes of a Native Son* (New York: Viking Penguin, 1993), 198–200, 132–33.

Colonel Stone Johnson

Born September 9, 1918, in Hayneville, Lowndes County, Alabama. Worked as truck driver for Bowden Provision Company and for Hormel Packing Company. Served as chairman of the Grievance Committee in the L&N yard. Organizer of guards for the Alabama Christian Movement for Human Rights (ACMHR). Vice president of the Alabama Southern Christian Leadership Conference (SCLC) and president of the Birmingham Alliance against Racism and Political Repression. *"It was from my activism with the union that I really understood the way racism worked. Then, in the 1950s, when the movement started, I was basically primed for it because I had already been doing this kind of work. This is what really motivated me. Shuttlesworth's uncle was the president of my local union, and he was in the undertaking business on the side. I had done a little extra work for the undertaker shop, and we got to be good friends. Morris said, 'Johnson, you know Shuttlesworth can't get anybody to watch his house and the church?' I said, 'Well, what do you think we ought to do?' He said, 'You've got a lot of influence with the men out here in the union, and during the meeting nights, ask some of the fellows to volunteer.' In the meantime, I had a good friend that was president of a mine local; his name was Will Hall. They called him John L. Lewis because he represented the miners union and he was real tough. The Lord fixed it for us to get together. We organized a watchmen group, and in those days you wouldn't have survived calling yourself a 'watchmen group' or a 'security group,' so we were labeled 'ushers' for the Alabama Christian Movement for Human Rights."*

Railroad Shops and the Civil Rights Movement

I was born in Hayneville, Alabama, in Lowndes County. Lowndes County is in the deep south of the Black Belt. I was about four years old when my parents brought me to Birmingham with my older brother, who was three years older than me and who is now deceased. I go back to Lowndes County regularly because it is like a haven to me. In Birmingham we lived in Travellick on Ellis Avenue, where we stayed for about a year or so. Then we moved to 1005 Sixteenth Street North, where we stayed from 1924 until 1946. We were the first blacks on the block, and there was a grocery store on the corner owned by Italians called Norman Schilleci's Grocery. There were not any repercussions when we moved into that neighborhood because Milton and Erickson Incorporated owned just about everything on the block, and my father worked for them. Most of the white occupants were renting, except four white homeowners on the block. There were white people living in duplex houses, and the real estate companies owned them. There were also two Jewish families and one Italian family living there. There was also a big millionaire who lived in a two-story house that had a servant house in the back. We called it the "big house," because the Joneses lived there, but the rest of it was rented.

My parents' education consisted of little for my mother, who was a housewife, and a lot for my father, who had several occupations. My mother did not go beyond the third or fourth grade, and my father received a degree in mathematics from Alabama State [College] in Montgomery. My father started off teaching school for thirty dollars a week in Lowndes County, then he got a job in Thorsby or Clanton—he worked in three or four little towns between Birmingham and Montgomery.[1] There were pipe shops all up and down the Montgomery thoroughfare, and the trains were very popular then. There was a plant in Verbena that he worked at a while also, because he knew that the closer you get to Birmingham, the more money you can make. From here he moved on up to Clanton, and then after Clanton he worked in a pipe shop in Helena, and then he started working with a company that built sidewalks. He worked with a cement finisher until he got his journeymanship and he became a full-fledged cement finisher. After becoming a professional cement finisher he started working in Birmingham, where he made it big with Milton and Erickson. One of the grandsons of this company is now a big contractor in Birmingham. Back in those days it started off with just two brothers-in-law who were farmers from Switzerland. My father did figuring for Milton and Erickson, and he could tell them the square footage of any job they had to do.

It was around this time that organized labor came in, and my father became the union representative for five counties: Jefferson, St. Clair, Etowah, Tuscaloosa, and Shelby.[2] He stayed on that job until he was eighty-six years old, because everybody wanted him to stay, until I begged him to quit. He was way over pension age by then, and he was a union official when he finally retired.

I graduated from Industrial High School, and I completed my education through correspondence courses. The school is now called Parker High School.

Dr. Parker was the principal there when I finished. People don't like for me to say it, but I experienced a lot of discrimination at Parker. If you weren't "high yellow" you stayed in the back. It was just like the rhyme, "If you black get back, if you're brown stick around." I was also discriminated against when I applied for an employment program for students whose families were not working. The National Youth Association of America sponsored this program, which was like the WPA for the young folks.[3] I had a buddy who was real light-skinned who applied with me at the same time in the office. Both of his parents were working, and this job paid thirty dollars a month to needy kids. He got the job, and they never hired me, and common sense told me why I didn't get the job. My buddy told me he also knew why I didn't get hired. I saw a lot of discrimination at Parker, even on the football team and with the majorettes.

In 1946 I bought a house at 708 Second Avenue North, one block away from Tee's Place.[4] It wasn't Tee's Place then, but it was the place where the Tee's boys were born, five brothers, the Taylors. This is where their home was, and right next to them was a building where an undertaker was. I bought the house really in 1941, when I was single, and I rented it out until 1946. We moved in and made a double tenement out of it, and my old man and stepmother moved next door, and we had one side. After a year or two we had it jacked up, and I put two apartments under it. When I moved there it was still a lot of whites in the community, even the church next-door that blacks eventually bought was a white Methodist church. Eventually whites migrated out of the neighborhood slowly as blacks started to move in.

In this community the Birmingham Police Department was all white, and most of the police were involved with the Ku Klux Klan.[5] The police were very overbearing, especially to blacks. Anything you let a person do to one race they will try it on another. I saw them beat white women just like they beat black folks when they tried to run away. They beat black folks without reason. If they felt like whipping you, they'd whip you, you did not have to resist arrest. A white person just figured that they weren't supposed to be treated like that, but they beat them too. You could make an error, like not saying "yes sir" and "no sir." If you just said "yes" and "no" like you were taught in school, then the man would take the club and hit you across the head. They had hoses they used to carry instead of billy sticks. They had heavy-duty hoses like water hoses, but it was industrial hoses that were reinforced. I saw them hit a lot of folks. They cut up real bad around here. You didn't have to go see a picture show; you could just watch the police when they came to the black community on Friday and Saturday nights.

As far as recreation was concerned, black people didn't have but two places to go in Birmingham, the Elks Club and the Masonic Temple. The City Auditorium was out of bounds, yet your tax money footed the bill. There were also industrial baseball teams, and these teams would play each other on the weekends. The black teams really didn't have anywhere to play. They had Sloss Field out in ACIPCO, and Perfection Mattress had two teams, one black and one white team. ACIPCO [American Cast Iron Pipe Company], TCI [Tennessee Coal and Iron], and Stockham Valve also had a black team and a white team. When integration came along they cut out the ball teams altogether. They would rather not play if they had to play with black people. As far as community organizations, they had some, but there was discrimination in those also, so I did not belong to any of them. Blacks would tell you if you didn't own your home then you couldn't join the Democratic organization. I owned my own home, but I wasn't going to brag about it. One other factor was class; I wasn't in the upper class, even though I owned my home.

My involvement in the civil rights movement started early in the railroad shop. When I was hired, March 31, 1942, I saw such a big difference in the treatment of men. I was previously working for just a minimum wage at Bowden Provision Company. There really wasn't a minimum wage; they paid you what they wanted to. I was a truck driver at the company, and they had an office in Hormel Packing Company. They did most of their buying from Hormel, and they let them have an office and let them store their goods there. The guy was real nice. He treated everybody the same, but he had some kinfolks who would call you a "nigger" in a minute. He would not; he knew your name. He'd find out your name, and he'd call you by your name. He would not call you "John," "Joe," "Uncle," and all that. His family, on the other hand, would call you anything. It's intimidating for a man to call you "Uncle" when he's older than you are. I quit working for this guy, not for any kind of race relations or treatment or anything, but finance. I wasn't making the kind of money I thought I should be making.

When I went to the railroad shop, all laborers made the same thing. They had a union shop. Black or white, all labor made the same thing. If you were the helper or the helper's mate, it was the same thing. Where the segregation came in was on the promotion. You could have a high school education and some college through correspondence courses, and a white man could be brought in right from a farm with a fourth- or fifth-grade education, and they would hire them. I've seen them bring them in by the truckload. Some farmer would bring in a truckload of people that he knew from Cullman or Huntsville or somewhere up in North Alabama during the wartime, in the forties and World War II, and they would hire every one of them. They would hire fifty men. They would be riding on the back of a ton-and-a-half truck like cattle, but they'd hire them even with an eighth- or tenth-grade education. They would hire them as helpers, and you were still a laborer, and you would know all the work, but you didn't get the preference that you should get.

They also had bad habits, like kicking. I've seen them kick fellows just like they would kick a dog. They called themselves "playing." I remember one instance where a young man who had just graduated from high school and was very intelligent got hired. I saw a foreman kick him and just laugh, and something in me just raged. I couldn't take it. I asked, "What y'all doing?" and I called him by his name, and he said, "We just playing," and just laughed. I said, "The ball field is unequal." I said, "If y'all playing, look like you'd kick him sometime to make it fair," and the foreman said, "That nigger's crazy." I said, "You'll see how crazy I am if you kick me," and he said, "Oh, the nigger is crazy, sure enough, I see he's crazy," but he never kicked me.

This was in 1942; I had been there about eight to ten months. I asked them did they have a union, and they said, "Yes, but the blacks are not in it." They would not exactly come out and tell you that blacks could not join the union. You were in the clerical department, and they had a clerk's union, Brotherhood of Railway Clerks. So I decided on my own to talk to a union representative because I had always believed in the union in the little jobs I had been on. You see, I had worked in both places, in the packinghouse and for Bowden Company. I worked for Hormel and for Bowden. Hormel had the CIO, and they hadn't merged then with the AFL. But anyway, when I went to this guy, he said, "Well, ain't no blacks in our union," just like that. So then I went to Mr. Lewis Berry, a black guy who was over the Firemen and Oilers. He said, "Come up to the union hall," and he told me when the union was going to meet, and he said, "We'll explain to you how you can get you an auxiliary."

An auxiliary is different from a full-fledged union. The Firemen and Oilers were a black union. Lewis Berry and George Henderson were the heads of it. They were the Brotherhood of Firemen and Oilers, which was a part of the AFL at that time. So they told me, "You have to have something out of your department, but we will get you a man down here to organize y'all auxiliary." They wrote to the headquarters, which was in Cincinnati, Ohio, at the time, and they sent a man, a field representative named Mr. St. John, a white man. He came down and talked with us, and he stopped at the Bankhead Hotel, and when we went to see him, we had to go to the back and get on the freight elevator to go up to his room. He organized a union for the blacks in the clerk department of the railroad. But that made them have dual representation, and they wouldn't give but one shop a district chairman, so that person would always be a white man, and they put us under his leadership. So if you had any kind of grievance, you would have to file it, and it would never be found justifiable. You would want to appeal it, but you had to go to the district chairman who was over the white union. This was also the same man you went to if you were trying to get a promotion. The same folks you were paying your money to were keeping you back.

But anyway, we organized, and Reverend Shuttlesworth's uncle, August U. Morris, we voted for him as the president, and we voted Regis Adams vice president, and just came on down the line. It was hard to get folks to accept positions because they were afraid the company would retaliate, so they gave Morris both positions. He was the union representative and the president for the first couple of years. We would always get together and have a little pow-wow away from the union hall. So Morris asked me, "Why don't you take the chairman of the protective committee?" And I said, "Well, I can't take it, you have to vote me in. . . . I'll accept it if you vote me in." He said he'd recommend it, and they did. I stayed there for twenty-eight years.

Reuben Davis was in the Brotherhood of Firemen and Oilers group with George Henderson and Lewis Berry. Reuben and myself got together so we could learn the rules and regulations because a lot of the fine print was hard to understand. However, when you have a roundtable discussion of things it really helps out a lot. Reuben figured up how a grievance is supposed to be organized, and he started writing one for all the blacks. We had a real problem with blacks being harassed by kicking from other workers, so we immediately started working to stop that. Before we got the kicking to stop, some of the white workers started kicking other whites. It was just like letting your dog bite your next-door neighbor, for instance. The dog will eventually go down the street and bite somebody else. He would soon even bite the police when he came by. The men that were doing the kicking were those usually in supervisory positions.

The first man I ever wrote up was named E. J. Bryant, a great big, old, fat white gentleman. He acted like he had a kicking machine the way he used to kick men. I saw him kick a black fellow named Higgins, who was seventy or eighty years old, who had a peg leg. I wrote E. J. Bryant up and took it to the master mechanic, who was the top man in the shop. The only boss he had was the superintendent, and at the time I wrote him up, we had a superintendent that was the toughest I had ever seen. This superintendent did not have any kind of manners, and he would use cursing for just about every word that he said. This superintendent's name was Richard McWilliams, and I wrote up E. J. Bryant to him. Mr. McWilliams is a little man, but if you did not see him you would think he was a giant when you heard his voice. He had a bass voice, and he really spoke with authority. He had authority, and the company gave him authority, and he used it. When the letter arrived to him the chief clerk opened it up first and read it. The chief clerk would read all the letters that came through, and if they discovered one wrote up against one of the foremen they would put it up in the file 13, and the master mechanic would never see the letter. The little reputation that I had built for myself in helping people assured the clerk that if I did not hear something from the letter, I was going to follow up on it. So they took the letter and sent for my supervisor, not my foreman, and told him that I had written the man up and quoted the first rule in the book, which was: "No horseplay, no wrestling, no scuffling, no drinking at any time on the company premises, or you will be dismissed." When he got the letter he called me in for a conference. My supervisor was a big man you could talk to. He was the superintendent for a big Baptist church in the community where the shop was. He was a discriminator too, but not as bad as some of the other folks.

I went into his office for the conference, and he said he preferred if we went outside to the warehouse to talk. He said he wanted to ask me a question without anyone else hearing it. He said, "Johnson, you know all those conversations we've had about saving a man's job?" I said, "That's right." "Well, here you have wrote up a man, and he's going to lose his job if we let this go through." I said, "We who?" He said, "You and myself. I'm your boss, and I'm his boss." I said, "Yeah, but I've been watching that fellow, and he treats these fellows like they are dogs." He said, "He ever done anything to you?" I said, "No, but I'm my brother's keeper, I'm head of the union. How can I represent a man and turn my head when he's kicking a man like a dog and the man being victimized is as humble as a lamb? I had to write him up," I said. He said, "Well, what would you do to take the letter out?" I replied, "Mr. Bryant would have to promise me he would never kick another black man on the company premises, and then I'll take the letter out. Other than that," I replied, "I can't do it." He said, "Well, I think we can handle that. I've already talked to E. J., so I'll call him."

He called him, and he was in another building about half a mile from where we were. The shop at that time was a five-mile shop, but when I left it was about a ten-mile shop. But anyway, this guy wanted to be a real heavy, but that was his boss. He said, "Tell Johnson I said call me." He came back and told me, and I said, "I don't want to see him. Tell him to call me on the warehouse phone. He wants to see me, I don't want to see him." So finally Bryant called and said, "Johnson, you want to see me?" I said, "No sir, I don't want to see you." He said, "Well, I heard that you wrote me up." I said, "Yes sir." He said, "Well, what did you write about me?" I said, "Everything you need to know has already been discussed with you. You don't know how to keep your feet on the ground," I replied. He said, "Well, the man didn't complain." I said, "But I saw it with my own eyes, and I represent the man. He didn't have to tell me or ask me," I said. "I wrote you up because it is unbecoming for a company employee to act like you act, especially with the position you have."

He said, "Well, what do I have to do?" "The supervisor has already told you," I said. He said, "Yeah, he told me, but I want you to tell me." I said, "I'll be glad to tell you. You make me a promise that you won't kick another black man on the company premises, and I'll take the letter out." He said, "Well, if it suits you, I'll promise that I won't do it anymore." I said, "Well, it suits me, and I'll go take the letter out."

I worked on the first floor, and the office was upstairs, so I went upstairs, and all the clerks stopped typing when I walked in. There were about ten to twelve clerks up there who were discussing what had gone on. I went to the chief clerk and said, "Good morning, sir." He said, "Good morning, Johnson, what can I do for you?" I said, "Well, I have a letter up here, and I have negotiated to take it out, and I want to do that now." He said, "Here it is. You are the only person that can take it out." I took the letter and threw it in the wastebasket. I never saw or heard of another black man being kicked. A bulletin was put out that read: "I mean what I say, if I catch anyone breaking rule number one, or any other rule, they got to go!"

When Reuben Davis came back from World War II they didn't want blacks in the steel gang. They talked about rebuilding freight cars for the Railroad Company. Those jobs paid good money, and it was a top job. Reuben Davis never did get one of those jobs, but he fixed it where the blacks could get them. You see, when you go to the army it's a proclamation. When you leave a job and go fight for your country, you are to be recognized by seniority and receive more money. So, Reuben asked for more jobs for blacks in the steel gang because no blacks had been going in it. The only people going to it were laborers that picked up scrap and moved it out the way when they tore the stuff off the cars. So Reuben was called a troublemaker, but all the men in Reuben's union were upgraded to helpers, and then from helpers to car repairmen or journeymen. A hate list was also put out, but not in writing but by word of mouth.

This goes back to what I was saying earlier about Richard McWilliams, the master mechanic that was fairer than anyone was, but who was a really tough guy. He said once that if you do your work in the union, then somebody would tell you what happened in personnel meetings. They would discuss how Reuben Davis was invading the job, white jobs for blacks, and he [McWilliams] showed his discrimination. He said, "I want Reuben Davis's job at all costs. If you have to lie on him, get his job! I want to run him off, I can't run him off for nothing, we've got to have something concrete on him." Reuben's foreman, Mr. McIntire, being a Christian gentleman, said, "I can't do it." He said, "He's a good worker, and I'd have to lie, and I ain't going to lie." Reuben Davis was a tractor driver. He was what you call a "push-up man": he pushed the cars on the assembly line in the big shed where they worked on them, and when they finished working on them he would push them out. It's three or four lines he had to push, but he was sitting there on his tractor what you might call "on the minute" all the time. As soon as he finished a line, and nobody could move a line but the foreman, and we walked both sides of the track to see if everybody was clear, and then he would tell Reuben to shove them out, and he would. He would shove another line of cars in there for them to work on. He wouldn't go along with the wrong program.

He had a redheaded foreman named Sam Hollingsworth. He said he was a labor foreman. He wasn't really Reuben's foreman ordinarily, but when the other foreman would be off, he would substitute for this guy to have a day off. He took on the responsibility to get Reuben's job, and he finally came out there one day when the regular foreman was off and told Reuben that he wasn't doing nothing there, and he said that he needed a man over there at the wheel shop, which was the most dangerous job in the shop. The rolling train wheels weighed up to nine hundred pounds, according to the car they went under. The wheels were standing up, and when one of them fell you had to have help to get it up. You had to use what was called a "wheel stick," and the men could catch it with their hands, and two of them would catch the stick, and they would pull it down and straighten the wheel up. Depending on whose turn it was, that person would catch it and roll it out on a flange.

We got a load of wheels that needed unloading. Reuben had better sense than to tell him that he wasn't going to do it. Reuben said, "I was just getting ready to come to you. I'm sick and want to go home." He said, "Oh, you refuse to work?" He said, "No, I'm not refusing to work. I'm sick." "Ah, you're refusing to work." So he wrote Reuben up, saying that he was refusing to work and to take orders from him. So they fired Reuben. Reuben stayed off a year, and his case went all the way to the National Railway Labor Board through appealing, and he had a union lawyer out of St. Louis, and they won the case in a year.

While Reuben was off he started teaching mechanics at Bessemer Tech or either Abram's [High School]. In that space of time they sent Reuben a letter in May, about May first, and told him he had his job back, but he was already teaching then. He wrote them back and said he would be back in thirty days. When school was out on May 28, Reuben came to work on June first and whatever they owed him, he got his money, and then he worked on through close to ninety days, and he gave them another notice. This notice stated that he was going to resign, and he went back to teach school.

It was from my activism with the union that I really understood the way racism worked. Then, in the 1950s, when the movement started, I was basically primed for it, because I had already been doing this kind of work. This is what really motivated me. Shuttlesworth's uncle was the president of my local union, and he was in the undertaking business on the side. They teased him because he was in this business. Sometimes he would drive a seven-passenger car to work, back when there really were only a few seven-passenger cars at the time. But anyway, Shuttlesworth's wife was named Ruby, and she was Morris's niece. They raised her, Mr. and Mrs. Morris. Morris's wife was named Adella, and she was a schoolteacher, and A. U. [Morris] was a clerk at the shop. It was only about three black clerks out there that were actually top clerks. One of the top clerks was A. C. McClenny, and he was very, very intelligent. He was a dispatcher. When all the train movements went out, he was the person who set up the schedule. McWilliams, when he came along [as superintendent], he stopped this black guy from doing all the white folks' work. You see, he worked second shift, and if anything were set up wrong at the first shift, he would straighten it out so that the paper work would go in right. When he left off of his shift he stayed there until twelve o'clock and one o'clock, and he was supposed to leave at eleven, and he would straighten things up and line it up for the third shift. So McWilliams told them, "You all are going to have to hire some intelligent white folks or get some black ones and put them on the job, because this man is working, and you are not even paying him." They didn't pay him for extra work; he was just staying there to help his fellow man, and he did it for years, to my knowledge. McWilliams told him when it was time for him to get off, leave on time, and do not come to work at 12:30 or one o'clock like he had been coming. He told him his job comes on at three o'clock. They did not hire a black man for the job, the white guy that had the job was an old man, and when he left, a young white guy who was well educated got the job. A. C. McClenny remained until he retired.

Anyway, after a long time I had done a little extra work for the undertaker shop, and we got to be good friends. Shuttlesworth was going to Selma University, and his wife was also enrolled. We would go down there, and I would drive the seven-passenger car, taking Morris down there, because I was one of his employees and he just used me for a chauffeur. Anyway, I met Shuttlesworth, and he was such a likeable fellow that we got to be good friends. When they bombed his house in 1957 or 1958 it was as if they had bombed my house.[6] It could have been my house. You see, if you stood up and talk straight without fear, the Ku Klux Klan would retaliate. They did not count the law. A lot of folks did not know it, but God says you got to reap what you sow. Young blacks don't consider the law now; they don't pay it any mind. The city is reaping, no special person, the city, the powers to be, because once upon a time the power didn't respect the law and they were the law. Now, these black boys and a lot of white boys will kill you in a minute. In this day and time when youngsters and teenagers fight, the first thing that comes in their mind is, "I'll kill you." The Ku Klux used that word and method through the years, and it's just reaping time.

But anyway, I went over to Morris's office that next day, and two or three days after that we were talking about what happened, and Morris said, "Johnson, you know Shuttlesworth can't get anybody to watch his house and the church?" I said, "Well, what do you think we ought to do?" He said, "You've got a lot of influence with the men out here in the union, and during the meeting nights, ask some of the fellows to volunteer." In the meantime, I had a good friend that was president of a mine local; his name was Will Hall.[7] They called him John L. Lewis because he represented the miners union, and he was real tough.

He was a coal miner, and he lived next-door to the Ballard House.[8] The lady that owned the house owned a taxi company. It had a special name, and it was two doors from St. John's Methodist church on Fifteenth Street and Seventh Avenue North. I went looking for Will Hall, and I told him the circumstances. We had another fellow who was a union-minded fellow named George Walker, and we all got together. The Lord fixed it for us to get together. We organized a watchmen group, and in those days you wouldn't have survived calling yourself a "watchmen group" or a "security group," so we were labeled "ushers" for the Alabama Christian Movement for Human Rights.[9] Ordinarily, we were security men, and that is the way we organized and started watching the church. It was a lot of men involved in this group, and they fixed it where you didn't have to stay but three to four hours when you first started off. I started off by watching Shuttlesworth's home and the church. The first parsonage was blown into splinters by the first bombing. That's when they left Shuttlesworth laying there on the mattress and God being who He is, just one of Fred's girls got a scratch on her cheek; no one else got any scratches.

They had got so bad out there, and J. B. Stoner was the chief bomber.[10] He would ride around all night in a Yellow Cab and that let me know that the Yellow Cab Company was tied in with the bombings in some kind of way. No driver could drive a car around with one man the entire week, all night, every night. I really did not know a whole lot about Stoner at that time. I had seen him on TV talking about black folks ought to go back to Africa, and they ought to be shipped there, and a whole lot of other stuff he said. But anyway, Stoner would ride around in that cab, and we kept seeing his face and remembered it. I never saw him walking until one Sunday evening, and then I saw he was crippled. Stoner had parked the cab around the corner, and we saw him limping by, one leg was longer than the other was. He had a shoe with a lot of heel and sole to lengthen it out and give him a kind of even walk, but he still walked with a limp.

We were sitting across the street at Mr. Robert Revis's house when we saw him. His front porch was enclosed, and there was a heater and everything. We would sit there on his front porch and watch the church. The next-door neighbor, Sam Smiley, had a garage in the back of his backyard, and we had men in the church at the back windows. But it's hard to see a person if he gets close to the building, which is what happened when they planted a bomb I am about to tell you about. At the Revis's home there was four of us sitting there: James Russell, myself, Will Hall, and another miner [who] used to sell peanuts. He ran a store out in Pratt City, and we just called him "peanut seller," but I don't know his name. But anyway, we were all sitting there on the porch, and one of Mr. Revis's daughters came in, her name was Lavonne McWilliams. She had come back home to stay with her parents. Her date brought her in around midnight in a Chrysler automobile; I will never forget it. When she got out of the car she said, "Y'all going to sit there and let the church burn up?" "Burn up, what you mean?" She said, "See, look at that smoke coming from the side of the church." That was the bomb. It was in a fresh paint can, and the fuse was lit, which made the paint smoke. We hadn't seen the smoke. They had someone set it there, and we didn't see that person.

We saw cars pass by, but this person must have walked up. There was an alley right behind the church, and they must have walked through there and dropped off the bomb. It was on a Saturday night, and a lot of folks were walking that night. We rushed out when we saw the smoke, Will Hall and myself. We got up close to it, and I said, "John L., that's some dynamite." He says, "I know it is." He was experienced with fuses that are in mines. He says, "Yeah, it's some dynamite." "Let's get it," he said, and both of us reached for it about the same time, and we caught the pail of the five-gallon paint can and walked it about eight to ten feet and set it in the gutter. The street wasn't paved then. It had a little ditch going by, and we set it down in the gutter of the ditch, and we backed off another eight to ten feet, and it went off. As we were going to the house where the watch station was, I said, "Somebody run in the church and tell those men to come out quick!" I knew there was dynamite around the church, and we didn't want the church to be blown away and kill everybody in there. We forgot about ourselves, because we were looking out for the other men. About the time that the other men got out the church, a fellow named Elijah Dawson, we called him Lige, came up and said, "What's the matter?" . . . BOOM! He was about ten feet from it, and he was the only one who got a scratch. A little shrapnel of steel hit him on the cheek. The bomb blew all the glass out of the church, and for five to six blocks around, dishes broke on the folks in the pantries and windows broke out of houses as much as seven or eight blocks, but the church still stood. I was standing about seven or eight feet from the bomb when it went off. As soon as I set it down and backed up at the same time, while we were doing that, those other fellows were coming out the church, and about the time Dawson got down there to see what was going on, and it went off.

We had a lot of fellows I could call by name that never did come back. But you can't think hard of a fellow, because nobody can take the fear out of your heart but God. It had just really frightened a lot of them to death, and when some of them went home and told their wives about it, the women didn't want them to go back anymore, but John L. and myself. It became real thin with men after that second bombing, but the men eventually came back. The Lord had always sent somebody else there. I can remember when it got real thin, and it was a fellow, I can't think of his last name. I had never seen him at Shuttlesworth's church, but he lived two to three blocks from the church. He and his next-door neighbor were buddies, and they would always come by there and speak. They were nice guys, it seemed to me. "How are you fellows doing?" We'd speak, "Fine, how are you all?" They started watching after they saw we needed somebody, and then eventually it built back up.

Bombings also occurred in an area of Birmingham called "Dynamite Hill," but I did not really have a station up there.[11] Robert Cole called me several times when the cars were driving by the houses. People never gave Leroy Gaillard[12] the credit he should have received. He had two-way radios in his station wagons, and he had a plumbing company. Gaillard furnished the two-way radios for the watchmen on Dynamite Hill. A lot of the time we would leave Shuttlesworth's house and go by Dynamite Hill and help them out. I know it was a stressful job, but we never really got tired, and I figured later on in life that God just wouldn't let us get tired. We were not really getting much sleep.

But before I go on, I must tell you that after the bombing, *Jet* magazine came along. Will Hall was on pension, and *Jet* magazine wanted to interview the both of us. I wouldn't let them interview me because of the job I had. I was not afraid, but I knew I had to use my head. They would have framed me and got my job. You see, they would put a smear on you like the folks tried to do the mayor of Birmingham, Richard Arrington. They have done everything in the book to smear Richard Arrington, but when God is in the plan, it is hard for you to smear a fellow. I watched it. In the Bible it says that Joseph was a chosen man of God to save his people. When God put a man in a position like Dick Arrington, you can't hurt him.

Anyway, when *Jet* came along, everyone came up to me and said that if I interviewed I would be known all over the world. I told them that I was working for a cause, not for an ego. God won't be in a plan that is based on an ego trip. But they wrote the story up in *Jet,* and I had a lot of criticism. People kept telling me, "Man, if I was you. . . ." "But you are not me," I replied, "And if I were you, I would be out there helping to watch Shuttlesworth's church," I told them. I even asked members of the church why they were not helping watch the church. Then a fellow that worked with me at the shop told the assistant superintendent that I was out there watching, so he could get my job. And that's what they would use. It was called a "backlash." A lot of folks were afraid. I never was afraid because I asked God to give me a good job, and the way he gave it to me [was] through my wife, and every once in a while she'd take credit for it. She'd say, "You know I got you that job out there." She was working for the master mechanic at that time, at his house. Theodore Cramer was his name, and he was quiet and easy, but he believed in discrimination too, 'cause he didn't believe in promotion. Anytime a man does not believe in paying you what you are worth, it does not matter how nice he talks. It doesn't really matter, because it is your livelihood that really counts. Anyway, my wife recommended me and would tell him about me driving on the road and going out of town all the time. I would come in so late all the time and work long hours with straight pay, no overtime and no vacation. So Cramer found out, and he told me to come out to the shop. I went out there, and he hired me. That's the way the Lord answered my prayer.

I was never arrested during my time I was involved in the Movement, but I was harassed. A lot of times I would leave Shuttlesworth's house on Sunday mornings, and when I left, the police would be waiting on me. If I went out Twenty-ninth Avenue, the policeman would get behind me and trail me. They knew my car, and the police would give me tickets because he claimed that I ran a stop sign. All the while I would be looking right at him sitting in the Bruno's [grocery store] parking lot. Bruno's used to be on Twenty-fifth Street and Twenty-ninth Avenue in a little burnt building. The policeman would be sitting on a three-wheel motorcycle sitting right in the door, and I could see directly in his face. I would have looked like a fool running a stop sign and simultaneously looking in a policeman's face. However, he still gave me a ticket. He would say, "Boy, you just ran that stop sign," and I'd say, "No, sir." "I'm a liar then," he'd say. I'd say, "I did not run that sign." He'd say, "Well, I'm gonna give you a so-and-so ticket anyway." He would give me a ticket for running a stop sign. I'd pay it, but that's what you had to pay. That is the price you pay for freedom.

The policeman followed me one day in particular. They had it set up good from Shuttlesworth's church all the way past where this policeman sat. When I turned on Twenty-fourth Street, where Southern Armature Company sat, there was a watchman sitting there in a little shack. They would stop you right there at the shack, and the watchman would come out there with a shotgun. This was all done to intimidate you and make you think they were dangerous and ready to kill you. The policeman would draw his gun and search you. They searched me many times along with the watchman standing right there. However, a lot of these companies did not know their employees were participating in this kind of behavior. The employees would use their own authority. When the big man or boss over the mountain slept—see, a lot of rich folks didn't even know the folks was being treated so bad—and then a lot of them had the same idea. But that's just the way it went.

Another harassment incident occurred one night when we had the mass meeting at Sixth Avenue Baptist. The church was sitting right where Cooper Green Hospital is now. I had a brand-new Buick and my old man and my wife and his wife and another person. There were five of us in the car. After the mass meeting we walked down on Fifth Avenue. There were so many people at the mass meeting that you couldn't get a parking space on Sixth Avenue. We walked down to the car and got in the car, and as soon as we did, the police pulled up on a motorcycle right up alongside of me. He said, "Gimme your driver's license." I got my driver's license out. "Your lights are too bright." He wrote me a ticket up for bright lights, and I hadn't even cut my lights on, but I had to pay that ticket. But that was the price we had to pay. A lot of people's eyes came open. You see, Wallace is paying the price for keeping folks from having their freedom. This is the reason why, when a man treats you wrong, you don't kill him, you forgive him. The boss man got the payroll, and he is going to pay off.

My wife used to drive, but she stopped when she saw the police intimidating black women, and she couldn't stand it. She said, "Y'all talk about nonviolence, and I hear Reverend Shuttlesworth and Dr. King say slap you on one cheek and turn the other." She said, "I read it in the book, but I couldn't stand it." She said, "If somebody snatch me out of my car and hit me across the head, if I don't have nothing, I'm going to grab them and bite them. I ain't going to drive anymore, because if somebody treat me like that, they would have me to kill, I can't stand that." She said, "I ain't driving no more," and she hasn't drove since. That was in 1963.

At the time of my initial involvement in the movement I was a member of Macedonian Baptist church, but I later joined Mount Calvary church because I visited there and they treated me with so much hospitality. My wife wanted me to stay where I was because she thought I was stepping down by going to a smaller church. I told her that I could serve in a smaller church more than I can in a big one. This church was not involved in the movement initially.

They did like other churches at first when the preacher said that people did not want the movement there, and they should not get involved in it. However, that preacher left, and we got a good country preacher named Prince Jenkins. He was as country-acting as watermelon, but he was real spiritual, and he was a young man who was interested in freedom, and he asked me, "Johnson, how come you don't get the movement to come to our church?" I said, "If the folks would accept it I would. The pastor before you said they did not want it and they would not allow it to come." He said, "I want it, and I'm going to talk about it today." He got up and said how much good the ACMHR had done and how he wanted them to come to our church. He told me that as soon as I could get them to come they would be welcomed. He said, "I'm letting y'all know now, the Movement is coming." Anyway, we started meeting at our church. I told the secretary, Miss Georgia Price, to communicate with Reverend Gardner[13] to arrange the places they would go. After that they started coming to our church.

My father and wife's reaction to my work in the movement was cooperative with my father, but my wife never did accept it. She went to all the mass meetings, but she was not as active as I was. She would still go to the meetings every Monday night, not missing hardly any days. Through all my work during the Movement, one of my really top motivations was Fred Shuttlesworth. He could explain God's idea of freedom so well that it would take away all the fear from your heart. His confidence in the Lord helped inspire other people also. One of his favorite quotes was, "If I was in an airplane without a parachute and God told me to jump, I wouldn't ask him no questions, I would just jump." When he would make statements like this, it was really touching to people. A lot of folks are afraid to preach the truth, but Fred was not. You would be surprised, if a preacher taught the truth, he had to go, even in the white church. A lot of people cannot stand the truth. The Bible says the truth would make you free, and that is what made a lot of people not free, because they did not want to hear the truth.

Some people said that Fred was a dictator and that he believed the Movement was his movement, but after working with him, I have a different opinion. Someone had to lead, and he was the leader. You can't have but one head. After Fred knocked a lot of the big trees down and got them out of the way, other people then came forth because of ego. When a man has an ego he will want the office without work. In other words, there is a lot of labor and a lot of sacrifice, and most people would not have done what he did. I have worked with him, and I am going to tell the truth. I have also seen him go out when a lot of people were in jail and needed money, he would go to New York, California, and all over the U.S. to get money for the Movement, even though he didn't have a lot of money for himself. He was a poor boy who was a long way from home, and a lot of other preachers would tell him that they would not put all that money in the Movement and not have any for themselves. Fred would say, "No, I preach in the name of the Movement. I was representing the Movement, and I'm putting money in there." This was God's plan. What the other preachers were ultimately saying was that if they were in leadership, the money would be going into their pockets. God paid Fred later for the work that he did. He is in good shape now because he got it honest, and he still has his integrity. You can't have anything when you obtain it dishonestly. He has it, and he is keeping it.

Edited by Laura Williams. BCRI Oral History Project, vol. 1, sec. 3 (Jan. 6, 1995).

Notes

1. Thorsby and Clanton are small towns just south of Birmingham on U.S. Highway 31.

2. Local 62 of the Operative Plasterers and Cement Finishers–AFL.

3. The National Youth Administration, 1935–1943, was a federal employment program for youth and students.

4. Tee's Place is now the Platinum of Birmingham, an upscale nightclub located at Eighth Street and Second Avenue North.

5. See Diane McWhorter, *Carry Me Home: Birmingham, Alabama; The Climactic Battle of the Civil Rights Revolution* (New York: Simon and Schuster, 2001).

6. The Bethel Baptist church was first bombed on Christmas Eve night, 1956. Glenn T. Eskew, *But for Birmingham: The Local and National Movements in the Civil Rights Struggle* (Chapel Hill: University of North Carolina Press, 1997), 131–33.

7. Will Hall, president of a UMWA local, was a relative of Asbury Howard Sr., a Mine, Mill, and Smelter Workers official.

8. A rooming house where the Birmingham Black Barons baseball team lived in the 1950s.

9. The ACMHR was organized in June 1956 as a result of the NAACP being outlawed from operating in Alabama. See Eskew, *But for Birmingham,* 22.

10. McWhorter calls Stoner "the most brazen church bomber of the civil rights era." See McWhorter, *Carry Me Home,* 71.

11. Dynamite Hill was located north of Legion Field and east of Birmingham Southern College, a white liberal arts college. Homes were bombed because black families were moving into this previously all-white community.

12. Gaillard owned one of the largest black construction companies in Birmingham. See Leroy Gaillard interview, BCRI Oral History Project, vol. 33, sec. 4.

13. Vice president of the ACMHR. All African American churches were not in favor of the movement. See Wilson Fallin Jr., *The African American Church In Birmingham, Alabama, 1815–1963: A Shelter in the Storm* (New York: Garland Publishing, 1997), 145–46.

Rev. Joseph Lewis Rogers

Born October 7, 1902, in Montgomery, Alabama. Lived in Birmingham most of his life. Worked as a carpenter, coal miner, timber cutter, and coke roller. First black checkweighman at Sloss Sheffield mines. Served as Local vice president of the UMWA. Served as pastor of Shady Grove Baptist church for more than fifty years. *"I was a member of the union when they got organized in '33. I was on the committee, and I was vice president of the local. We had a white president and a black vice. Whatsoever a man was qualified to do, they were trying to get him to do that job. . . . My job was to sit up on the top where the coal come out and weigh it when it goes across the scale. . . . I didn't like . . . that strife when I came down off the truck. . . . [T]hey threatened me . . . because . . . they didn't want a black man to have that job."*

Unions, Ministry, and Movement

My parents are from Montgomery, Alabama, and I was born there also. I lived there about fifteen years before we moved to Birmingham. I used to visit my aunt here before we moved here. When I came to Birmingham I had finished elementary school. I was sixteen years old. I went to work at Gimmick's Pipe Shop in North Birmingham. My job was keeping the furnace heated up. My next job was at the Ice House. I rolled coal there to keep the furnace rolling. It was a big furnace there, and I had to roll enough coal in the day for the night fireman to fire it during that night. I stayed there for about four months.

After that, I went to the American Radiator. I was an assistant to the foreman. The company made radiator heaters. I was assistant to the foreman and would have to take in new flashes and take out old ones—keep the sand clean to form the mold with.

After that I went to the coal mine. In the coal mine I was loading coal. I worked in the coal mines twenty years.

I was a member of the union [UMWA] when they got organized in '33. I was on the committee, and I was vice president of the local. We had a white president and a black vice. Whatsoever a man was qualified to do, they were trying to get him to do that job. I was the first black checkweighman in Alabama in 1937.[1] My job was to sit up on the top where the coal come out and weigh it when it goes across the scale. I enjoyed seeing the coal roll across the scales and giving them just weight, but I didn't like it so well, that strife when I come down off the truck. Well, they threaten me and all that type of stuff because they didn't want a black man to have that job because, number one, they had never had one in the state of Alabama. But I was supported by the union. I worked there about one year. After that, I left Lewisburg and went to Republic Steel. I was at Republic Steel from the latter part of '37 until '43.

My job at Republic Steel was the coke roller, loading coal, and a committeeman. We were working by the ton. Making around about two hundred dollars a month, which was pretty good. The [Steelworkers Organizing Committee–CIO] constitution give a person a right to a job regardless as to what it was, if they were qualified for it.

I lived in North Birmingham. There were several plants in North Birmingham. There were several stove foundries, and there was U.S. Pipe, what is Jim Walter now, it was Drummond's then. Now, that was a great place to work, and they had several foundries there where you make stoves. My neighbors worked at different jobs. Some mined, some worked in the foundries, and others in factories, things like that.

The Alabama Christian Movement

Shuttlesworth was my friend, and I got involved in the movement through him. We worked together in the churches, and then we worked together in the movement. He pastored one of my neighborhood churches. I became a pastor in '43. I was a member at Shady Grove Baptist church. The same church I'm pastoring now. That was my membership church, and when the pastor died, I had been preaching about two years, and they made a choice of me, and I been there ever since.

I was president of the Finance Committee of the Movement. I had to raise money, and I would take the money to the bank.

I attended just about all of the mass meetings. The only reason I didn't attend would be if I was out of town. Mass meetings would seem like a church mostly because all of them were looking like religious people, the way we operate was just like a church. We would have a meeting, singing, praying and lifting an offering, and speakers. It was set up on a Christian base. Most of the people were Christian people. They wanted to change many things, where other people could get jobs and where they should have them, such as changing at the depot, changing bathrooms.

Police were usually at the mass meetings taking notes of what we were doing. I never went to jail. I don't know why I didn't. Folks all around me, but I never did go to jail. I got them out of jail when they got in jail.

I got interested in it after Rosa Parks refused to give up her seat.[2] Then Martin Luther King and Shuttlesworth got together, and it was necessary. Members of my church were very active. When I first got involved, my church lined up, took part, and went to jail, just like the other people did. We had meetings at my church. Shuttlesworth and I worked together in our churches. He was just like a brother: anytime I need him, he'd come, and anytime he needed me, I would come to the rescue. If he had to go somewhere, needed some money and didn't have enough, he'd call me and he'd go.

Lots of things failed in the Movement, but it wasn't too much. Birmingham has changed considerably. When I first came to Birmingham, you find a dead man on the street or on a railroad most any day. But it don't happen like that now. Some were chalked up like the train rolled over them, and some threw in water and some in bushes and like that, but mostly somebody would get killed every night.

Miles College played a great part. Dr. [Lucius] Pitts would turn them loose and let them march.[3] Miles played a great part. The students were active. They were ready to go anytime you'd say "go." Marching, marching. We had some regular people, you know marching on the street. But when we got ready for that march, well, they were there.

Well, if I did have the ability to change one thing [about the Movement], on the annual days such as Easter, Christmas, Thanksgiving, I would have them quit going to the stores. Don't buy them. Teach your dollars some sense. Some black folk slipped into stores to buy, but later they quit slipping and went ordering it by mail. I would ask them not to go in, but if he went on in, we wouldn't bother them. I started it on our church. The members were spending a lot of money, unnecessary money, and I told them, "I don't want nobody on Easter with a new outfit," and the people saw how much money they were saving on Easter, and they said they were glad that I insisted that. One man told me I saved him about three hundred dollars.

I've been there fifty-seven years, but that's my membership church.

Edited and abridged by Horace Huntley. BCRI Oral History Project, vol. 3, sec. 2 (Mar. 2, 1995).

Notes

1. The checkweighman was an elected position of great importance. He checked the weight given by the company weigh master to every load of coal brought up by a miner to ensure that the miner was properly paid for his work.

2. The Montgomery bus boycott, 1955–56.

3. Dr. Lucius Pitts was president of Miles College. See the interview with Harvey Lee Henley Jr. on the importance of Miles College to young black workers.

Lloyd Harper

Born December 1, 1926, in Marion, Perry County, Alabama. One of eleven children. Moved to Birmingham in 1946. Worked at ACIPCO. Member of the ACMHR. *"A lot of times we had people come in and try to get the union. In '58 and '60 I was involved in that. The reason I pushed for it was because they were still crushing the black man, keeping him down, and still you were doing the work. They would bring a white man in one day. At that time I was oiling. They would bring a white man in and say, just hired, and say, "Lloyd, this fellow here was hired today. We want you to show him the work." But he's my boss. I had to show him the work, and he was my boss, and I didn't like that too well. Someone told us that if you got a union, a union will stop all of this. And I went out in '58 and '60, and somebody came to me, and we got started trying to get a union in. It was the UMW."*

Bringing the Movement to a Nonunion Company

I'm from Marion, Alabama, that's Perry County. It's eleven of us. I'm the second oldest. They all depend on me. I'm the only one here now in Birmingham. I have one brother who lives in the home house, but they depend on me. My father was a farmer. We bought it around '35. Before that we sharecropped.

We were able to buy because the government gave people on a farm the opportunity to buy their homes, and they gave them the money.[1] My dad was one that always wanted to try his hand, and they gave it to him, so he went. My mother went to about the sixth grade. Neither one went to college. She helped Daddy on the farm. And with that many children, I don't think she had time to work out. She had a pretty big job at home.

I remember normally that Mama and Daddy were the type of people that were sort of strict. They didn't allow us to have our way. We mostly stayed around home and worked on the farm. I can hardly remember back to the first grade, but I do remember about the first or second year in school. It was an old school that we went to. It wasn't nothing like . . . it was actually an old building with one teacher, through the sixth grade. I only went to the sixth grade. After the sixth grade I think I started working with a dairy farm. And from there I got drafted into the army. I guess I was sort of slow in learning, I didn't learn as fast. I was about eighteen at the time that I was in the sixth grade.

Like I said, Mom and Dad were sort of strict on us. A lot of folks didn't want to go to the army. But to me that was a way to get away from home. It was a thing that I wanted to do, and I was glad. I went to Fort Benning. Mama and them had to take me from home. It was cold that morning on the wagon to catch a bus. That was the first time I had been out of Marion, when I got on that bus heading for Fort Benning, Georgia. I was eighteen years old.

When I arrived at Fort Benning, I guess it was something I had never seen before. I had never been around that many people. Something was just strange. I guess the training that Mama and Daddy gave me, that's what kept me into it. It gave me an opportunity to be on my own, and that's what we looked for. I felt good. That was May 1945.

After basic training I went to Germany. I took basic training in Fort Benning, and I went to Salinas for a while—Salinas, California. Then they gave us that opportunity. They said that if you reenlisted, they were getting ready to send us to Germany, or they said if you reenlisted you could go home and stay home for about a month. Then when you came back, you would go to Europe, to Germany. So I took that opportunity, and I reenlisted. I came home and stayed for a month. After that, I left and went back to camp, and they sent me from there to Germany.

I'm one that tries to look ahead and try to see things that will benefit Lloyd. When I got over there it was a thing that you could do, there was work in the kitchen, or you could go out on the airstrip every day. If you worked in the kitchen you worked all day. You were usually in there at five in the morning, and you worked all day, but you were off the next day. If you went out there and worked on the field every day, you had to go every day. So I chose the kitchen. It came out on my discharge, it says "Cook." My children jump on me and say, "Daddy, you can't cook water." I was mostly KP. I didn't do much cooking. I was mostly cleaning the pots and the pans and things like that. I served one year and six months. When I reenlisted I hadn't been in but six months.

Germany was exciting, actually. Very exciting. I liked it. [I] got a chance to see the world. I went up to Stuttgart a time or two, and I think that was one of the main places in Germany. It was just being out. [I] had an opportunity to be with different people. When I went in we were still a segregated world. And the army was segregated. You were still black at that time, but you got a chance to be around people, and it just felt different.

This what I guess what you call a learning experience. When I left home I was under Daddy's thumb, and I couldn't tell him where I was getting ready to go, and I'm the oldest boy. I had a sister older than I was, but she was still at home. So when I get home [after service], now I have an opportunity. In my mind, I'm coming to Birmingham where my uncle, James Whitehead, is. He's my mother's brother. I was going to come there and get a job at ACIPCO. That was my thinking. All I do, I go home, stay home, I get out on November 2. November 18 I was in Birmingham trying to get a job. So that's what my thinking was: now I know I got to go to work.

I got a job with ACIPCO. I had to go back home and get mother to sign for me because I wasn't quite old enough at the time for them to take me. I was still considered a minor. I think you had to be twenty-one at that time to go to work. When I first went there, my uncle was there, and he was in the YMCA, and that's like I say, he was in a job that seemed to me that had an opportunity to help folks. In other words, he was sort of a stepping-stone, and I knew that. Everybody knew him, and it was an opportunity for him to introduce me to the folks and tell them I had a nephew coming and he would like for me to have a job. I lived with him for about six months. I was still single.

I married when I was twenty-five. I had been working four or five years when I got married.

After leaving my uncle's, I lived up there on Twenty-fifth Avenue North in Birmingham with a Mr. and Mrs. Sanders. They had a boarding house, and I lived with them.

I was started off as a grinder, grinding Ford axles. I think if you see some of these tractors now, they have an axle on the front of it, that's one of the axles that we were producing at that time. I don't think they produce it now, but those are some of the axles I started grinding. Grinding with a grinding rock, grinding the rust parts off and making it smooth. That's what I was doing at that time.

At that time you had color lines, and you couldn't go but certain places. There was black, "colored" work and "white" work. You didn't go over here and do this. You could do all you could into the "colored" line of it, and that's far as you could go.[2]

When I got married, we started renting at that time. We rented for a few years. I forget now when we bought our first home, but I believe it was right around '60. I went to ACIPCO in '46. ACIPCO didn't have a union, but they sort of worked with you to keep ahead of the other surrounding companies in the area. That kept people sort of satisfied. In other words, if U.S. Pipe was making a certain amount of money, ACIPCO was normally making two or three pennies more than the people that were doing the same type of work. Then, we had better benefits at ACIPCO. We were getting a bonus at that time, and nobody else was getting that. Every three months, if you made a profit, they would give it back to you in a percentage. That's one of the things.

A lot of times we had people come in and try to get the union. In '58 and '60 I was involved in that. The reason I pushed for it was because they were still crushing the black man, keeping him down, and still you were doing the work. Normally, we do the work. They would bring a white man in one day. At that time I was oiling. They would bring a white man in and say, just hired, and say, "Lloyd, this fellow here was hired today. We want you to show him the work." But he's my boss. I had to show him the work, and he was my boss, and I didn't like that too well. Someone told us that if you got a union, a union will stop all of this. And I went out in '58 or '60, and somebody came to me, and we got started trying to get a union in. It was the UMW [United Mine Workers of America].

Well, we didn't get the union, because at the time I was the main source—black. We had one or two whites trying too at that time. But if you know white folks, if they get dissatisfied they will get somebody else to do their dirty work. And when things get a little better, then they are ready to turn their back. And I told them, "Now, if you get Lloyd, if you're not going all the way, don't mess with me. I'm not one that is going to start and stop." I said, "If I go, I'm going all the way, whether I like it or no." And at that time, when the vote was taken, it was only blacks sitting there. I had one fellow to sit with me at that time, John Culpepper. I think he left ACIPCO right after. He left on his own. They didn't bother him. But that day it was only black, and I think they didn't have any whites that sat with us. They had all turned back at the time. I didn't want it, but I told them I was going all the way because a black union at ACIPCO wouldn't have meant nothing. It was just all black. It wouldn't have been anything because they would have run you off. Well, we lost by about five or six hundred. We went from six hundred to three hundred, I think it was.

There were other efforts after that. The next effort came along, and actually the president wanted to know what they could do. You know, a lot of times when things happen, folks want to find out what can be done to better the situation. I got up a committee. It was about two whites and two blacks, and we went to talk with the president. We told him what the things were. Before that, you could walk in the boss man's office, and he would say, "I got a record on you, and if you don't straighten up, your record is going to get you out of here." Well, a lot of times he wouldn't open it up. He didn't tell you what was in your record. He didn't tell you how you got your record.

But he could have written anything down in there, and you didn't know about it. I told him then that what we needed was them to let us know when they put something in our record and what it was about. We needed better jobs. They promised us then that they wouldn't have hidden records. They would pull that out, and they did.

The next time the union came up I was totally against it because the way that they were doing it. They weren't completely right, but a union wasn't going to help us in the other situation either.

Normally, white workers thought they were being mistreated from their work hours. They thought that they weren't making enough money. They were making some money, but they should have been making more, and they figured if they had got a union in there they could have been making more money on the hour than they were. That was the main thing. But after they got into it, they found out what this union man thought. He said, "If we get a union in there, the blacks are going to get as much as the whites, and they are not going to be different." That's when they started having private meetings, and that split the workforce by race.

[So] at ACIPCO you didn't have a union. At that time they had an auxiliary board. That would consist of twelve blacks. They were elected for a two-year period. The blacks voted for the blacks. Then you had a board of operatives that was white. Now, we had to vote for them, but they couldn't vote for us. We would go in with our complaints that our folks gave us, give it to them, and then they would take it further. A lot of times the president would meet with us about our complaints, but you know how they were sometimes. He would listen, but you didn't have any power. But it was a sham. A few years later somebody filed a suit, and now they're all together. You don't have two different boards. I was on that board. The year I ran, I ran three years straight before I got elected. My slogan was, "If you want a man with courage, vote for Lloyd Harper." I stayed on about twelve years.

[At the time of the Montgomery bus boycott] I started collecting money, and that was dangerous at that time. If they knew about you collecting money for things like that, you could have lost your job. I started collecting money. That's when I met Shuttlesworth and Billups.[3] I came upstairs in the Pythian Temple building one day. I guess I had about three hundred dollars that I had collected from folks to send to Montgomery. So in a way I was involved in that. And the night that they organized, I was there.

The night they organized [ACMHR] they were at old Sardis [Baptist church], on the top of that hill up there. Well, it was very exciting because the man, the Sardis preacher, he was the one doing the most hollering. I can remember how he hollered, but I think he was the first to jump and backed out right after that. There were a lot of folks at that meeting.

I was in all of the meetings. I'm sure I went to Monday-night meetings like I could go to church. On Monday night I knew where I was going. A mass meeting was very exciting and very . . . a thing that looked like it was getting people together. It looked like it was something that was trying to get people's minds changed from one thing to another, and that's what we needed, because we didn't have a leader at that time. We needed something to help us to get off the way we were going, and we needed a leader. Fred Shuttlesworth was that leader at that time.

I don't know exactly when, but I was a registered voter because I went down to register to vote. I had already been once. They asked me had I been here before, and I told them no. I got registered that time. It had to be during the Movement because they were the ones doing the pushing. The first time I went I think all the questions or something, I couldn't pass them. I didn't pass them, and I didn't know all the senators and whatever they were asking, I didn't know. I think it was the probate judge, who was the senator from Alabama, and stuff like that. During that time I didn't know, I just went. But the next time I think I had it all. I was ready for them. But they didn't want me in there if I had been within six months, so I sort of fibbed. I told them, "No, I hadn't been down here before." I went on through, and I passed.

Well, they were asking at the Movement meeting for folks to do some things to help to promote it or to try to get folks into it. They were asking folks when they had just started, and I think one or two had rode the bus, and they had had some incidents. So I decided—it was in January, because my last child was born on January 1, 1960, and my other two children, Sharon and Edward, we went to see their mama that Sunday—when we come back, I said, "Well, we're going to ride the bus." So we parked our car downtown, and we caught the bus. When you catch a bus and you drop your money in that change thing, and you asked the driver, "Oh, I dropped too much money, and I want my money back." He said, "Your bad luck. You dropped it in there, that's it." So we dropped our money in the box, and this white man was sitting on the side, started raising so much sand. He asked the driver, "If you can't get him off, I'll get him off." Well, we were sitting on the front seat, and I asked my children, I said, "The bus driver says, 'How about you moving back?' I said, 'No.'" I asked my children, "Are y'all satisfied?" They said, "Yes, Daddy, we're satisfied." So I said, "Well, we're satisfied." So that's when this white fellow said, "If you can't get him off, then I'll get him off." The bus driver asked me, "Would you please get off?" I said, "Well, if you get me my money back, yeah, I'll get off."

He gave me my money back. And the next bus came along, and we caught it. We didn't have any trouble from the next one from the whites except a little grumbling, but we had one black lady in the back. I think she knew me, and she hollered, "Harper, won't you come back here where you belong?" I said, "Well, we satisfied up here, Miss, and we going to sit up here." So we sat there, and we came on out to Acipco, that's where we were living. Then I went back downtown later and picked up my car.

But in the marches, when the dogs were out there, I think I was down there one day, but I couldn't afford to go to jail because of ACIPCO. I was in the crowd, but I didn't participate in the marches. I knew if I went to jail, that was one thing ACIPCO was waiting on, and I didn't get into that.

I did the same thing for this effort in Birmingham. I would pick up dollars. I would get to folks that were actually afraid or weren't going. You know, you had some people that weren't going. I'd get money from them, and I would turn it in. If I couldn't make it that night, I would probably give it to Lola[4] or something like that for them to turn it in. I didn't have any difficulty in collecting money. They didn't mind giving it. A lot of them were afraid to go, or at least that's what they said, but they didn't mind giving money.

I knew both Dr. King and his wife. She was from the same town, Marion. I knew her. I met him during the time of the Movement. I met and talked with him and let him know that I was from Marion and I knew his wife. But Shuttlesworth was one that we knew each other from the start. The first time I met him and Billups was upstairs when I carried that money. That's when I met Fred Shuttlesworth, so he knows me personally.

I was a member of New Pilgrim. I went to New Pilgrim after that because I met Smith[5] in the Movement, and I went to New Pilgrim. I had been at Sixth Avenue.

Reverend Smith was very active. That's all I can say. I don't think we ever had a meeting at Sixth Avenue as far as I can remember.[6] I think Reverend Goodgame was there. I joined New Pilgrim the day they buried Goodgame. He was against it [the Movement]. I know that he talked about his turkeys that he wouldn't be able to get since the black folks were doing the things that the white folks didn't care much for. And now he wasn't going to be able to get his Christmas turkeys and stuff like that that they had been giving him.[7] He was one of the big men, and white folks were giving him turkeys. And since the "niggers" had gotten messed up in that now, they were going to cut his turkeys out. He was against the Movement. That was one of the reasons I left Sixth Avenue, because if I'm following you, but you're not doing the thing that I think is helping me to move up, then I don't think I need to follow you. And that was one of the reasons that I left, because Smith was in it. I wanted to follow somebody that was leading in the Movement.

My baby was born January 1, 1960, and I think about that time every Saturday night from twelve o'clock to day, I was guarding the church up there and Shuttlesworth's house. I did that every night, and I think I was gone the time when my wife was there, and I didn't know when the baby was going to happen. Sometimes I think about that now, but she didn't have any blame. She didn't say nothing about it. But every Saturday night from twelve o'clock, that was my guard night. I think that was one of the things that I contributed to, and I'm proud of it. Well, it was organized. You had folks there every night. They had different hours. Every night they were there. My night was Saturday night from twelve to seven in the morning, and that's where we stayed.

Normally, we sat and watched and walked around some. We had the porch there that we watched off of. I can't think of the man's name with the house now, that we watched off of. But that's where we watched. He had a screened-in porch. That way we could have a wide view of the church and the house. We had shotguns. I didn't see any strange thing happen on my time.

The day that Sixteenth Street Baptist was bombed, I was headed to Marion in my automobile when I heard the news. I couldn't drive. It shook me. It was very disturbing. I knew the photographer.[8] I knew him because he was in the Movement all the time.

Segregation and racism have been dealt with, but not effectively enough. I'm to the point now where I can go eat where I want to. I couldn't go eat then. I couldn't go nowhere. I had to sit on the back of the bus. That bothered me, and I needed to do something about it. But anywhere I go now, I can go in and sometimes when the family goes, my wife loves fish, and if there's anywhere they sell big fish, or somebody do good fish, she's going. We go up to Cullman somewhere up there every once in a while. It's about twenty-eight miles up that road. But when we walk in, the only blacks in there is us. But we don't feel like a nobody. They welcome you when you come in and when you go out, no problem. So what are we going to fight for now? I go where I want to, in a way. But segregation is still here. It's still in certain jobs. I guess if you start a thrust, you still going to have that.

I think that Birmingham and the Movement did a very good job in that day, but the only thing about it, when we get to a point, we stop. In other words, we have gotten somewhere, but we don't keep going on this road that we should be traveling on. We should still be fighting this segregation thing, and I think now this affirmative action thing is something that was helping us, but I think they are pushing it aside. Somebody needs to be doing something about it, but nobody wants to make a move, and it's just going to be a thing that will die because not enough of us are pushing it.

My opinion of the Million Man March is that it was a very good thing. I think that it's something that when you can get that many people together, that many black folks together, then it's beautiful. I hope that something will come out of it that's productive.

Edited by Horace Huntley. BCRI Oral History Project, vol. 16, sec. 2 (June 12, 1996).

Notes

1. The New Deal's Agricultural Adjustment Act provided cash payments to farmers for plowing under their crops. Large landowners benefited most. Between 1935 and 1940, however, the Resettlement Administration and its successor, the Farm Security Administration, did lend money to some southern tenants and sharecroppers to help them buy their own farms; about 21 percent of these loans went to blacks. William H. Harris, *The Harder We Run: Black Workers since the Civil War* (New York: Oxford University Press, 1982), 99–101; Larry A. Greene, "Blacks," in *Encyclopedia of American Economic History*, vol. 2, ed. Glenn Porter (New York: Scribner, 1980), 1009.

2. See Luther McKinstry interview in this volume for a discussion of the same problem at U.S. Steel.

3. Fred Shuttlesworth was president of the ACMHR, and Charles Billups was one of Shuttlesworth's assistants.

4. Lola Hendricks, the corresponding secretary of the ACMHR. See her interview, BCRI Oral History Project, vol. 1, sec. 4.

5. Rev. N. H. Smith, pastor of New Pilgrim Baptist church and secretary of the ACMHR. See his interview, BCRI Oral History Project, vol. 9, sec. 4.

6. The Movement was allowed to hold meetings there after Rev. John T. Porter became pastor in 1962.

7. Companies and wealthy white employers often made Christmas donations as a paternalistic gesture.

8. Chris McNair, whose daughter was one of the four little girls killed in the blast.

Elias Hendricks Sr.

Born January 14, 1924, in Boligee, Greene County, Alabama. One of thirteen children. Moved to Birmingham in 1941. Worked at Armour Packing and served as chairman of the grievance committee for the United Packinghouse Workers Union. Member of the ACMHR. *"My role was to handle grievances across the table. You sit down on one side of the table, and I'm on the other side working out an agreement for whatever kind of situation you got. And I can do that. But I can't have people calling me everything and doing everything to me and keep calm. I don't believe in nonviolence. I believe in self-defense. A man ain't nothing but a man."*

Fair Wages and Yours to Keep

My parents were raised in Boligee. When you go down Highway 11 you go through Eutaw. It's twelve miles on the other side, going west towards Mississippi. My parents had thirteen children. I was number six. Growing up in Boligee was awful at that time.

There was no money. You know, fifteen people had to eat at one time. We only farmed. We had to rent the land. At that time, that was all that people were doing. If you weren't cutting logs, you were farming.

I first started school when I was six years old. It was a pleasure to go to school, and I was a very apt child, and I learned fast at that point. I didn't get very much education, and I say that very humbly, because as soon as I got big enough to run I had to go to work. I had to work diligently to try to keep eating. Therefore, I didn't get the hours in the classroom that I needed to get, which I would have loved to have picked up. But you go back again to the numbers. You're talking about fifteen folks when you talk about the family. Fifteen folks got to eat. There could not be much time spent elsewhere at that time because it was during the Depression time.

On the farm you go to work as soon as you can do something. If you can't do anything but pick cotton when the cotton gets ready, you do that, or you do whatever you can do. We worked sunup to sundown. At the end of the crop-growing season you might have garments for everybody, but they soon wore out beyond what you could put on and go out in public with. I remember times when we wore our clothes in the daytime and washed them at night and wore them the next day because there was no clothes.

[Mother] would get up earlier. It was nothing for her to get up and serve us breakfast about seven o'clock, so she would have to get up two to three hours earlier, because she had a lot of food to cook. We would get the food and take off to the field. Going to the field was just a necessity. I didn't necessarily like it, because it wasn't comfortable enough to like it. I wanted to get out of the field. That's the reason I left Boligee at the age of sixteen.

I come to Birmingham. I had some people, an aunt, my daddy's two sisters were living here. So I came to stay with the oldest sister.

I was the first to come to Birmingham. There were some that left before me, but they went other places. Kentucky, a place called Verda, Kentucky. It's a mining area where they went to work in the mines, my two oldest brothers. Well, I never wanted to work in the mine. And I tell you, I never did. The conditions were of such that you just didn't encourage people to work there.

I worked construction for a good while. Then I started to work at the packinghouse, for Armour Packing Company. I spent a lot of time working for Armour. It wasn't any substance to it, because the packinghouse was the big company, and they were able to pay a little bit more than the rest of the people. And I enjoyed it. I worked there until they closed the plant, twenty-something years ago.

I served in the union. I was the financial secretary for our district union. The headquarters was in Atlanta. I worked there as a butcher until it finally went out of business. Any jobs that had a union was paying fair wages. If a guy didn't have a union to insist on them giving minimum wage, they would do whatever they wanted to. So everybody wanted to be in a union, so what little you did make, it was yours to keep rather than somebody just reaching in the pocket and get whatever they wanted. Payday they might just decide they want some of your money.

I was drafted into the army in World War II and served some time overseas. I worked for Armour a while before, so when I came out of the army, I had a job with Armour, and I went back. That's when I got involved with the union. I had some military training, and along with some other training I was able to get, I was in a position to handle that sort of thing.

But Birmingham was still like Birmingham. There was nothing to write home about. We were in an environment that just wasn't conducive to decent things for black folks. Everywhere, whether you were in the union or out of the union, you still was one of those people when it come around to it. I think when the decision was made back somewhere, the *Dred Scott* decision,[1] they said that a black man had no rights that a white man have to respect, and those guys lived up to that kind of thinking, that kind of training, and they were able to get away with it.

I lived right there down the street, between Third and Fourth Avenue and Fourteenth Street.

My oldest aunt lived there, and when I came to Birmingham I lived with my oldest aunt until I went to the military. And when I came back I spent a few months with my oldest aunt. I was still single. I went back to Armour, and I decided I wanted to buy me a house. I never rented me a house. I bought a house. I've never been a renter. All of my adult life I've been in a house that I bought. The first one was out in the Acipco area. I got the chance to have a house built in a little place called Ellsberry Park.

On the question of race, as the little boy would say, "Don't even talk about it." There was bad people and worse people, because our organization was always integrated. White people at that time felt that we had no right that the white man had to respect. They dealt with us in that vein. Well, the organization . . . we had a very liberal union, and our advantage was most of the members were black. There were white members there, but most of the membership was black. And our headquarters was in Chicago. Those kind of things kind of played it in a way that it wouldn't have been, had it not been for these.

At a point, black men basically controlled the union. We were always into something. I was, for a long time, chairman of the grievance committee, which handled the grievance whenever a problem came up. It was our job to settle it, and I happened to be the president of our local union, as well as the district financial secretary-treasurer of the district union, with its headquarters in Atlanta.

There were cases, but we kept ours under pretty good control, and the reason why we kept it under control, our headquarters was in Chicago. Chicago at that time was like, people would say, "It's heaven there," and that sort of thing. If we got into a little racial problem, we could expect the international union to come and straighten it out. They came in so much because those kind of things happened. At that time, those white people felt, and I still feel that a lot of them think, that we had no rights that they had to respect. But the union would deal with the situation based on the facts in the case. We had the handbook right there, and the handbook says this is it.[2]

There were a lot of repercussions due to my union activity. I'm trying to figure out the worst situation. When they finally decided to integrate the union, because they had separate bathhouses and separate everything, we decided to integrate and make it all one thing. Naturally, as the secretary-treasurer, I had to lead the way, and I was the first one they put in jail. The company had me arrested, and naturally the city fathers and law enforcement folks were glad to do it for them. That was back in the forties.

I was tentatively involved when the Movement first started. I had a problem that I always had to deal with. I had a temper, and certain people could say certain things, or they would do certain things, and then I'm going to come back. I don't care what nobody say. Realizing that, I kind of stayed out of the heat of things. My coworkers saw to it that you could do some things, but you can't do this thing because you can't take such and such a thing. I respect them for that. I have to agree that at a point I would overdo. So I listened to them.

Demonstrations I didn't do. I never went to a march. My family demonstrated, demonstrated, and demonstrated. But I knew some of the things they did to my sisters and brothers. If I was out there getting beat, it would be, okay, no: it wasn't going to be okay. If you stepped on my foot . . . I knew how much of that I could take. When they were in jail, they just threw them in there and treated them like they were animals. They could take it, but I knew myself well enough to know that I could do some things, but there are some things that I can't do. So I stayed out of that sort of thing.

My role was to handle grievances across the table. You sit down on one side of the table, and I'm on the other side working out an agreement for whatever kind of situation you got. And I can do that. But I can't have people calling me everything and doing everything to me and keep calm.

I don't believe in nonviolence. I believe in self-defense. A man ain't nothing but a man. Everybody understood that. I understood how I felt about it and didn't mind telling people how I felt about it, and they finally gave me a name. He's a fool. So I wore the name very well. I had to work where I could work. I knew myself, and I knew some of the things that the guys did to some of the people, that it wasn't the kind of thing that I was prepared to accept. So I tried to keep myself out of it.

I went to some of the mass meetings, but when they got to the nitty-gritty and go to jail for so many days, no. That wasn't my bag. My family was good at it. They could do it. But I couldn't do it. I know my limit. I know how far I can allow anybody to push.

The civil rights movement would have not been able to do a lot of the things that they were able to do had it not been for the labor movement, because they [unions] could get in some doors that black people just couldn't get in. They were, incidentally, helping us the only way that they could. I think they did more of providing things and actually getting behind doors and talk about things and talk about how to get from here to there. That sort of thing.

Edited by Horace Huntley. BCRI Oral History Project, vol. 20, sec. 5 (Aug. 30, 1996).

Notes

1. *Dred Scott v. Sanford,* U.S. Supreme Court decision, 1857. See Colin A. Palmer, *Passageways: An Interpretive History of Black America,* vol. 1, (Fort Worth, Tex.: Harcourt Brace, 1998), 190–92.

2. On the nationwide influence of Chicago workers in the United Packinghouse Workers of America, see Rick Halpern, *Down on the Killing Floor: Black and White Workers in Chicago's Packinghouses, 1904–54* (Urbana: University of Illinois Press, 1997); Roger Horowitz, *"Negro and White, Unite and Fight!": A Social History of Industrial Unionism in Meatpacking, 1930–90* (Urbana: University of Illinois Press, 1997).

Rosa P. Washington

Born July 8, 1912, in Davenport, Alabama. Worked at Birmingham Greyhound bus station and witnessed police and mob actions against Freedom Riders. *"At nine, ten o'clock, somewhere along that time, a big, burly, heavyset policemen with a K-9 on leash and his billy stick and [hand]cuffs jingling on his hip came in the station. A well-dressed tall man was with him. I believed him to be a detective, and they passed me, but just before they got out of earshot from me, I heard one of them say, 'Tell me . . . I hear one of these little niggers will be praying this morning. I want to hear what he is going to tell God when I turn this dog loose on his black ass.' That brought a shudder. I just started spot sweeping and running, trying to hear what was going to be said or done."*

"A Job Where White Folks Work and Not Ride Around Kicking Dirt on Me"

I was born in a little town called Davenport, Alabama, about twenty-five miles south of Montgomery. My father was from the same town. He was a sharecropper farmer, and he had three brothers in that area, which is why he hesitated so long to move to Birmingham. The youngest brother came to Birmingham and went to work. My father, he didn't come until I said I wanted to see white men work rather than riding around kicking dirt on me. My mother, on the other hand, grew up in a little town called Sandy Ridge, not too far from Greenville, Alabama.

My parents were very diligent, hard-working people. My daddy didn't go any further than the third or fourth grade. My mother went to the fifth. They had two children, one boy and one girl. My brother and I are thirteen years apart, he being the oldest and I the baby.

One day during my childhood, while I was still living in Davenport, I was playing in a large cotton basket. My parents were hoeing, and the owner of the farm came riding by on his big stallion horse. He rode up beside my basket where I was playing and threw candy in the basket to me. The horse he was riding kicked dirt in the basket on me. I became angry, jumped up, and turned the basket upside down and went running down the road calling my daddy. The man was right behind me with his horse, and daddy didn't like that. My dad asked, "Why are you chasing her?" He said, "She didn't want me to give her candy. She poured it out because the horse kicked dirt in her basket." And I asked Daddy, "When are you going to get a job where white folks work and not ride around kicking dirt on me?" My daddy really wanted to please me because I was his little girl. I told him [the owner] I didn't think that he was doing any work; he was just riding around to harass me. My daddy dropped to his knees and locked his arms around me.

My mother had always been after him for a while to leave and come to Birmingham and find work. When she got to the area where he was still holding me, she asked him, "Why you holding that child like that, and she's screaming, and both of you wringing wet with sweat?" He jumped and looked at her as if she dropped out of space. He didn't realize who she was, and he took a deep breath and let me go. When we got home to dinner, he just kept looking at me. He cut his eyes at my mother and looked at me again. He said to my mother, "Can you handle the farm at harvesting time? I'm going to Birmingham and look for me a job. I don't intend for my girl child to ask me the question that she asked me today." My mother responded, "What?" He told her that I said, "Why couldn't you get a job where white folks work and not drive around kicking dirt on me?" My mama was glad. She told him, "Well, don't worry, just don't worry." But she felt like getting up and hugging me to death for telling him that. She was ready to leave the farm and sharecropping behind. So when harvesting time came, he came to Birmingham and was fortunate enough to find a job.

I was not quite eight years old when we moved to Birmingham. When we came to Birmingham, the first job that my father worked was in a plant called ACIPCO. My daddy rented a house for a year in Acipco.[1] He said he couldn't get the kind of house he wanted, but he bought the property later and built an expensive house. He had the intentions of eventually selling it, leaving the South when I started to high school. His health prevented him from doing that. He worked at ACIPCO from 1920 to 1931 until he had a stroke. My mother never worked outside the home.

The Acipco community was the common scene in those days of hard-working people, and most of the homes were rental property. There were a few homeowners on Twenty-sixth Avenue and further up. The area where I lived, the alley divided my area from the whites after you passed Twenty-ninth Avenue or Twenty-eighth Alley. Everyone on that side was all white. Quite a few of the people that lived there worked for ACIPCO. Some worked at Dickie Clay plant or at the Ensley plant.

I attended a school called West Acipco School. I thought it was fantastic because we had a school building. It wasn't quite large enough for all the classes, so [from] the first through the third [we] went to school in a church nearby. The school was actually owned by ACIPCO initially. Then, in the later years, I don't remember exactly what year, but there was a Mr. Walker, and he was living in a two-story building, and when ACIPCO changed and turned the school over to the public school system, he made those men move out of that building. Then they deeded the school to the Birmingham school system; that building was called a "domestic science building." This is where they taught you table manners, boys how to escort girls in a building, and how to put the chair up to the table and let the girl sit down to eat. They taught us to make beds and how to clean houses. They taught sewing and some shoe repair.

When I finished Acipco, I went to Lincoln. I guess you would call it a middle school. I went to Lincoln from the ninth through the tenth grade. Then I went to Industrial High. Industrial High at that time was termed to be the largest high school in the world for black folk. I thought it was great. Professor Parker was the principal of the school, and he always stressed, don't soil these uniforms. The girls wore blue and the boys wore khaki until they got into the twelfth grade. After that, the girls had to wear white and the men wore dark suits, blue trousers or blue suit. We were immaculately dressed at Industrial High.[2]

"Don't Get Hurt about Your Color"

Back in those days in Industrial High School there were a number of areas that one could sort of concentrate in. There was dress making, beauty culture, carpentry, shoe making, tailoring, and printing. I was interested in dramatics. In the eleventh grade, I was in the training for the leading-lady part—every part had two persons to see which one would handle it the best. I was given the part, and I was so proud of being the leading lady. "The mistress," as it was called. I would perform before my family and friends on the school grounds. My friends, they would say, "Rosy, you got it, you got it!" Edna Elliot and I had the same part. When I would practice, the teacher would usually reply by saying I had done well. Then Edna would come up. Edna didn't remember her lines in some instances, then the teacher would tell her that she wasn't putting enough action into it. When it was over, Mrs. Wyatt told me,

"Rosa, you performed beautifully, and I admire the way you have learned and studied. But this part is for a white mistress, and you are too dark for that part. I'll give it to Edna."

Children now would have thrown a fit on her, but I didn't. I picked up my books, and I tried to keep from crying as I went across the campus. When I got to another classroom, I met Mrs. Mahalia Morris, and she was a very dark woman. She taught math, and she called me "Acipco Skinny" because I didn't weigh ninety pounds. She said, "Acipco Skinny, what's wrong with you? You act like you're about to explode." I said, "I'm all right." She stopped me. She said, "No you're not. What's wrong?" Then I burst out and started crying and told her what had been said to me. She said, "Don't let nobody put you down. Dry your tears." And she said, "Everybody knows that I know this book that I carry [referring to the math book]." She was teaching math and algebra. She said, "I found an error in this book that the company had to recall when I sent it to them. I got big bucks for it. I will defy anybody to do more with the teaching of these subjects than I can." She responded, "That's what you do. Don't get hurt about your color. God made us all."

That experience had an impact in my life for a while. While I was in school and as a youngster I felt put down because for years the lighter people tried to put the darker-skinned people aside. At that time, Parker had [more] lighter-complexioned and fair-skinned teachers than they did darker teachers. This was because that's what Professor Parker stressed according to some of the teachers. This had an effect on some of the other children. Some would often say that they felt it, too. Our majorettes and your various other teams mirrored that kind of mentality to some degree. But if you were really good, they had to acknowledge it and allow you to be on the team.[3]

During that time our community's relationship with the Birmingham Police Department was absolutely horrible. Whenever they would come in the neighborhood, if it were next-door, you could hear them banging if you were in your bed because they always knocked so severely hard. Some young men told me that they would roll down the window and ask them some questions and then roll it up so they wouldn't be able to get their head out, and then they would beat them on their heads.

After I finished Industrial High School, I worked as a means of saving some money to go to college. My father had had a stroke; he couldn't afford to send me. I met this young man who had come down from Pittsburgh to visit his father, and we fell in love. He asked me if I would marry him. I told him I wanted to go to college. He said, "Well, if you marry me, I'll take you back to Pittsburgh and send you to Penn State." But after we were married, he took me up to Penn State nearly every Sunday and Saturday for whatever they had up there for entertainment. He'd take me up there for that purpose only. I told him, "I'm tired of going up there just sightseeing. I want to go in." He said, "Well, when I can get a better job I'll send you." The second year we were up there, he contracted tuberculosis, and I didn't get a chance to go to college. After years of our marriage, he passed, and I moved back to Birmingham. My father had also passed. My brother had a tragedy in the family, and the mother of his children died. They had five children, and I was left to take care of all the children. I was home a year and a month, and again tragedy struck; I lost my mother in death. I was crushed because so many tragic things had happened in my life in such a short time.

After all this I went to work at Newberry's [a five-and-dime store]. My mother was on welfare, and I had to report her death, and when I reported it she was only getting twenty-five dollars a month, and they asked me was I working. I said, "Yes." They asked me, "How much do you earn?" I replied, "Seven dollars a week." Then they stated to me, "Well, that's more than we allow for a family your size." So they cut me off. I told them, "I'm just keeping my brother's children, and they are not my children." They said, "We'll have to cut you off, and you support the children on your own." That was extremely rough. Six people were to be taken care of on seven dollars a week.

Need to Work and Retaining Dignity

At Newberry's I was a maid. There was a dress shop there then, and I worked there. On Mondays and Thursdays I had to work at the manager's house. When I worked, they would go party and come in at one and two o'clock and take me home, and yet I was still expected to be at work at the same time at the store as usual. So when the maid quit at my manager's home, she kept having me washing back and forth from her home to mine. She continued to tell me that they would let me work at their home after the maid quit, and I told her that I couldn't stay as late as I had already been there. I asked for more money, and she said she couldn't pay me any more money because when I worked there I got three meals a day. Whereas if I were at the store, I would have had to pay for my lunch and eat my breakfast at home or bring my lunch to work with me. So giving me three meals a day, in her opinion, would supply that income. They kept working me like that until a friend of my family moved from the farm, and I carried her on the job. She [her boss] kept her [her friend], and I continued going to work on Mondays and Thursdays.

One morning when I got there, I was making my breakfast, and I told her that I couldn't get there at seven because of my responsibilities. I would come at the same time I went to the store, and she asked me, "Rosa, why is it that Mamie has to be here at seven o'clock to get Manny's [her husband's] breakfast to get him off to work, and she has had her breakfast? You show up at nine, and you making your breakfast." I said in response, "I beg your pardon?" I understood her, but I wanted to see if she would repeat it, and she did. I said, "Well, these were your plans. You told me you couldn't pay any more money, and three meals would be a supplement to my salary." "Don't stand there and do your proper talking and bucking your big eyes at me. When you got to work with them five youngins, you get to work when you can." I also told her, "If you can show me God Almighty's handwriting on the wall, telling me I got to work for a poor-ass Jew like you, I'll be here till hell freezes over."

She said something else snazzy to me, and I reached for her. I forgot that I had put the clothes that were soaking on a barstool—she did not have a washing machine, so I had to wash them by hand. As I reached for her, the water and clothes went all over the place, and the girl that was working said to me, "Don't you do that! What's the matter with you?" I told her, "Take your hands off of me. If you hadn't flapped your lips, she wouldn't know what to say to me. Let me get out of here." So I grabbed my work clothes and made a dash for the door. The white lady told me, "You needn't show up at the store." I said, "Who would want to show up at that store? I'm sick of you Jews," and I left. I had children, seventy-five cents between heaven and hell, the poor house, and me. On the top of all that, I had to use a dime of that money to get home.

When I got to town I used a nickel to call my date to tell him that I would be available to go and see Duke Ellington, who was coming to town that night. He said, "Well, child, let me go get the tickets before they go up at ten o'clock." After that I went home.

That night I went to see Duke Ellington. When I woke the next morning I said, "My gosh, it's Thursday, and I'd rather wait until the first of the week and go see about a job." So I got the children their breakfast, and I went back to bed. At about ten o'clock, my best friend through the years came to see me. She said, "Girl, what in the world is wrong with you? I called the store, and they say you weren't there. I called the house, and the woman almost hung up in my face telling me you weren't there." So I told her what had happened. She told me, "Well, God bless you. The Lord takes care of fools and babies. With this heavy responsibility you have, you have walked off of your job." She continued to tell me about how her boss at Greyhound, Mr. Townsend, had been observing me. He had made the statement that "I admire that girlfriend of yours that comes here. She does not wrestle and tussle and chase the porters. She just stands around and waits until you can talk to her, and she is very courteous and polite." He told me one day, "You keep hanging around here,

I'm going to put you to work and not give you a dime." I said, "Well, we'll see about that."

He told her to come and get me and see if I would work. I left home and got to the station at eleven o'clock. When I got there, they sent me to Dr. Thuss for a physical, and he didn't show up until 4:30 to give me an exam. When he arrived, he told his nurse that that day had been one hectic day, and he was so tired. He started to pull off his coat. She quickly said, "Don't undress yet. Greyhound has someone here." He said, "What's wrong with him?" She stated, "It's not a he." He then said to me, "Come here, Catherine." That was my friend's name. The nurse said, "No, she's not Catherine. Her name is Rosa, and I don't know anything about Rosa." So when I walked in, she told him I was to be there for my physical so that I may be hired. He said, "Stick out your tongue." He put a paddle in my mouth and had me say "ah," and he took my pulse. Then he said, "Do you have a hernia?" I said, "No." "Do you have hemorrhoids?" I said, "No." He wrote me out a statement saying that I could be hired. He told me, "You go on. If they don't hire you, I will [hire you] here and give you another exam." They hired me, and I worked at Greyhound for thirty-seven years and four months.

"Don't Jump My Gun"

At Greyhound I was a maid. My duties were to take care of the white and colored waiting rooms. My responsibilities were also to keep the baggage room and the ticket offices swept. This period I am speaking of was a time that this society was totally segregated. This is how it manifested in this bus station.

There were separate waiting rooms, separate bathrooms and restrooms. The larger part of the ticket window faced the white lobby, and there was one small window that would serve the blacks. The agents sometimes would just stand there and wait on all the whites that were in front of them and not take turns and turn around and wait on those at the black window. The only ticket window exposed to the black area was about a two-foot square opening. There were three or four ticket windows for the white people on the white side of the station.

The white waiting room had about six toilets and washrooms. Two of them were washrooms where you paid a quarter to go in, and you could stay for as long as you wanted and wash up in a face bowl. The other washrooms, there was a face bowl out for the entire public to use. In the colored waiting room, as it was called then, there were benches with dividers on them. Sometimes there were two armed chairs available, so if you ordered food, you ring a bell for your food, and they would bring the food to the black passengers, and they would sit there and eat. If there were more people ordering, they would have to sit on those benches and eat their food.

Sometimes the white people that I worked for would jump my gun, and I would be a very outspoken person if they pushed me too far. To give an example of what I mean about jumping my gun, we had a mop pail that you had to use to hold the water. The bucket had a lever, and we had to push down on this lever and pull up on the mop to wring it out. It had been broken for about three months, and the manager kept promising and promising to get it fixed. One day, the thing popped loose and hit me on my leg, and it was so painful. As dark as I am, the mark on my leg was just fire-red, but it didn't break the skin. I went in the office, and I told him, "Mr. Drennen, look at my leg. What are you going to do, wait until that scrub bucket injure us? We have been tying it with rope and string and whatever else we could find to keep it together. I don't want my leg broken." He replied, "Oh, I just forgot." I said, "Well, if you give me the money, I'll walk down to Wimbley and Thomas on Morris Avenue and Twentieth Street and get the bucket." But I was too black and proud to walk that far carrying that heavy bucket. I used a dime for trolley fare. When I got back, I gave him the receipt for the bucket and counted out the change, and I told him I used a dime for transportation. He stated, "What are you talking about? I didn't authorize you for transportation. That's company money." I said, "Well, I'll tell the company that you didn't give us supplies, and I had to go get it, and I think I'm entitled to transportation." He told me, "You are going to give me my dime!" And I turned and walked off from him. Every so often he would ask me, when he would see me working, to give him back his dime. I would just look at him, smile, and walk off.

I was cleaning the white lobby, sweeping in the lobby, and a white woman's baby soiled. She asked me to go and get her some wet paper towels or whatever to clean the baby. When I brought her the soap, wet towels, and some dry ones to clean her baby, she gave me two dimes and a nickel as a tip, and I thanked her. Mr. Drennen was standing not too far off, and he called me. He said, "Rosa, come here." When I walked over to him he said, "I saw that woman give you two dimes and a nickel. Now give me my dime." I said, "I don't have your dime." He said again, "Give me my dime. You owe me a dime for the money you took out for trolley fare." I said, "I couldn't afford to walk six blocks carrying that heavy bucket, and that's why I used the dime." He stated, "Well, what are you talking about? There are hundreds of colored women who would be glad to walk not only six blocks but six miles for the salary you are making." I jabbed the broom handle in his chest and told him, "Well, the first one that comes along, tell her to start sweeping." He handed it back to me and made the statement, "You better get this floor swept." So I went on and swept the floors. He didn't bother me about the dime any longer.

When I finished sweeping, I went to check the ladies' lounge. The cashier and owner of the restaurant came dashing in behind me. She said, "You better be glad that Mr. Owens is a kind-hearted gentleman. Any other boss would have fired you with your sassy talk." I said, "If I was slinging hash for you, I guess you would have fired me? But before I let anybody drag me down I would crawl the street on my hands and knees and pick peanuts out of elephant droppings." She said, "Well, Miss Rosa." I replied, "Thank you," and went about my business. For the life of my stay there, she referred to me as "Miss Rosa." It was highly unusual for a white woman to say "Miss" to a black woman.

Another incident took place when the Traveler's Aid booth [attendant] was in the lobby, and one day she called me to come to her and said, "Rosa, I want to ask you something. You're intelligent, and I like to talk with you. Which of your people do you have the most respect for?" I replied, "What did you say?" Then she stated, "Which of your people do you have the most respect for, the lighter-skinned or the darker-skinned?" I said to her, "Be they white, black, mulatto, Indian, Sioux, or Crow, the people that do most for humanity are the people that we look up to." She replied, "Thank you, Miss Rosa." I was "Miss Rosa" to her from then on. I would not back off any of them. I didn't take anything from anyone. My father always told me, "Whoever you are talking to or whoever is talking to you, you look them in the eye. Don't get an itch somewhere, or some dirt on your foot, squirm, or look off. Look them in the eye."

In 1961 I moved from Acipco to a community called Enon Ridge. My community was not active in the Movement. I had to join the NAACP through my church, Thurgood CME church on the corner of Center Street and Sixth Avenue. When they allowed us to vote, I registered to vote. The process was a simple process for me. We were eligible to vote, so we went to the register's office, and they asked us questions about different political areas. I also attended some of the mass meetings of the ACMHR. Dr. King preached a couple of sermons at the AOH Church of God that was located on Seventh Avenue and Eighteenth Street at that time.

I was still working at the bus station in 1961. There was a group of students from the North that came, and they were called the "Freedom Riders." I was sweeping what they called the white waiting room then, facing Nineteenth Street. The entrance to the black waiting room was facing the back. I was so nervous and tense because I had heard that they were coming, and it was Mother's Day. There were two front entrances. One would let you out, and the other one was supposed to be the enter door. When I heard the doors, which made a *sss* sound, I looked around and saw those young blacks coming in. Some went in the dining room, some went in the men's room, and four went in the ladies' room. When they went in, the white women rushed out as if a wild animal had gone in there. They acted as if they were traumatized.

When the news got back to the manager of the restaurant, he came running down. He ran towards the restaurant, stopped, and snapped his fingers as he was passing the water fountain, turned back around, and yanked the wiring out of the wall so there would be no cool water. He then rushed down to the restaurant, and when he got there the blacks were in there, so he tried to get them out. He had a worker stand at the door to not let any more in, and those that were in there were trying to order food. He demanded that the workers remove the food from the steam table and leave the menus out for the whites. That brought tears to my eyes. Black and white hands prepared the food, and both black and white hands were removing it. Yet black and white could not sit in the same room and eat that food. The only Freedom Riders I saw were all black, although I was later told that some whites came with them. This same day, some of them were attacked by an angry white mob, but I didn't witness that. Their bus had been set afire in Anniston.

We had a commissioner form of government back then. Bull Connor was the commissioner over the Birmingham Police and Fire Departments. The news was broadcasting about the Freedom Riders coming. So he went to the city-limit line and waited for them. When they got there, he flagged the bus down and stopped it. He then boarded the bus and told them not to come into Birmingham—they weren't welcomed here. He had a regiment of policemen with him. So they turned around and told him that they will be back. This is exactly what they did. Then Bull Connor brought his regiment to the bus station. They were out on the loading zone where the buses came in. They were cursing and saying ugly things about what was going to happen when the damn "niggers" get to the station. That made me tense and afraid because I couldn't tell if anyone was mean enough to throw a bomb in the station to kill me and everyone else. I waited nervously.[4]

The four girls that went into the restroom really scared the whites to death. This one little white woman sat near the door where she could see the track and get to the restroom before time for her to get on the bus. She looked up, she said, "Well, here's them damn niggers." She rushed into the lounge, and I tried to console her. I stepped forward to console her, and she let me know that she didn't want to be bothered with the Freedom Riders, nor with me. I worked the relief shift, and I was supposed to get off that day at 3:30, but I chose to stick around a little longer, even though I knew I had to be back the next morning at seven o'clock. When I got home I was so nervous, and I didn't rest well.

When I arrived that next morning they were still there. I brought my breakfast and lunch to work with me. When I went into the ladies' lounge to clean, three girls were in there gagging, perspiring, and half crying. I asked them, "Have you had any food?" They said, "No, ma'am." I said, "Well, I brought my lunch and my breakfast, I'll share it with you, or I'll get permission to go to the A&P up on the corner and get you some food or some juice." They both stepped forward and looked me in the eye. "No, ma'am. Thank you. We will not accept your food. We are dedicated to change. And if you give us food, you're helping to defeat our cause." The four of us embraced each other, locked arms, and cried.[5]

About nine, ten o'clock, somewhere along that time, a big, burly, heavyset policeman with a K-9 on leash and his billy stick and handcuffs jingling on his hip came in the station. A well-dressed tall man was with him. I believed him to be a detective, and they passed me, but just before they got out of earshot from me, I heard one of them say, "Tell me . . . I hear one of these little niggers will be praying this morning. I want to hear what he is going to tell God when I turn this dog loose on his black ass." That brought a shudder. I just started spot sweeping and running, trying to hear what was going to be said or done. A little bit after they got out there, a young black man, I wish I knew who he was, stepped up on the float, that's the wagon used to push the luggage, locked his hands behind his back, and raised his face towards heaven, and he prayed. I don't remember all of his prayer, but this he said: "Dear God, we keep their houses, we take care of their children, we prepare their food. Please, God, tell these pharaohs to let your people go. All we want is to choose our place to sit down." That touched that police officer and me too. A little bit later, both of the white men came through the station with stern looks on their faces. The fat one was batting his eyes. I can't swear it was tears, but he was patting his face as if there were tears.

The students stayed there until later on in the evening. But later on, Attorney General Robert Kennedy called the station and told some of the officials to get the Freedom Riders out of Birmingham and go to Montgomery, where they were supposed to continue their traveling. Mr. Hunt and Mr. G. J. Owens were the officials who got the call, as the other employees told me. Attorney General Kennedy called and told them to get them on their way, and a bus driver by the name of Joe Cabinero took them on to Montgomery. I was told that the policemen escorted them out of the city to the city limit.

My working hours didn't allow me to march during the Movement. Although I once did walk down to Booker T. Washington's school on my lunch break, and I witnessed the fire department turning the hoses on the children. They had them connected and tried to spray the children with the forceful water, but nothing came out. I witnessed that attempt from the fire department to hose the marchers. This experience couldn't help but bring tears to my eyes. I was saddened and almost afraid to walk the street alone. Some whites were arrogant toward all blacks.

But the change came. Mr. Herman Hardy was a porter, and they got him into being assistant supervisor in Greyhound. In '63, up until the Freedom Riders, everybody black was classified as porters, maids, and cleaners. We were all considered as being class-B employees. Ticket agents, baggage agents, express agents, and office personnel were all white. As a result of the Freedom Riders, this all changed. But in order to get into these higher job classifications, the employers had a question-and-answer elimination program. I tried to get my best friend, who got me the job, to take the test. She was leery about taking it, but she got sick and couldn't. I told her I was off and I would come to see her, and she asked me to stop by the terminal and get her a sick claim. While I was there, it hit me like a thunderbolt. When I turned around and I saw the manager, I asked him if I could take the test. He said, "Well, Miss Rosa, you're older now." I said, "Both of us are ten minutes older than we were when we walked in here." He said some more remarks. I said, "Are you telling me you're not going to allow me to take the test?" He stated, "No, I didn't say that. Well, you're not like the porters. They have been exposed to it because they have to handle the baggage." His secretary was a racist. The entire time we were talking she was just bowing and looking and cutting her eyes at him and at me. So he told me that three or four porters had taken the test, and they failed. After telling me this, I said again, "You're not going to let me. . . ." He responded, "Yes, you can get it." He just kind of chuckled and said to me that it is going to be kind of hard.

When I finished taking the test, he said, "Well, what time do you come to work?" I said, "I'm off today." "Well, I'll have it graded when you come back." I said, "I'm off today, and I can stay here until you get time to do it." To pass the test, you needed to score a sixty-four. Well I passed the test—I made a sixty-nine. I was a maid. So now I was supposed to go to the information department where the jobs were previously all white.

They had at the same time a bus driver who had bad health. They had him to stop driving buses and he was put in the baggage room to work. When he learned that I had passed and the shift was posted, he started watching me. If I went out to the dumpster, he'd run and peep to see where I went. If I went to go around to the colored waiting room, he was peeping to see where I was.

Some of the other fellows would make comments saying, "He's watching you, he's watching you." So one day I started out, and he saw me going but he didn't see where I had gone. He ran back and looked to see if he could find me; he couldn't see me. I hid down in a telephone booth. He came to the window peeping and while he was peeping out of the window a customer came up, a shipper. He started writing the shipper up. It was three minutes to four o'clock. I had to sign in before four o'clock. I signed the sign-in sheet, and he saw me—he came running back there. "You needn't be signing them, you needn't be signing. I'm too old to be working back here. I'm tired of lifting all this mess. I'm going into information, you're not going." I said, "That's your privilege," and I turned and walked off.

When I was in that area they continued to mistreat me. When the luggage or packages from the waiting room were too heavy, the men would tell the customers through the window that was exposed to the white waiting room to come around inside the baggage room to pick up their luggage. But when I started, they told me I couldn't do that. I had to lift it. They disqualified me on those grounds because I couldn't lift the luggage like I should. But God took care of that. He wasn't there two months before they called him in, and I went to information. So I would eventually get the position that I was supposed to have. But in the beginning, because of that white man, I had to go into the baggage area to work.

So after he left, the shift was open. My vacation was coming up in about two or three weeks after. They let somebody work double shifts until I returned from vacation. When I got back, one of the black men had passed the test—a porter. They put him in the information area. When I came back, I asked, "How did he get in there, since I had more seniority?" They told me blah, blah, blah. So in return I went to the union representative. He told me, "Well, when Wednesday comes, you just go on in there. You're qualified." Wednesday rolled around, I went in there, the guy, whose name [was] Johnny Green, was sitting in there. The supervisors who were monitoring us heard our voices, so they called Johnny out and decided that one of the ticket agents would help me in that area instead of him. The other woman that worked in the information booth with me would meet me every morning so I could share my breakfast with her. She sat with her back to me and was so hostile and ugly to me even though she ate my food.

While working, I tried so hard, but they wouldn't let me take a manual home to study. One night I was seeing a relative off, and I was carrying her luggage, and Mr. Jim Nalley, who was a very liberal man, saw me. He said, "Rosa, where you going?" I told him. He said, "Well, I want you to come into the dispatcher's office before you leave." When I went in, he said, "I hear that they are thinking about disqualifying you, but if anybody can do this job, I know you can. You have a pleasant voice, and you read. You can see, and I know they did not treat you right. They gave you two days' training rather than two weeks of training like they gave everybody else. I'm going to have you know what you're doing when you leave here tonight." I stayed, and he told my husband, "You can sit down over there, or you can go back to your car and lay down. But when Rosa goes out of here, she is going to know how to find her routings." He kept me in there from 9:15 until he was off at twelve o'clock.

The next morning, I was off, and my husband woke me up. He had prepared breakfast. I told him, "Oh, you so smart, you fixing breakfast, and it's not Saturday morning." He had always made breakfast Saturday morning. He said, "Yes, if God put Mr. Nalley into your life to strengthen you to keep your job, I'm your husband, I'm going to stick closer than he did. You're not going to do anything today but eat, sleep, and stay with that book." Mr. Nalley gave me a discarded manual—what they called the Russell Guide—and told me how to use it. When I went back to work the next day, this woman that had been sitting with her back to me said, "Huh, what happened to you? What kind of smarty pills you been taking?" I said, "I took the Lord in prayer, and he sent me a friend."

What Mr. Nalley did for me helped me to retain that job for fourteen years and four months. That's where I retired, October 17, 1977. The blessed part of it is when I retired, Mr. Herman Hardy told me to choose any place in the city I wanted to go to dinner. He and his wife would escort my husband and I. I chose the restaurant I wanted, which was The Club.[6] We went to The Club, I was seated where I could look all over the entire city and see the view. I finally got my reward.

Edited by A. Michelle Craig. BCRI Oral History Project, vol. 5, sec. 2 (Apr. 14, 1995).

Notes

1. The residential community was named after the company.

2. For a discussion of pride in the school, later called Parker High School, see Lynne B. Feldman, *A Sense of Place: Birmingham's Black Middle-Class Community, 1890–1930* (Tuscaloosa: University of Alabama Press, 1999), 127–32. See also the interview with Reuben Davis in this volume.

3. For more on color at Industrial High, see the Colonel Stone Johnson interview in this volume.

4. This part of the account appears to be based on hearsay. For historians' descriptions of the encounter, see Glenn T. Eskew, *But for Birmingham: The Local and National Movements in the Civil Rights Struggle* (Chapel Hill: University of North Carolina Press, 1997), 156–58; David J. Garrow, *Bearing the Cross: Martin Luther King Jr. and the Southern Christian Leadership Conference* (New York: Harper Collins, 1986), 156–57.

5. The students from Nashville did have a hunger strike after they were arrested May 17, 1961. See Andrew M. Manis, *A Fire You Can't Put Out: The Civil Rights Life of Birmingham's Reverend Fred Shuttlesworth* (Tuscaloosa: University of Alabama Press, 1999), 270–71.

6. A previously segregated exclusive club atop Red Mountain, overlooking the city of Birmingham.

James Greene

Born July 19, 1925, in Birmingham, Alabama. A postal worker and union representative for the National Alliance of Postal and Federal Employees. Active in voter registration in Birmingham. *"They would send you home for no reason, trying to fire you several times. You would be sick, and they would want you to bring almost a doctor back there. So you would have to file a grievance with the union. So if we couldn't solve it here, we would send it all the way [to headquarters], and then we would get three representatives to come to Birmingham. Then in coming to Birmingham they would have a trial. Without a union there would have been chaos. The union definitely helped. The union saved a lot of little things rather than any white making an accusation against you. With the union, that made a big difference. Even with the union representative walking through, that made a big difference."*

All-Black Union in the Post Office

I was born in Birmingham, in Sherman Heights, across the bridge from Ensley. My father was born in Birmingham, but my mother was from Troy, Alabama. I have one sister, no brothers. There were just two of us. My sister is the oldest. My father went to about the third grade. My mother was about the sixth grade. My father was a steelworker at TCI in Ensley.[1] My mother was a housewife, and she never worked outside of the home.

I started first grade at Council in Ensley. I was there for first and second grade. Then I left and went to Sherman Heights; it was the TCI school at that time. I went third grade through the ninth grade there. I started living with my grandmother so I could go to a school in Sherman Heights. At the TCI school I remember we had lunches and a lot of things to play with. Before the county had taken over, we had practically everything you wanted to play with. Athletic departments were fair. There was quite a bit of difference when the county took over because all these things that were added were now taken away.

Sherman Heights was a community where everybody knew one another. There wasn't too much there. We had one hydrant in the middle of the road, and the restroom. We didn't call them that then. We just called it the toilet. They would dig a hole and set it over the hole, and whenever it filled up you would move it to another spot. We didn't pay it any attention because that was the way we thought it was supposed to be. We had the best teachers. I remember most of my teachers. One that I remember, Mrs. Carter, was at Council [Elementary School] and then got moved to the TCI school. She was there and the principal, Mrs. Arrington. Professor Lawson was there for a long time.

Well, see, when they first . . . when the county had first taken over, they went all the way through the twelfth grade. The TCI [school] went all the way through the twelfth grade. After the county took over, I don't remember what year it was when they stopped, but they moved the tenth through twelfth to Westfield [High School].[2] Going to Westfield, you had to catch the bus. You had a time limit, and you had to make sure you were there at a certain time. When I was at TCI school, I had about six or seven blocks to walk. It wasn't a problem. We would walk and be on time. Well, actually, where I lived I could catch [the bus] if he stopped for me. I had to walk four or five blocks to catch it and going in the other direction. Most of the time he would stop. I would try my best to be there.

My parents brought us up kind of strict. They wanted to know about me and what I'm learning. I'm proud of them. I couldn't do what others did. I had a lot of work to do. We got a little business, and I had to work there. We had a grocery business over in Sherman Heights. I had to go work in the store. I also got a job working downtown, 'cause I needed the experience. I worked at Tutwiler Hotel as a porter. Porter was the white man's job. They only hired me, but I couldn't touch a bag. It was the white man's job to touch the bags and take things upstairs. I just ran errands. I wore my suit with my name on it. I couldn't go upstairs. I had to stay downstairs. This was while I was in high school. I would leave high school and catch a jitney instead of catching the bus back home my last year at Westfield.[3] I would catch a jitney from Westfield to Fairfield for a nickel and then catch the green bus for a nickel for the ride downtown. I think they went up to a dime, but when I first started it was a nickel to ride downtown. Then when you get ready to come home then you catch the trolley, streetcar, whichever, and you pay seven cents. You come home, and then you get off and walk to Sherman Heights.

I finished Westfield in 1944, and that summer I went to [Alabama] A&M [College] in Huntsville.[4] I had taken up vocational trades. I had taken up sheet metal and foundry, and I had taken up something else, I'm trying to remember. There was foundry and sheet metal. Then when I came back for the winter I went to Miles.[5] I was there for two years, and then the army called me. Then I had to go and serve. At Miles I had planned on studying chemistry because I was going to go into the field of medicine. After I went into the army, I tried to get into the medics. I worked two days in medics, and they closed that section down, so they put me in the trucking company. I didn't get a chance to learn in the medics. So when I came back I had to change my major and minor. I went to math and history.

When I joined the army, I left Birmingham and went to Fort Benning and had my training in Anniston. I left Anniston and went to Camp Stone in California and then left there and went to the Philippines Islands, Manila. While I was there I went to Manila, Philippines Institute. The war was over. I was a replacement soldier. I replaced the fellows that had been fighting. The Philippines was beautiful. One thing I liked about being in the army, when I was in the Philippines, I was just like the white man that was here. See, I was the big man then, even though I was black. The Filipinos respected us as being rich. They would give you all the courtesy that we were giving to the other [white] people while I was here. So it was beautiful in the Philippines. I learned to speak the Tagalog language.[6] I stopped speaking English. I spoke nothing but Tagalog.

At that time we were segregated. Not too long before we were integrated. Even though, there at one time, I was in the hospital and I was the only black, but they . . . it wasn't a problem, they accepted me there. All the honors that were given to a soldier, well, I learned about it early while I was there.

In the service I was a truck driver, and truck driving, during the time I was in the service, was easy, but it was dangerous. If you were an all-right Joe, you could make it, especially if you would get caught out by yourself with the truck.

I got out in 1947. I went back to Miles College. See, I had to come back on account of my people at the store wanted to take a vacation. So I had to come back and took my old job, and then I went back to Miles. Then Miles, we were getting ready to start training to teach the people how to vote and how to fill out the application. See, at that time you had an application to fill out, and you had to know all about who was the president of the United States and his cabinet and . . .

We left from the school . . . there was a group of us, after training others, had gone, and then before then they wouldn't register you unless you had property. See, although at that time I had some property, so I didn't have a problem, other than they only asked me two questions. One I believe was who could vote, and then there was who could not vote. So I answered those and by . . . they had a large group of people from Miles College that wasn't quite as bad at it, 'cause most of us passed.[7]

After that, I had gone and knew how it was. Then we would meet at different churches and start people. They would bring all the material to the church, and then there we would explain how to fill out the application. We had sample applications. We had every question that there was at that time. So, it was . . . most of the people, they learned. They wanted to learn. You take my church and most all of the people there that went, all of them passed. At that time you paid a poll tax. You have to catch up from the time you were twenty-one whatever age you were when you started. You had to pay. They would make you go back and catch up for every year. I was trying to think how much, I knew it was $1.50, I don't know that at the beginning if it was three dollars, but I'm not sure of that, but I do know it was $1.50, because at that time I had to catch up and pay for my age. I believe I was about twenty-four or twenty-five, in other words, it was April of 1950 when I passed, and my wife, she came a little later than that. At that time I was staying where I'm still living now, at 57 Sixteenth Court, that's Vinesville. I moved there in 1949.

During that time I knew most of the ministers, but being . . . see, I was a federal employee, and we were restricted in not getting involved in the city. I worked at the post office, and we had practically the largest black union in the United States. See, we had the National Alliance of Postal and Federal Employees.[8] That union was somewhat like the NAACP. Our home office was in Washington, D.C., and we had some of the best lawyers that you could have at that time. Whenever we had a problem they would definitely send help, or you would cable them and get some help. We had a lot of problems back then.

Our workers' union was all black. At that time you couldn't join any white union. You had to be in the black union, and our union would handle cases if you were in the army, navy, or whatever. If the department you were in was federal we could handle it. I worked with the president, Joseph Spencer. At that time he was the president, and I worked out of his office. I was the contact man over the union. I was a union representative. I was the recruiter whenever anybody joined or came to the post office. I went other places recruiting you to join the National Alliance. Black folk came into the post office and most of the federal government, somewhat, after 1953. Before that, we had some black carriers in the post office because we had quite a few fellows that left Miles [College] and came to the post office. They tried to get me to come, but I had a good job at that time. I was a projectionist. I worked at the motion picture theater. We had a union, it was a black union, and we supplied all of the black theaters with operators.

After I came back from the military, my teacher, Mr. William Jackson at Westfield, told me about becoming an apprentice. I became an apprentice and learned how to run the theaters and make out schedules and whatever the theater needed. I started at the Palace Theater in Ensley. Then I left the Palace and went to the Miles Theater in Fairfield because I was going to Miles College, and it was closer. It wasn't on the campus, it was downtown in the city. We had all the black theaters around here: the Carver, the Famous, the Frolic, the Grand, the Champion. Well, the union provided operators for all of the theaters. At that time I figured I would stay with the theaters 'cause they were there.

When TV came in, we were under the impression it was coming to the theaters. All these off-shows that they would have they would zoom into the theaters. But then instead of coming to the theaters, they boxed it and put them in little boxes what you call the television. This was in 1944. I started studying on the side. RCA put out some booklets, and some of the fellows went to school and started studying about the theaters. [When] I came back from the service I was pretty well up on it.

Well, after all of the theaters were closing, I had [worked at] the Palace and the Miles theaters and came to the Champion and then went to the Joy Theater on Sixth Avenue before it closed. It was on up there by Leonard's [a black-owned café in the neighborhood of Titusville], across the street from there. Then I came to Eighth Avenue Theater in Smithfield [a neighborhood in Birmingham]. Then I left there and started working at the Famous and Carver [downtown], but then I figured . . . I had a family at that time, with two kids. I figured I needed to do something. Well, I was working at the VA [Veterans Affairs office] also. I always had two jobs. When they opened the VA up, I got a job there because I had knowledge [of] what was going on at the VA. In the housekeeping department, in maintenance and truck driving, and so forth, I had a lot of knowledge. I went and filled out the application, and I put on my resumé what I knew about things. When you fill out an application and you know what's going on, well, you know the business that you are filling out for. They'll be looking for you if you know what's going on, and I knew what was going on. So I had two jobs there, I was the elevator operator, and I was in maintenance. I knew about knocking down walls and helping the electrician and all that. I got the job just like that.

I went to the post office in 1955. I left the VA, and they just transferred me on over to the post office. I didn't want to teach, so I didn't take teacher's training [while at Miles]. So I went and got a job at the post office. I would take a lower job, but I figured I could move up. I went there as a mail handler. I worked about ten months as a mail handler, and then I took a comprehensive test, and I made a passing grade. I went regular and then became a regular clerk. The clerks distributed the mail and put it in the little holes that you got. At that time we didn't have zip codes. I'm trying to remember what year we organized. Well, the union was organized in 1913, and I'm trying to figure out what year we had brought it to Birmingham. We had brought it to Birmingham somewhere in the fifties.

The movement was going on all the time, you see, from the forties. We had a representative come from Nashville and Chattanooga because that's where it originated. Then we had a representative come from the home office, which was in Washington, D.C., and set us up. That was the first year, but I didn't join that first year because I was on probation, so I didn't want to get involved.

The group that I came in with, we didn't have any problems. The only problem we would have would be the grievance problem, where you would be mistreated on certain jobs and so forth. You weren't treated the same way the white clerks were. You, during that time, didn't have much association with them. If they were at a case sticking mail, and you were robbing that case (meaning you're taking the mail out) they would stand up. When the hole would get filled up, then you would come and get the mail and put it in a tray, but they would stand up. It was a long time before they accepted even the change when we would change it, but they would do things, and we would have to file grievances.

They would send you home for no reason, trying to fire you several times. You would be sick, and they would want you to bring almost a doctor back there. So you would have to file a grievance with the union. So, if we couldn't solve it here, we would send it all the way [to headquarters], and then we would get three representatives to come to Birmingham. Then in coming to Birmingham they would have a trial. Without a union there would have been chaos. The union definitely helped. The union saved a lot of little things rather than any white making an accusation against you. With the union, that made a big difference. Even with the union representative walking through, that made a big difference.

I was a union representative. The union title was the National Alliance of Postal and Federal Employees. With the union when they . . . I don't know what year it was; we didn't have anybody in small-business administration. We didn't have nobody in the defensive, and we didn't have anybody in as an air-traffic controller, or whatever department of the federal government. We didn't have any blacks in around here, and they had to put some in right away. They would send two representatives, one from Washington and maybe one from Atlanta or some other large office, and then they would come to our union. Most of the time the president would be out of town, and I was the contact man. They would bring all the applications, brochures, and whatnot, and then I would have a talk with our brothers and sisters. We didn't have too many sisters at that time.

It covered all federal agencies, and during that time whatever your agency was, if you had to file a grievance and if we couldn't handle it here, we would send it on to Washington, and then they would find somebody and then send it back here. Then also our insurance, if you were in the army or navy you could join our insurance. We had a pretty good insurance company. Well, with my army time and my VA time and my post office time, I was there thirty-five years.

When we brought the ladies in, the black ladies, there was always mistreatment of the ladies. They would stand them up all day, and then if they asked to go sit down, then they would send them home, but they wouldn't send no whites home. So, then, whenever this happened they would come to me, and then we would go over and talk to the supervisor. As time went on, they would do that, but I was able to squash things, then they wouldn't have to go home. A lot of times I would do that. After I got further, well in my later years, I had moved practically over in the management department, and I was the finance clerk, you know, payroll clerk. Then I got a different training. So, I found out then that if he doesn't have it, don't give it to him, and if he's got it, take it. The way that they were treating us is another matter. They knew they were wrong, they just wanted to give us some problems. So, this is what I was told. Sometimes the blacks would get the big head and get mad and fly off the handle and say things or do things they shouldn't. So, if I could get to him, I would try to save him.

Federal employees had some difficulties when it came down to really being active in getting involved in the movement. I couldn't march or anything, I just could stand on the side and look and watch them. I would work through with my church.

I witnessed the demonstrations all the time because I'm always downtown working, not too far from here. We'd leave home in the morning, and I was working in the afternoon. Then there was a lot of times that I would do things also in order to, like, when you've got a lot of whites that used to be standing on the outside, then I would walk in the middle of them, then they would move. Also, I was one of the first to integrate the lunch counters at Lowe's Restaurant [then located in the retail area of downtown Birmingham]. After they had declared that, you know, let's integrate the restaurants and Newberry's and other desegregation businesses.

Then Lowe's was not too far from the post office, and then I knew. I said, "Whenever it comes out, I'm going." Then the fellow would say, "Man, we're going to have to come and get you." I said, "I'm going," and I had one young lady to go with me the first day, Mrs. Margaret Johnson. She said, "I'll go with you." Then we went on down. The first day they didn't serve us.

Then we went back the next day, and the manager was there, and he waited on us. Then we sat in the first section of the place, and all the whites went to the back section. So we did that for about three or four days, and by Friday we decided we'd get some more, 'cause we were sitting up front where there was two seats, and they had about three or four more tables with just two seats, and we didn't want to go back in the back. So the last day, Friday I believe, we got a couple of more, so we could go in the back. Then we went in the back, and everybody moved up front. Some just got up and left and left their food and everything. So we stayed in there for quite some time.

This wasn't organized at all. We were just going for lunch. We had to do something. We couldn't march, but we could be in the meetings. I attended many of the meetings. Also, after they bombed the church [Sixteenth Street Baptist], then all of the church doors opened in Fairfield and all around. King and his group would come and be in our church for maybe an hour, and then he would go to another church, then another. I think he came to our church twice, which was Mount Olive Baptist church in Fairfield. Our minister, James Sarris, was very active.

I never did hold an office in the union because I was always the representative for the grievance man. I never had any time because I was doing that or I was the contact man. So at that time I was always backed up. After I had moved back up in the post office, when I went into finances upstairs, and this was a section by itself, then I had to give up some of that downstairs because I wasn't able to do any grievances. But I did attend the meetings, and also whatever the union was doing I could take an active part.

As a part of management, I kept my membership in the union. At that time the union had integrated, and we had four or five unions in the post office. See, you had the mail handler's union, and you had the carrier's union, and then you had the two clerk's unions, and then you had the supervisor's union. Everybody had a union. So whatever you were working, you joined that union.

The efforts of the union and the movement were almost similar. As the movement outside moved up, then the post office would move up. We fought all kinds of cases that dealt with people when they were wrongly treated. We had all kinds of cases all over the country during that time, but mostly here in Birmingham.

Now what happened in the post office, the home office in Washington after we had applied for some help here, there was a . . . what we call Boon Pop Team. It was a team of people from Washington.

I'll have to look that up and get the other name for it. They came here, and they would listen to nothing that the postmaster on down would say. They gave the ultimatum of what it was all about, and then they left. Now, I was at the terminal [station], and we were definitely segregated. The first black that moved in the locker room with the whites was Emmitt Green.

This was the railroad post office. See, you had the city and then the railroad. See, the railroad handled all the mail going anywhere in the world, and the city just handled the mail going through the city. So wherever Emmitt was, or where his locker was, they wrote on his locker, "This is a coon's locker." When he washed his hands and his face on the mirror they had "a coon washed here," or whatever restroom part he used they would write "a coon was in here." Those signs would stay up for about two or three days. At that time we had found out about it, and in turn we called the Boon Pop, and they came back through there, and the representative came, and they looked at all of this, and they went out there and told the foreman to wash this off. Then they cleaned it off, and they said if it ever happened again we are going to do some changes. It never happened again.

These weren't union people, these were government people coming through to make sure of all the changes, including the segregated water-fountain deal. They were taking them down.

One water fountain remained, because if you had two, we would still be drinking out of the one. So they were taking those down. It was quite some time before the whites would accept, you know, because even after that, the city and the terminal station merged together. It became one, and when our seniority numbers merged I was 380 something out of about two thousand.

So that put me in a pretty good position. When the first building came out, you could get a job at a window unit, those window unit jobs and so forth. Yeah, I bid for Ensley, and Hooker bidded for the city. Hooker was maybe two or three before me, 'cause he came in before me. Most of us that came in around that time stayed together. Whatever was done, I would push them into their job. Hooker got a job in the city, and they closed that window. Rather than to let him work there they closed it.

It was downtown on Fifth Avenue. They closed that window, and I don't know how many windows were down there, but they closed that one. The window out there in Ensley, instead of giving it to me, they gave it to a fellow named Keiser who was a few digits over me also. He was a white fellow. He didn't want it, but they gave it to him, and then when it was time for him to go to work he didn't take it. See, after that I had taken my second bid. I had two bids. I put in for number one and lost it, and so they gave me the number two bid, which was [handling mail destined for] Florida. Which means I was the first black man that had the case to work in Florida, you know, down in the city. Only whites used to work all of those cases. Then I had to go down there to the city, but when I transferred, the foreman greeted me, and he was glad to have me, 'cause when I put it up, it's put up. You have to take an exam on it, and you have to take the whole city in Florida, and you pick out a hundred cards, and you have to do those hundred cards within five minutes.

They would pick out a hundred cards, and you've got your case before you, where these cities . . . where they go. It's just like Birmingham, but in Birmingham you can put Ensley, Fairfield, all those cities that Birmingham can handle in the satellite offices in that particular section. Like Montgomery, whatever is close to Montgomery you can put those in there. With Florida I made a hundred, so they had seen my record.

See, when records go before you, that's what I tell people, when you got a good record it helps, especially if they look at it. They knew they were getting a hundred-percent Florida man. I came down, and it was nice. I didn't have any problem with it.

In the post office that you see now it's a lot of stress. The stress is, I don't know why, but it comes from the high up. Not here on this level but from Memphis or wherever. What they do is they look at records, and they figure that we ought to do better, and then you are already stretched out, and then they send it down. The pressure was from the top. See, with this, I'm not saying they are dumb for this, but then when we come out in the black, they take the bonus from the top, but you don't get it down here. I remember once when I was in the office, I had to go to the postmaster's office and get the mail off his computer, and he had in there that we were using too much sick leave. By me handling the sick leave and by me handling the time and all that, I didn't see it. They weren't abusing the sick leave, but it came down. I knew he was going to give out a memo about it.

I didn't talk about the city of Birmingham. Now, the city of Birmingham, I was here, I was downtown here from the age of ten on up, off and on, and I worked downtown most of the time, even though I worked at the house store too. But here before the integration came, Fourth Avenue was beautiful. I worked at the Champion Theater, the Frolic, and the Famous, I was here every day. I would leave school and come. The people, they were here going to the movies, going into the restaurants, and we [black people] had businesses all down Fourth Avenue. I had a business on Fourth.

I had one I started. I opened up a lounge on Eighteenth Street and Fourth Avenue in 1968. Then in 1971 I opened up a restaurant on Fourth Avenue next to the Famous Theater. It was nice, but they wouldn't allow you to go beyond certain areas. You couldn't get the real estate company to rent to you, and even after that you couldn't get a license. See, because I tried to get all kinds of licenses, but they wouldn't let me have one. I couldn't go across Eighteenth Street. When Bohemian Bakery closed, I tried to get next-door. This was about 1970, but they wouldn't let me have the building. I was going to put up a restaurant. I hadn't put up my restaurant on Fourth Avenue. I had two places that I was checking. I was checking on [A. G.] Gaston,[9] and I used to talk to him all the time. He said he had a place if I didn't want the place I got. He had a place that used to be an answering service. I didn't take it. He used to tell me what to do and how to do it. We had a good relationship.

There were a lot of black businesses down there and a lot of good friends. We can talk about the theaters. The whites owned the theaters. I never worked in any of the white theaters. We didn't start working in the white theaters. It was a long time before we integrated. After the union was dissolved, some of the blacks started working in the white theaters.

Edited by A. Michelle Craig. BCRI Oral History Project, vol. 32, sec. 1 (Jan. 28, 1998).

Notes

1. Tennessee Coal and Iron, a subsidiary of U.S. Steel.
2. Westfield was a TCI coal-mining town west of Birmingham.
3. A jitney was a privately owned automobile that served various communities just as taxicabs did.
4. Alabama A&M College was a state-supported school for blacks in Normal, Alabama, established in 1873. See Henry Chase, *In Their Footsteps* (New York: Henry Holt and Co., 1994), 23.
5. Miles College, in Fairfield, was established by the Colored Methodist Episcopal church in 1898. See Jimmie Lewis Franklin, *Back to Birmingham: Richard Arrington Jr. and His Times* (Tuscaloosa: University of Alabama Press, 1989), 38.
6. See Mark Donohue, *A Grammar of Tukang Besi* (New York: Mouton de Gruyter, 1999).
7. As a result of the Boswell Amendment to the Alabama constitution ratified in November 1946, blacks attempting to register to vote faced hostile examiners who asked ridiculous questions. See the introduction to this volume.

8. See Gary M. Fink, ed., *Labor Unions* (Westport, Conn.: Greenwood Press, 1977), 294–95. The association's initial jurisdiction was black railway mail-service employees, who were barred from the Railway Mail Association–AFL. It expanded to cover the entire post office in 1923 and all government, commercial, and industrial employees in 1965.

9. A black millionaire businessman. See A. G. Gaston, *Green Power* (Troy, Ala.: Troy University Press, 1968).

Ludie Mae Martin

Born June 1, 1929, in Bullock County, Alabama. She lived in Montgomery, Chicago, and Youngstown, Ohio, and presently lives in Birmingham. Served as chief steward for the International Brotherhood of Teamsters, Local 743, for twenty-three years. Member of the Coalition of Black Trade Unionists and the A. Philip Randolph Institute. *"Let me tell you. When I became a steward, you had to sign out if you went to the bathroom. I started raising hell. The workforce was a majority black women. When I first became a steward, there were quite a few Italians, Polish people, and when I left, there were about as many Spanish as there were black. When I first became steward, they had two seniority lists. One for the women, one for the men. The men were always paid more than the women. Now, you know I had to argue about that one and straighten it out, which I did. The longer I stayed there . . . the more respect I got from the people, from the union, and everything else. I was called the mother of my local because at union meetings I was the only one to get up and raise hell about whatever."*

"The Mother of My Local"

I was born in Bullock County, Alabama. The nearest little town was called Winelevel, which was not in Bullock County, but that was the nearest town. Bullock County is where I was born and raised. I'm number eleven out of a twelve-child family. We're six boys and six girls. My mother was born in Pike County, which is down the road a bit. My father was born in Bullock County. His mother, who was Maggie, they were all from Bullock County. She was the one that would explain to me how she was the child of the slave and all of this. I didn't really pay her too much attention. She would tell me about when the Yankees came down through there and started freeing the slaves. The Yankees poured the syrup out on the ground and made the Pickets, who were the slaves' masters, dance in the syrup. We always thought that Grandma was crazy, that she didn't know what she was talking about. We would laugh at her because we didn't think this was true. I wished I had listened a lot more as a little child. They said Grandma's mind was bad, and [while] my brothers went to the field, my older sisters were all married, and my job was to stay home and watch Grandma and make sure that Grandma didn't get away. Grandma would sit there and tell me all of these things, and I didn't have sense enough to retain it. I didn't think it was nothing of importance at that time. She would tell me about a lot of things that went on because her mother was the cook for the Pickets, and she was the little girl. The Pickets had a young boy named Fred, and they would always go out and play with each other.

[My parents] did not own their land when I knew about it. They were renters, and they rented from some people. It was coincidental these people were named Boswell, too. The white folks were named Boswell, and my daddy's name was Boswell. I don't know if there was any connection between those two sets of Boswells or not. They rented, and they did the farming. If they made money, they made money, and if they didn't, they didn't. Most of the time they didn't.

During World War II, four of the brothers went away to the service. All of my sisters were already married and away. When these four brothers went away to the service, when they came back from the service, my father was dead, and my mother was trying to get them to stay there and help her raise a farm. I never will forget, my brother Murray told our mama, "I'll do anything in the world to help you, but I'll never tell a mule to get up if he sat in my lap." So they moved into Montgomery. By this time I had gotten married to Henry Lee Davenport, and we didn't move to Montgomery right then. About a year later is when I moved to Montgomery, me and Henry Lee, to be near my mother and brothers and all of that.[1]

The only school that I attended was called Mount Olive School. It was a little one-room shack with a big heater in the center, where they would put wood in the fireplace, in the stove, to make the school warm. We had different teachers. One teacher taught everything. My first teacher that I remember by name was Miss Tennell. She taught reading, writing, arithmetic, math, and all of that. She taught everything in all the classes. The school didn't go no further than the eighth grade. That was as far as I was allowed to go in school, because my parents would never let me come off to Birmingham to let me live with my sisters, or something, so I could go to school. They tried, and my brother Clemmy, we call him Clemmy but his name was Albert . . . by the time they thought they were going to get me off to school, Clemmy wrote Papa a letter and told him not to let me go off up there to school because "Ludie Mae is fast" and she'll wind up getting pregnant, and "Papa you ought to keep her at home." Papa wouldn't let me go to school. I never got no further education. Some certificates I did for the University of Illinois. Then I got my GED in Illinois.

So, after eighth grade I got married. Thought I was grown. I repeated the eighth grade one year because I didn't want to stay at home. I just went back and went through that same grade again. See, I got married when I was sixteen and didn't have no business getting married then. I thought I was grown, and I did. See, my daddy had died, and that's the only time in my life that I had ever prayed to die was when my daddy died, because I didn't think I could live without my daddy. He died in September, and I got married in January. Wasn't in love, just did it.

Growing up, though, before Daddy died, it was rough, really rough. I never will forget some of these white folks. They respected my daddy, because he was the Worshipful Master of the Masons, but a lot of other people caught the devil. Things would go down, but if my daddy would go in and intervene for them, the white folks would leave them alone. I never will forget, I guess I must have been about ten or eleven years old. Mr. Thompkins's wife had a baby, and he got on his horse and came down to my daddy's farm to ask my daddy if I could come up there and help his wife, who was Mrs. Louise. She had just had this baby. My daddy said to him, he said, "Ernest, get back on your horse, get out of my yard, and don't come back here asking for my child to help you no more." I couldn't understand it. My daddy said to me, 'cause I asked him, I said, "Papa, why you wouldn't let me go with Mr. Thompkins?" He said, "Ludie Mae, sit down and let me tell you something. You don't never go and work for no white man in his house, 'cause he'll work you to death, and he'll use you."[2] I couldn't understand what he meant when he said "he'll use you." I kept asking Papa, and he said, "He'll make you go to bed with him, and don't you ever do it." I made up my mind then that I wasn't going to do it, because my daddy said don't. So I never wanted to go to nobody's house to work, but I didn't have the education to do any other thing.

By me being a girl they always would never let me know what was going on. They would kind of shield me, and then I would ask my brothers what had happened. That was when the family down the road from us, they were making whiskey. They caught them down at the whiskey still. This was a black family, and the sheriff beat them up so bad. Nobody would ever let me know about all of this, because they were protective of girls at that time. I would ask my brothers. I said, "What happened to Pappy Jack and Mr. Tanner and all of them?" They were down there making whiskey, and the sheriff come down there and beat them up. They killed old so-and-so. I forgot the man's name, but they killed him and just threw him in the woods. Nobody never came out and investigated it or nothing. It was just another man got killed.

When I moved to Montgomery I was pregnant with my first child. I moved up there, I think it was March, and my baby was born in May. I thought moving was a big thing, really. We were moving to town, and my husband had got a job doing plastering. I was two doors up the street from my mama, and I just thought this was the greatest thing ever. By September of that same year, after the baby was born, my husband and one of my brothers, Nathaniel, decided they were going to do better than what was going on in Montgomery. So they went to Youngstown, Ohio, where my sister Sara was living, and got a job in the steel mill. That was a big jump, I thought. By November, Henry Lee had sent for me to come to Ohio. I moved up there, and I thought everything, the world was free. I could go up there now, and I didn't have to be under all these segregated rules and things. I thought it was going to be happiness, but that was where I found a lot of misery. My marriage at this time was going bad.

The rest of my family was there in Montgomery. My health went bad, and I had to have surgery. My mother came into Youngstown to help me. She carried my daughter, this was after my son was born, and she carried the baby back to Birmingham because I wasn't able to see about this baby. I told my mama, I said, "As soon as Dr. Shirt lets me travel I'm getting out of here, and I'm coming home."

[Youngstown] wasn't much different from Montgomery. Even though it didn't say that you were segregated from everything, the people themselves segregated themselves. You went your way, and the white folks went their way. You did what you could do, and they did what they could do. You know you weren't supposed to do certain things, and you didn't do it.

The law might've said there was no segregation, but the custom was you were still segregated. The blacks lived on one side of the river, and the whites lived on the other side of the river.

I never worked until after I left my husband and went back to Birmingham and I got a job working as a maid at Pizitz, the department store. I first got this [other] job, I was going to work over the mountain in somebody's house.[3] After I had worked there three days my son got sick with pneumonia, and this woman's baby was sick with pneumonia. I stayed at home with my baby and took care of him. When I did go back over to her house to go to work, she chastised me, 'cause she said, "You know my baby was sick, and you know I had to go to the country club, and blah, blah, blah. . . ." I said, "Let me tell you something right now, my baby was sick with pneumonia, and I stayed at home and took care of my baby. I don't care nothing about you having to go to the country club." So she said, "I'll fire you right now." And I said, "No, you can't fire me, 'cause I quit." I came on back downtown and applied for a job to work at Pizitz and went to work that same day. That was in 1952.

I wasn't a registered voter at that time. When the *Brown v. Board of Education* came about, I had quit Pizitz because I wasn't making nothing but eleven dollars a week, and at Wheeler Business College I had went to work as their maid. That's all that we could do was be a maid.[4] It was between Nineteenth and Twentieth Street on First Avenue, upstairs, and I was the maid. I went over there, and this teacher had been trying to teach me how to type, but the day of that decision, she didn't tell me why she could no longer let me practice typing in the evening. She didn't tell me about the decision, but from then on I was getting, I thought, pretty good. She never let me go in the typing room and type no more after that.

I lived in East Birmingham, at 1418 Sipsey Street, you know, where the creek would overflow. I lived in a three-room house, shotgun house.[5] I thought I was doing alright. I had three rooms: living room, bedroom, kitchen. Me and my children. In my community the women usually worked in somebody else's house. Some of the men worked at Stockham, and some worked at ABC.[6] Men had the heavier jobs, and women worked as domestic work. After I got that job with Pizitz I never went in nobody else's house to work. I remembered what my daddy said, and I only spent three days in my life doing that.

You would ride that streetcar to work for seven cents, and you would ride it back home for seven cents. You weren't paid a whole lot of money. When I went to work over at Wheeler Business College, where I was making twelve dollars a week, I thought I was getting rich. I lived here in Birmingham from 1950 to 1956. Me and Mr. Martin had separated because he became an alcoholic, and I couldn't stand it at that time, and I moved to Chicago. Worked different jobs. The first job I had there was working for Slenderella International.

That was a reducing salon. At that time nobody could work for them that weighed over 135 pounds. If you went over 135 pounds they would give you ten days to take it off. They would give you an hour a day, on their time, to work on their machines to get that weight off you. If you didn't get that weight off, you got fired. Only women worked there. I was working at this reducing salon, something happened. I had a fall and got hurt and messed up my back by slipping on some water. Because I applied for worker's compensation from this injury, I got fired. It didn't bother me. I just went on and got me another job.

I lived on the South Side, 42 East Sixty-sixth Street. I lived in Chicago from 1956 until 1963. I was real crazy at that time. If I was at work and you made me mad, regardless of what it was, I quit that job and go get me another one. At that time it was easy to get a job. You would be out of work for maybe, sometimes a day, and sometimes you could go on that same day and get you another job. So it didn't bother me.

In July of 1963 we came home for our first family reunion. When we were in Montgomery, this Dr. Jones told us that he thought my mother had cancer. He wanted to operate on her again. He wasn't sure, so all of us decided that, all of the sisters and brothers got together and decided, no, we didn't want her operated on no more. If she had cancer, that would be just something we would have to live with, and I was the only single one out there. I had made up my mind that if my mother had this cancer, that I wanted to be close to her, because when she had gotten sick in 1959 I wasn't able to come home because I couldn't afford to take my children out of school and I couldn't afford to leave them with nobody. All I could do was send money home to my sister to help with my mother. I said, "If something else happened, I'm going to be here myself to see my mama off." We all decided that we didn't want Dr. Jones operating on her no more. This was in July, and I went back home, back to Chicago, making all my plans on coming home to see about my mama. The day President Kennedy was buried is the day I moved out of Chicago. I came back to Birmingham and even tried to make another go with my ex-husband. You'll do anything to make ends meet at that time. I got my mother and brought her to Birmingham, where I was, so I could see about her. I got me a job over at the box factory. That was one of the better jobs, but it was hard, it was hard.

[I got involved in the union] after I moved back to Chicago in 1966. I had done what I said I was going to do, come back home and see about my mama. My mother died on the sixth of June, and I just said, "I'm going back to Chicago." I figured that I wouldn't have to hammer at that box factory no more, 'cause that was some hard work. I got back in Chicago on a Saturday night, and my nephew went out and was telling folks that my auntie was back, and she's going to need a job. That same evening a man called me about a job, to come down to his place, it was a lamp and shade factory. I didn't feel like I was ready to go to work. The next day he called me again. So I said, "I'll be down there later on this evening." When you really didn't care . . . I went down there that evening, and they put me to work right then. He showed me how to start off doing silk shades. I stayed there. Then, a year or so later, somebody, Hamilton Lamp and Shade, bought this company out. We moved about four blocks away, but we were still with the same people, all of us were still with the same union: Local 743, International Brotherhood of Teamsters.

After we had moved over there, you had new bosses and all of this. They weren't messing with me, but they were messing with other people. Being the big mouth that I was, I would always jump in and say whatever was necessary to be said to get the monkey off my back. Finally, when they voted in the pension instead of a raise, I was so mad with them. We needed to make some money. Here they are voting in a pension. Didn't know at that time that it was going to be the best thing that ever happened to us. Right after that, this steward, Wilma, had a heart attack. I wasn't at work that day. Then, when . . . you know how people take up collections on the job? They took up a collection to send out to Wilma. They gave it to this other little steward. Three weeks later, come to find out that he had never carried it over to Wilma. You know how women get in the bathroom, they talk about it, but nobody was going to do nothing about it. I wasn't even there when they took up the collection. I called the union office and wanted to know if anything could be done about this situation. The business rep told me to come over, that he wanted to talk to me. I went over to the union office raising all kinds of hell, because they had took up this money for Wilma, and Herman didn't carry it over there, and nobody was doing nothing about it. They said, "We didn't know nothing about it, how could we do anything about it?" I said, "Well, I'm telling you now what happened. They took up 150-something dollars, and he didn't carry it over there." So they said to me, he said, "Ludie, I'm coming out to that company tomorrow morning. Can I ask for you when I get up there?" I said, "Yeah, you can ask for me, 'cause I'll tell you what they said." So they came out there, and he asked for me, and I went out to the lobby where he was, and they called for Herman. They questioned him about this money. Herman started saying that his wife had the money. They told him that, "I'll come back tomorrow. You go home and get the money from your wife and bring it back here so me and Ludie can take this money over to the hospital to Wilma." Come to find out, Herman was lying, they had spent the money. Then the company wanted to loan Herman the money to replace it. I said, "No, get it out of his paycheck. If he stole it, he's supposed to repay it." It was funny. They got the money. I don't know how the money came up. I don't know the full details, but Dave Hayes [the business rep] said for him to give me that money so I could take it over to the hospital. He wouldn't give me the money. Dave Hayes came back out there and gave him twenty-four hours to give that money to me. So we got the money, and me and Dave carried the money over to the hospital to Wilma.

Then Dave came back out there another time to talk to me. He came out in the department, and all of the women wanted to talk to him, yakety yakety yak. They told Dave Hayes they wanted Ludie to be their steward. I wasn't the representative then. I was just a blabbermouth. Dave said, "Ludie, I appoint you as a steward." I said, "You can't appoint me to nothing. You can ask me if I will accept this until some later time." He said, "Whatever you say." Then it rocked on a couple of weeks. Then Dave kept coaching me on what to do and how to do it. Everything that would come up, I would call him. I said, "Dave, I don't know nothing about your laws, but I don't want to work on no appointed position. If you want me to be your steward, I think you ought to have an election." He said, "You think we ought to have an election?" I said, "Yes, 'cause I don't want to be put up here and said that I'm doing your job if I wasn't elected." He said, "Okay, we'll have an election." So they set up an election, and there were three other people that ran against me. I said, "It don't make no difference. If I don't win, I don't want to do it. If they win let them do it." So out of six hundred and something people, these three other people got a total of eighteen votes, and I got the balance. Well, I said, "I don't mind working." Then I told him, "If I'm going to be the steward, I know you've got some kind of classes, or something or other, that you can teach me what to do." So they set me up where I would go to school to learn how to be the steward and learn how to do certain things. I guess I must have learned it a little bit too good, because it got to the place if I saw it in the book, read it, and learned it, and if the union was wrong, I was just as much on them as I was on the company. I thought this is what you were supposed to do, and I kept doing it.

Dave got fired, 'cause I didn't know what I was doing. I complained about the company was taking advantage of people, some people, they were taking dues twice a month. I didn't know no better, but I complained, because I thought it was wrong. Once you were a steward, you got paid a compensation of twenty cents a member to represent these members, and you got that once every three months. So Dave brought my check out there, and I forgot how much it was, but it wasn't what it should have been. I complained to him. He was about half drunk, and he told me that if I wanted to know any more on that, I would have to see the president. I said, "Well, thank you." He had no more than left the building and I called the president. I wanted to know what was wrong. He said, "Well, Ludie, I'm sure they sent you whatever the company sent in." I was telling the president how many people were on my seniority list, and he was telling me how many people the company had paid for. The company had paid for 112 people when it was supposed to be paying for five hundred and something people. So the president told me, he said, "Ludie, when you get off of work, come over here and bring me that seniority list, and we'll find out what's wrong." So I did. I went over there that evening and carried the seniority list. When Dave Hayes came back in, I was sitting up in the president's office with the secretary treasurer and showing the seniority list has these many people and the company had only paid for 112. So they didn't tell me nothing, but the president told me, "Give me that check you got, and I'll make it right." The next morning the secretary treasurer was at the company when the office opened that morning. They went over their books and come to find out they had stole a lot of money. Dave Hayes had accepted a lot of that stolen money. I still didn't know what was wrong.

Then, about three months later, I was over at the union office, and Dave Hayes had gotten fired. I was raising hell about something else. I heard this other man say that "they better give her what she wants, or she'll get you fired." By this time, I had made buddies with some of them over there. I went and asked Roy, my buddy, I said, "What are they talking about? If they don't give me what I want I'll get you fired." I said, "I've never gotten anybody fired." He said, "Ludie, I can't talk about it now." He said, "When you leave here, you go to this tavern there on Thirteenth Street and Michigan Avenue, and I'll be over there to talk to you. I can't talk about it in the office." I went over there, and that's when he came in there and told me that's how Dave Hayes had gotten fired. It was because of what I did. I got scared after that, but I didn't get scared enough to quit. I still fought for the people. I wasn't going to change.

I stayed there until I went on disability in 1990. That had happened back in the seventies. The longer I stayed there and done it, the more respect I got from the people, from the union, and everything else. I was called the mother of my local because at union meetings, I was the only one to ever get up and raise hell about whatever. After I retired, when I retired and got ready to leave Chicago, they set up a retirement party for me. Something they had never done for any of their other stewards. That was part of what had happened, and I have to show you this. At this retirement party [that] they set up for me, I received a whole lot of plaques and a whole lot of money.

Let me tell you. When I became a steward, you had to sign out if you went to the bathroom. Can you picture signing out to go pee? I started raising hell. You didn't go off the clock, but you signed out. Everything you did, it was really just a sweetheart contract. I didn't know what had happened. In my first contract negotiation I argued for what I thought was right, and I got most of it. Come to find out, Hamilton got kicked out of the Lamp and Shade Association 'cause they agreed with me and let me get all of these different things. The rest of the companies thought they let me have too much. Well, all I was arguing for was whatever I thought was right for my people. They needed some more money, they needed an increase in their pension, and they needed work rules that were reasonable to work under.

The workforce was a majority black women. When I first became a steward, there were quite a few Italians, Polish people, and when I left, there were about as many Spanish as there were black. When I first became steward, they had two seniority lists. One for the women, one for the men. The men were always paid more than the women. Now, you know I had to argue about that one and straighten it out, which I did.

By that time they were so in love with the way I fought, they didn't care. It was just great what I did. I filed a grievance on equalization of pay. They had to bring the lower-paid employees with the higher-paid employees. When we merged the seniority list, then, you had where I would fight for the time. If you got more time and you have been here longer, then you deserve more by way of pay. I just argued for what was right, and that's what I always did.

My union has always been, from day one, one of the most liberal unions in the whole International Brotherhood of Teamsters. When it wasn't feasible for, you know, you weren't supposed to do certain things, our union would fight for it. They would help you fight. I [was] always ready to be out there leading the fight for what was right, and I did it all.

Chicago was a tough town for some unions, not all unions. Teamsters was one of the strongest unions in the city, so we didn't have a problem. Some of those weaker unions might've had problems. Then, after 1972, when we started the coalition of Black Trade Unionists, was when Chicago tried to ostracize us, but we were too big for them to ostracize us. See, one reason we had to form the Coalition of Black Trade Unionists is when McGovern was going to run for president, and the AFL-CIO was saying that they were not going to support nobody. We felt strong enough that we separated and went out there and said we are going to support McGovern. That was at the birth of the Coalition of Black Trade Unionists.

That's when we had to stand up as a group of people to defend what was right. In 1971, when we started organizing the Teamsters Black Conference in Miami, Florida, Fitzsimmons sent our president out and wanted to know was these Negroes crazy, or drunk, because we didn't feel like we were getting our fair share of what was going on. The more they fought us, the stronger we got, and we grew and we grew and we grew. As being part of the Coalition of Black Trade Unionists personally, I didn't feel like the women were getting equal treatment. Me and about four or five other women would argue every year, get the microphones and complain, 'cause we weren't getting our fair share. We tried every trick in the book to change the system. Finally, in 1977, we got it through where we had a women's division, so we could be heard on women's issues. Now we only do the women's luncheon and we have a workshop on that day on nothing but women's issues. Now we are stronger than the men.

Another instance of rabble-rousing was when Ralph Metcalfe was our congressman in Chicago. The year before he died is when Mayor Daley and them had decided that they did not want Ralph to go back to Congress. We as a people decided you can't tell us who to send to Congress. Being the person I was, I got with every radical group in the world to send Ralph back to Congress, which we did. The A. Phillip Randolph Institute, the Urban League, and everybody else, we worked overtime and sent Ralph back to Congress and gave Mayor Daley a heart attack. Then, Ralph wasn't there very long, he had a heart attack and died. That's when I became involved with the A. Phillip Randolph Institute, 'cause they do voter registration, voter education, and get out the vote, and that's what I was interested in. When I ran up with this group, I figured, this is my place in life, let's do it. That's what I always wanted to do, help somebody to get registered and get them out to vote. We can get them registered now, but we can hardly get them out to vote.

Today we are not as far as we should be, because believe it or not, black workers had to fight harder and be smarter just to get where we are today, because most unions are controlled by the white majority. That's where our union Local 743 was different. We had a majority of blacks there. All these years I've spent my life for giving us good jobs and a better future.

Edited by Horace Huntley. BCRI Oral History Project, vol. 33, sec. 3 (Mar. 11, 1998).

Notes

1. While discussions of black migration usually emphasize movement from the rural South to the urban North, the vast majority of the BCRI interviews discuss movement from the rural South to the urban South.

2. As a domestic servant in Georgia told a correspondent from the *Independent* in 1912, "'a colored woman's virtue in this part of the country has no protection.'" Quoted in Jacquelyn Jones, *Labor of Love, Labor of Sorrow: Black Women, Work, and the Family from Slavery to the Present* (New York: Vintage Books, 1995), 150.

3. "Over the mountain" represented the most exclusive white neighborhoods, including Mountain Brook, an enclave of the rich.

4. For historians' discussions of domestic work, see Cliff Kuhn, Harlon E. Joye, and E. Bernard West, *Living Atlanta: An Oral History of the City, 1914–1948* (Athens: University of Georgia Press, 1990), 111–22; Tera W. Hunter, *To 'Joy My Freedom: Southern Black Women's Lives and Labors after the Civil War* (Cambridge, Mass.: Harvard University Press, 1997).

5. A house where you could stand on the front porch and look straight through to the back porch.

6. Stockham Pipe and Fittings; ABC was the coke division of the Drummond Coal Company.

Harvey Lee Henley Jr.

Born April 6, 1937, in Kemper County, Mississippi. Family moved to Johns, Alabama, in 1940. Worked as scaleman at ACIPCO. Worked to end job discrimination at ACIPCO and participated in the ACMHR. *"I was really concerned about the labor aspect of the Movement. The place where I worked, we had a real problem out there about discrimination. Anything that you did out there at the time was a bold move, because people were afraid. If you attended the mass meetings, you would be reported to the company. . . . [I]f you were arrested [for demonstrating] and stayed in jail more than three days, you were automatically fired. If you worked at these shops and factories, had a family, you probably were not going to get arrested. But you would do anything else that you could do. That was my position."*

Black Power at ACIPCO

I was born in Enondale, Mississippi. When I was three years old we moved to Johns, Alabama, which is about twelve miles below Bessemer. Johns was a coal mining camp. There were eight children in the family, and I was number four. My parents had about an eighth-grade education. My mother used to wash and iron clothes for white people. Though living in the mining camp, my father did not work in the mines. He was a lumberjack. He cut the props for the coal mine. We didn't stay in the mining-camp housing. Our house belonged to the man that owned the sawmill, and that's how my father got the contract with the coal mine. The man that we rented from allowed my father to contract with the mine on a sharing basis.

Blacks and whites worked in the mines and in the sawmill. Both lived in the camp, though we were separated by about a block. There were black churches and white churches. You had a white community [elementary] school and a black community [elementary] school. The only recreation we had was swimming down in the creek. We played click 'n' wheel, roll a wheel, roll tires, and that kind of stuff. Black and white children played together until we got to a certain age, and then people started teaching that [the black kids] got to say "mister" or ["miss"] to the sawmill boy or girl. There was no organized recreation facility at all.

Johns was a one-horse town. We had one [traffic] light and one policeman. He was white. We called him Gun Rust. He wore a big pistol on his hip that reached all the way down to his ankle, and we said it was rusty because he never used it. He drove a 1947 Plymouth. Usually when he tried to arrest someone for a traffic violation, they would always lead him on out of town. [Residents' cars were usually faster than the police car]. After I moved to Birmingham, I returned to Johns, and Gun Rust got in behind me. I outran him once in my 1956 Ford, and he told my father. He said, "Harvey Lee, that boy of yours coming down here running over our town. Next time he come down, you bring him over here." My father tried to persuade me to go see him. I never did.

Gun Rust was suspicious of anything that was out of the ordinary. One year, Reverend Norwood [a minister from Birmingham] was preaching a revival at one of the churches down there, and Reverend Norwood always drove a big long Cadillac car. So Gun Rust come through there and saw that Cadillac car sitting out there, so he came in the church and wanted to know what was going on, and we were running a revival. But I guess if it had been Martin King or somebody, that he was going to arrest everybody in there. But, anyway, we were running revival, and that was good, so he didn't say anything about that. But, no, we never had any trouble out of the law. The only thing that the bootleggers down there, they had favoritism. He would let [some] bootleggers get by, and he would arrest the other ones.

[Though Gun Rust was not much of a threat to us, the Klan was.] Their object was to terrorize the community, keep fear in people. They used to have these caravans to come through the community. It was a hundred cars, sometimes with a big cross on the truck and the white sheets and hoods on. I will never forget, one night my uncle had just bought two chickens. He was coming back home and saw those cars coming down the road, and there was a bridge there. So he got up on that bridge and jumped in that water, and the chickens went one way and he went the other way. That shows you the amount of terrorism that they were creating.

When the headlines came out in the paper about Autherine Lucy attending the University of Alabama, and headlines such as the Supreme Court making a decision on integrating schools, then they start that demonstration.

There were two white high schools that we were closer to, but we were forced to go to Westfield.[1] We rode the bus to Westfield, which was about a forty-mile round-trip each day. I have a lot of praise for Westfield High School simply because the teachers there were concerned, and when you left there you really had a good basic education. You didn't have any problem getting into any college. There was complete discipline in the classrooms. The boys would slip off to the woods and smoke cigarettes. But the principal, Mr. Reeves, would come up there and run them out. If he caught you, you would be punished with whipping or suspension.

After high school I volunteered for the army. I went to Fort Jackson, South Carolina, Fort Bragg, and then to Fort Benning. I served two years, and upon my discharge, a captain spoke to those of us who were returning to the South and said we did not have to go to the other side of the fence again. And I realized what he was talking about. But when I got back to Alabama—I think in '58—they had moved the signs on the bus that said "Black" and "White," but they still had black seats from back to front and white seats from front to back.

One day when I was commuting from Johns to Birmingham, I paid my money, but blacks were already standing from the back, so I got in the front door and was standing about halfway in the bus, and this white soldier motioned for me to go to the back. I was standing ahead of where two white women were sitting. The soldier told the bus driver, "You got a nigger up here in the front, [he] don't know where he's supposed to be." Then the bus driver started looking through the mirror, and he started pointing back to the back. I didn't move. I said, "It's no room back there, I can't get back there." So he stopped the bus, and he said, "You got to go back there now." I said, "No, there's no room. I paid my money, and there's no room for me to get back there." Two black women told me to go on back there, go on back there. I said to them, "No, I'll just get off the bus." So I got off and walked to Roosevelt City. My aunt took me home.

That one incident started me thinking about what they were doing in Birmingham with the Alabama Christian Movement for Human Rights, because these were the things they were meeting about at the mass meetings. So I decided to go to the mass meetings. I felt good about what I was hearing, and the people looked like they were really ready to do something. This gave me the opportunity to get information and take it back to Johns. There was limited success in getting people to participate in anything in Johns because they always thought that the Lord was going to change things. You had a few old people that got involved in voter registration and education. But as far as attending mass meetings from Johns, Alabama, very few people did that. But I did start attending the mass meetings.

I moved to the Powderly community in Birmingham in 1960. I was not a registered voter, but that was one of the things that was stressed in the mass meetings. Asbury Howard Sr. and his son ran the voter-education campaign in Bessemer.[2] I went and got some of the information, and a lot of it was stuff that you would learn in high school about the Constitution. Then you would have to pay your poll tax. But the first time I went to register, I did not pass. There was a written test, then an oral test where this guy asked me who was the mayor of the Mississippi town I was born in. I was three years old when I left there, and I am not sure they even had a mayor. I thought this guy was going to pass me. He had black hair and he was red, I thought he looked kind of like a Jew. He didn't look southern.

The next time I went, this woman asked why I failed the last time. I told her, and she said that the man should not have failed me for not knowing the mayor of Enondale. She checked it off and gave me my certificate, and I was registered to vote.

I was really concerned about the labor aspect of the Movement. I had gone to work out at ACIPCO. We had a real problem out there about discrimination. And anything that you did out there at the time was a bold move, because people were afraid. If you attended the mass meetings, you would be reported to the company. I was reported, and the superintendent said, "Harvey, you involved in that mess going on down in Birmingham?" I said, "I'm not directly involved, I'm an observer." He said, "Well, Harvey, we don't need that kind of stuff. You too good a man to be tied up in that old communist stuff." I said, "I appreciate your comments and you feeling that way about me, but I don't know the difference in a communist and you. I associate with all kinds of people. Now, whether you think I'm being influenced by somebody, I can think you being influenced by something." And he got mad and said, "Well, you just keep on going and observing." I said, "That's good. But don't have no problem with me associating with people. I know how to go in and out and take care of myself."

I was involved with the Movement in several ways. I encouraged the men to give contributions to the Alabama Christian Movement. Davis Jordan, Edward Hicks, and I would ask the guys for a contribution, and we would get it to the Alabama Christian Movement. If the supervisor had caught us, that would have been a reason to fire us. I was warned once about passing out leaflets in the shop. I demonstrated at city hall once and was present at L.R. Hall when a white guy said he wanted to shake Dr. King's hand, and instead he slapped him. The guy was grabbed, and Dr. King said, "Leave him alone." Dr. King told the guy that he loved him, and he did not press charges against him. I was at the Palm Sunday March but was not arrested. If you worked at these shops and factories, had a family, you probably were not going to get arrested. But you would do anything else that you could do. That was my position.

You see, if you were arrested and stayed in jail more than three days, you were automatically fired. Less than three days brought a reprimand; the first offense was two weeks off. It was called defiance of law. A second offense meant discharge.

My family was supportive of me, but never involved. I was the most progressive in the family. I had a brother who died at the age of thirty. He went to school and became a civil engineer. When he returned home he was a Muslim. I mean, he just didn't like white folks at all. Although I was always gone from home, my wife didn't say anything. She supported me. I was a member of Mount Herman Baptist church in Johns. When I first moved to Birmingham, I joined First Baptist in Powderly, and later I joined New Pilgrim Baptist. At First Baptist some people were involved, and some were afraid of the possibility of their church being bombed. There was no resentment to the Movement at First Baptist, some people were just afraid.

The mass meetings were educational for me. I learned that before there was an EEOC there was a Commission on Equal Employment.[3] At the meetings they had people telling workers about their rights. As a result, we started filing written charges against our company, ACIPCO. They had black jobs and white jobs. When I first went there, a black man could work only as common laborer or as a round man. The round man rounded the mold. That's the thing that would shake you to death. That was the highest paying job a black could get. Investigators came in to check out our complaints. But these government agencies, and I have dealt with all of them, they give you the runaround. But we kept writing those letters until finally we did get a good investigation. That was in 1963. In 1964 the Civil Rights Act was passed, and it had what was called Title VII, which had to do with equal employment. Where the commission had tried to get good faith agreements, Title VII gave us access to the courts.

The president of ACIPCO had meetings with the employees. They were segregated meetings, and he told the white workers, "Y'all ain't got to worry, ain't nobody going to come here breathing down our backs. We are going to go on and do things just like we been doing them." White guys continued to get the best jobs, and we kept filing charges. So in 1963 the company implemented the California Achievement Test for Mental Maturity. That was supposed to be our relief, but we couldn't pass the test. This got the government off the hook, and they said, "The white people are passing this test, and you can't pass it. Therefore, you don't have no complaint." But the white people weren't passing the test. They were given the test to take home and schooled on it.

We then developed the Committee for Equal Job Opportunity, a black caucus at ACIPCO. The company had always been unorganized. It was a peculiar setup. The company was said to be family owned, where the employees are supposed to have equal shares. We are supposed to get a bonus every three months because of our profit sharing. The founder of ACIPCO was apparently a good guy. Some of the older people said that he really had the idea that industry should operate according to the Golden Rule. But since then, the company fell into the hands of these honkies that come out of the woods and just took everything back. That's why we had to start filing charges with EEOC.

People like Andrew Young and Stokely Carmichael representing SCLC and SNCC [the Student Nonviolent Coordinating Committee] were trying to recruit people for their organizations. If you are working in industry, you really could be supportive of any kind of movement. They would meet with us and talk about labor's untold story. Andy Young came and talked with us and said that "Black Power is what you all are doing here. You have formed a caucus in this all-white shop." We were viewed as troublemakers. When the sit-ins were going on downtown, we were sitting in at the ACIPCO restaurant. Those were bold moves because we didn't have no union, and the only representation was the Committee for Equal Job Opportunity. As a result of our sitting-in, they had to tear the wall down that divided black and white workers while eating. We would come out of the shop, all sweaty and dirty, and go to the restaurant and sit next to white people who were dressed in suits. Once, a big white carpenter, weighed about three hundred pounds, tried to intimidate us by standing at the cash register with his hammer. The manager was standing there with him, but it did not frighten us. The Movement caused that show of strength. The Movement caused the people to develop a consciousness that it was time for us to do something.

I participated in at least three union campaigns. But management had the ability to manipulate the situation with money. If you were supposed to get a bonus and you hadn't been getting one, they would start giving you one. In 1975, when we had the union campaign going on, we hadn't got a bonus in three years. When they started seeing union cards being passed out, they started giving a bonus and gave a bonus for three years until it stopped all vestiges of that union campaign. We were successful one time in getting enough cards signed and I believe to win the election. But the company had about three hundred people that were supervisors and are not supposed to vote. But they allowed them to vote and threw the election off.

An older fellow told a story about a CIO organizing campaign. He said they had already gotten the union, wearing the buttons and everything, and said the president of the company found out that blacks were the ones that was doing the most campaigning to get a union. So he had a meeting with the black folks and said that he had a big tub sitting over there with a bunch of bow dollars in it.[4] And he had a black Jesus up on the wall. He said the president come in crying, saying, "Gentlemen, that man up there died for all of us. We have a good place out here to work. Now these foreigners are going to come in here and take what we got. I can't let them do it. We can't let them do it." And those people started getting a handful of bow dollars and come out crying. They lost that election.

The labor movement was racist, too. They always had their separate things. Labor unions couldn't do what we were doing because they were controlled by the national office. We could file charges, and we could say things even about the labor movement itself. They could have been more involved, but they wanted to do their own thing. They don't want to come in and join you in the overall effort, but they want you to support what they do.

We got one of the first affirmative action plans written on paper at ACIPCO. But if you don't have the national government supporting you, it don't mean anything.

I think that '63 was the apex of what the Birmingham Movement was all about. It raised the consciousness of a lot of people. People developed a political consciousness, their religion took on more meaning, they developed courage and a feeling that they were heading somewhere and they weren't going to turn back. I think we need to reassess that sometime and see where we got off the track. And that's why I say we need to go back to what our foreparents did and see how they dealt with these situations. We got to get ourselves closer together because we are similar to the same problem now. I think we are going to reverse, or we are going to repeat what we went through.

Edited by Horace Huntley. BCRI Oral History Project, vol. 7, sec. 5 (June 21, 1995).

Notes

1. Westfield was a TCI coal mining town in western Jefferson County.
2. Howard was a leader of the International Union of Mine, Mill, and Smelter Workers, the NAACP, and the Bessemer Voters' League. See the interview with Asbury Howard Jr. in this volume.
3. In 1961 President Kennedy issued Executive Order 10925, which required equal employment opportunities in federal employment and in companies with federal government contracts. It also created the President's Committee on Equal Employment Opportunity. Herbert Hill, *Black Labor and the American Legal System: Race, Work, and the Law* (Madison: University of Wisconsin Press, 1985), 380.
4. Silver dollars were referred to as "bow dollars."

Reuben Davis

Born December 18, 1923, in Birmingham. Served in the navy. Worked at L&N Railroad as a tractor operator and served as Local 1044 representative for the International Brotherhood of Firemen and Oilers. Taught in Bessemer school system for thirty years. Fired from L&N because of union activity. Served as county commissioner for Jefferson County. *"Mr. Hosea Hudson is someone I know who was an avowed Communist. He lived in East Birmingham, in the Greenwood area. At the time, you would wake up in the morning, see little leaflets on your porch, and never know how they got there. Someone was always spreading information around. I once heard Dr. Ballard, a Birmingham physician, say at a church service, 'Anytime a black man made any move toward progress, they would brand him as a Communist.' In my opinion, the American government was not fearful of communism—they were thinking that communism would advance the cause of black people."*

The Long Struggle for Economic Rights

Both of my parents are from Montgomery County. My dad came out of Tuskegee around Mount Meigs, Alabama, and my mother was born in Montgomery. They married in Montgomery, and I was born in 1923. I have an older brother, born about 1917. Somewhere around 1915 or '16 they moved to Birmingham for better employment.

My dad had been living on a farm around Mount Meigs. His father died early. And so he had one brother and several sisters and his mother, who lived to be about 115 years old. She stayed there and educated two of her daughters on that farm, and finally my uncle and my dad went to Mount Meigs and brought my grandmother back here. But my dad worked in the coal mines for a short period of time, he and his brother. His brother stayed with the mines until around about 1950. He left and went to Detroit and started working for Chrysler. My dad got scared and came out of the mine.

My father's education was limited. I think he went maybe to the primary grades. My mother was similar. Education opportunities were very limited for both of them. My mother never worked out of the home. She was a housewife and a mother. I have two brothers and two sisters. I was the knee baby. They had to give me a title because when they started to call my baby sister "the baby," then that created a problem for everybody. So they said I was a knee baby. My brother was the oldest and my sister, then I came in, and then my other sister.

I was raised in Collegeville.[1] I was born within about five miles of where I live today. And the strange thing about it, I've never had a change of address other than during military time. I never had any intention of ever leaving Birmingham. Even during the crises and all the hardship that we were going through, I still felt that Birmingham was the place to live. I never did leave.

When I was growing up, the only white people to live in Collegeville were Italians. According to the census tract, there were eight thousand black people living within less than a square mile that went from the L&N Railroad down to U.S. Pipe and then from that to Birmingham By-Product. People in the community then had a variety of occupations. In the mornings about 6:30 you could see men going to work in different directions. L&N was to the east, U.S. Pipe and ACIPCO was to the west, Sayreton Mines was to the north, and then you see ladies going to Norwood,[2] which was where the ladies worked as maids and cooks.

I remember at the time that black ladies would carry baskets on their heads. They would put the clothes on their head and walk to Norwood to their jobs. In the evening they would come back, bring those clothes, wash and iron them, and carry them back. I also recall that Montgomery was noted for women that worked at some black farmer's garden. They would go and shell butter beans and peas all day long, but they were graceful. They could walk with a bucket of water on their head and not waste a drop. I've never seen a white woman with that. I remember that black women had a tendency to be graceful. Some of the teachers at Hudson [Elementary School] would teach young girls to walk with books on their head. Somehow, we don't look that way now.

Anyway, I started school at Hudson, there in Collegeville. I was a mama's boy, and I didn't like being away from my mother. My first day at school in first grade, Miss Hill was my teacher. I had a middie blouse on, and they had greased me up with lard, had me all shiny. I just knew I wanted to be at home with my mother. There was a young fellow in front of me who said, "Miss Hill, may I be excused?" And so she said, "Yes." I saw him walk out. I said to myself, "That's the way to get out." So, when he came back I asked if I could be excused. She said, "Yes." I didn't stop until I got home.

That afternoon, my mother was hanging curtains. And so I made up my cry just before I arrived to our home. And she jumped up and said, "What's the matter?" I said, "Somebody took my lunch." Well, this was early—before lunch period. She said, "Wait a minute." She went in and got a switch and went across my neck all the way back to school. My mother said, "I'm going to give you to Miss McQueen." Miss McQueen was a Birmingham City truant officer. When they called the roll, if anyone was absent that was supposed to be in the classroom, those names were turned over to Miss McQueen. She would visit the homes and find out what was happening. Miss McQueen told me that if I didn't stay in school, she was going to take me to Mount Meigs to the boys' reformatory school. So I was no more problem. That was a holy day for me because I learned then that I had to go to school.

When it was time for me to go to high school, Parker was overcrowded. Parker High School was identified as the largest Negro high school in the world. And Ullman, which used to be a white school, was vacated. I had to go to Ullman for two years and Parker the other two to finish high school. One thing that was real strange to me as a lad: I had to ride Norwood streetcar to Eleventh Avenue South to walk about three blocks to Ullman. Well, I would pass Phillips High School[3] on the bus, and I was curious, "Why do I have to pass a school going to school?" I raised that question. But I found out that our teachers really weren't sensitive to their responsibility of enlightenment. I think they were controlled or something. They never could discuss such issues as that.

I don't think the school system, as such, was interested in the education of black people. They had to have a school just for the sake of having one in name only. If you got an education, it was a by-product. But fortunately, we had teachers that were sensitive to our needs, and they did what they could. At that time, if you didn't do what you were supposed to do, or do it in the way that you should have done it, then you had a problem. Parents supported the teachers.

The thing that stands out in my mind most about my high school experience is the fact that there was pride. We had to wear a uniform, you had to have your shoes shined, and everyone who attended Parker High School had to go to general assemblies. We would have programs, and they were an enrichment to the student body. There was a sense of belonging and a sense of pride that stayed with me. All the students that graduated from high school with me have been successful. One friend of mine that lived in Collegeville,

Clifton Casey, was in the air force at Tuskegee, and he later retired as an inspector of the Detroit police force. He was also the first black person, or first person to fly a helicopter for the City of Detroit police force.[4]

I wanted to play football in high school, but I was too small. Coach Collins had selections from all over the city, and therefore he could pick all big boys. But I really wanted to play football. I also loved to skate. The only paved street in the whole community of Collegeville was where my family lived. We loved to skate on that street during the Christmas holidays.[5]

When we would skate, sometimes the police would come by, for no reason, in those red cars they used to drive. The kids would run off because police officers were known to call you to their cars, wind the glass down, and then, once you put your head in, wind the glass up so you couldn't get it out. Then they'd hit you upside the head. So we'd run when they drove up, even though we hadn't done anything.

We didn't have a very good relationship with the City of Birmingham. Actually, the only service that we received from the City of Birmingham was a man that was called "the ten-gallon-can man," who would take the cans from the outhouse and dump those cans. That's the only service we had. No garbage service. Jerry was our man. He had his wagon and a mule, and he would come in the alley, and you had this tin can in the outhouse. My job at home was dumping the slop jar in the ten-gallon can.

After high school, I went to work. I really didn't have any reason or any encouragement at all to go to college. When I finished high school in 1943, there was no incentive. No matter how much education you had, you were limited to certain kinds of jobs. You could be a preacher. You could be a school teacher. You could sell insurance, work on the railroad, or be a postman. Those were the only jobs available. I wanted to be a railroad engineer, and so, as soon as I finished high school, I went to work.

At the time, my dad was working for the railroad as an oiler. He oiled and lubricated each channel. The oilers' responsibility was to put oil and packing in the channels to keep the train boxes from running hot. You see, if the box ran hot, it could cause a wreck. The black men were helpers, and the white employees were inspectors or car men. The black man would oil the box, and the inspector was supposed to come back to make sure it was properly oiled. If the box ran hot, the oiler, the black man, was held accountable for it. A lot of them lost their jobs because a box ran hot or because the train had to pull out one of the cars. That was one really strange thing about the system there, because the inspectors were supposed to see to everything being done right. But if anything went wrong, it was always said to be the helpers' fault.

My dad didn't want me to work for the railroad. He wanted me to go to

Tuskegee, but I didn't want to go to school. I didn't see any need for it. I was interested in getting married, I wanted a family, I needed a job, and I was seriously interested in being a railroad engineer. I lived not too far from the L&N main lines. If you are familiar with Vanderbilt Crossing—there's a fish market there now—that's where the main line was. I would see the passenger trains and the freight trains going north and south. For some reason, my mind locked on the power of that locomotive, and I wanted to be the one to pull that throttle, I really did. But it never occurred to me that a black man couldn't be an engineer.

I started out as a laborer after my neighbor, Mr. Lewis Berry, recommended me. I wanted to start at the bottom and move on up. I found out the engineer's job wasn't for me, but I kept working there for several years until I went into the service.

When I was drafted in 1944, I wanted to be in the army rather than the navy. This is because I had learned to swim in Village Creek, but I couldn't see myself swimming in the ocean. However, they sent me to Fort Benning, Georgia, gave me an aptitude test, and decided that I would be in the navy. I noticed that if you had less than a high school education, they would send you to Great Lakes, Illinois, which was a naval base that trained seamen for various crafts aboard the ship. If you had a high school education or above, they would put you in the steward's branch of the navy. The stewards cooked, made beds, and cleaned up the rooms or areas of the officers. So they put me in the steward's branch, and that's what I did during the entire war. I was in the same outfit as President Kennedy, who was what they called a dollar-a-year man. That meant that he wouldn't accept a salary from the government, but they had to pay him something, so they paid him a dollar a year. He was in PT 109.

Anyway, I wanted to be a naval officer and felt that I was eligible for that. I had 4.0 conduct, and I was willing to take training. At the time, there was pressure to have a B-12 program so that blacks could become naval officers. Secretary of the Navy Knox stated that before he would allow a black man to become a naval officer, they would fly the flag at half-mast. Finally, they did fly the flag at half-mast, and they began to have black naval officers. I never did get a chance to get into that area, because I had some serious problems, hatred built up in my heart.

I was disgusted the whole time I was in the navy. I was made to shine officers' shoes, to make their beds, and to serve them with a little white coat on. I learned to do this at the training facilities in Newport, Rhode Island. On our sleeves, we wore a little white moon with bars below it to indicate the rank, but white sailors had a crow with ranks under it. We weren't allowed to wear a crow.

At Newport, I had some experiences that changed my whole life. A steward who ranked as a petty officer was over us. One night, this steward informed me that I was assigned to work in the officers' club from eight or nine o'clock until early in the morning. They would pay you extra money for that, but I told the steward that I didn't care to work. I said, "Give it to someone else." He said, "You have duty up there." I said, "I don't care for the money." He said, "You got to go." I said, "If I have to go, when the bugles are sounding taps, I'm hitting my rack." You see, I knew I had to get up at five o'clock that next morning to go in the galley.

That night, I went up to the officers' club and carried drinks from the bartender to the officers. They were dancing and drinking with their guests and whatnot. When I heard the bugler sound taps, I had a drink in my hand. I put it down on the table and walked out. I went by the executive officer's office, wrote a note, and explained to him what had happened concerning the stewards and stewards' mates getting up at five o'clock in the morning to go to work and then working until two and three in the morning at the club. In the note, I told him I didn't care to work at the club and that I didn't think I should be forced to do it.

The next morning, my name was called out to report to the executive officer. I went to his office. The steward was there, too. The executive officer asked me to explain what I had written on the note. "Well, sir," I said, "I explained to the steward that I didn't care for the extra work, and he insisted that I go up. So at taps, I knew I had to get up early in the morning to work in the galley, so I just come up and went to bed." The executive officer asked the steward, "Did you tell him he had to work up there?" The steward said, "Yes, sir." The executive officer said, "Well, I'm telling you, he didn't have to work up there. But Davis, you didn't handle this the proper way." And so that settled that part, but within the next two days I was shipped out. They shipped me to the Pacific, to Pearl Harbor. They determined that I was a troublemaker, and they shipped me out. That was a serious change in my life—I had decided that I was a person.

I was in Pearl Harbor for seven or eight months, then they shipped me back to Newport for about two weeks. After that, I was sent to Europe. So I served in both theaters of war. After I came back from Europe, there was still fighting in Japan, and they were going to send me back to the southwest Pacific. I told them I refused to go. They shipped me to Fargo Building in Boston, and from there they sent me to New Orleans, where I was discharged.

One of the first things that I did when I returned to Birmingham was register to vote. When I had been in France, I had tried to vote for President Roosevelt's reelection but had gotten a letter saying, "Dear Alabamian, you are not on our list of qualified voters, and you have to apply to be qualified before you can vote."[6] I was discharged from the service on the ninth of December in 1945, which was a Friday. I registered to vote that next Monday without any problems, and they asked me no questions whatsoever. When I qualified to vote in Collegeville, more than eight thousand black people lived within less than a square mile, but only eleven of us were qualified to vote. Two of those eleven were doctors—Dr. Mitchell was a surgeon, and Dr. Macklin was just a medical doctor. There were a few miners that were qualified to vote, but just eleven men, and I was one of those eleven.

I found the ballot to be powerful. I immediately joined with the Progressive Democratic Council, and I knew that, sooner or later, the conditions in the political arena would have to change. Some of the people involved with the Progressive Democratic Council were Mr. J. R. Hatchett, Mr. L. F. Berry, Mr. Mobile, and Mr. Bart Washington. Each of the communities had a Civic League that was a branch of the Progressive Democratic Council. Members of the leagues would get together, examine the backgrounds of all of the candidates, and then choose the best one to vote for. There were no blacks to vote for. Around this time, I was in my early twenties, and I was elected president of the Civic Youth Federation, a group of young people within the Civic League.[7]

Dr. R. B. Macklin, a doctor in the North Birmingham area, paid for our letterhead. As president of the Civic Youth Federation, I wrote letters to and visited the Italian stores in the Collegeville area during 1946–47, telling them that if they hired a black clerk, then we would assist them in getting more business. I was able to get a black woman hired at one of those stores behind Hudson School.

At this time, the Collegeville community had no connection at all with city hall. There were no sidewalks, and the only paved street was Twenty-seventh Avenue, since it was frequently used by industrial workers coming from North Birmingham to East Birmingham. Around this time, I called Birmingham City Hall and asked the city to put a streetlight on Thirty-fourth Street and Twenty-seventh Avenue because that was an area where it was dark. The only streetlights in the Collegeville community were located near the Italian stores. The rest of the community was completely dark. The man I talked with at city hall was fair, and he told me he would look into it. The next thing I knew, the streetlight was there.

When I came back to Birmingham, I began working at the L&N Railroad again. However, this time I was pressing for a higher job because I'd seen black men in the navy operate cranes and drive trucks—jobs that weren't available to black men in the shops where I'd been. I wrote a letter to the master mechanic, asking for apprentice training as a machinist. The master mechanic summoned me to his office. He said, "Davis, why do you want to be a machinist?" Then he said, "I'll give you a leave of absence to go up to Nashville." There was a school in Nashville that taught dentistry, and he wanted to make a dentist out of me! I told him, "I can't leave Birmingham. I have a family here, and I want to work the top job I'm qualified for."

Through the GI Bill, I applied for the job as an apprentice machinist. The government would guarantee me an opportunity, but they left it up to me to find somewhere to work as an apprentice. I went to Tuskegee to take an aptitude test, which I passed. When I came back to the shop, I realized that I had a fight on my hands.

L&N never did give me an apprentice position. I ended up in court fighting this. I'm pretty sure I'm the first person who filed a discrimination case against L&N because of this. It was 1946, and I knew that I was representing a lot of men in that courtroom, a lot of men that were in the same situation that I was in. I never asked anyone to testify with me or sign a petition, though.

When I went to court, L&N used Mr. Mulvaney, the foreman at the roundhouse, as a witness. At the time, I was working on the coal shoot, putting coal and water on the locomotive engines that were kept in the roundhouse. Mr. Mulvaney testified in Judge Lynn's court that I was "hotheaded," that no one could tell me anything. You see, the promotions at L&N were supposed to be based on ability, merit, and seniority. They admitted that I had ability and seniority but argued that I didn't merit the position because I was a "hothead." Judge Lynn, who was appointed by President Roosevelt as a district judge for the Northern District of Alabama, ruled against me. I think if I'd had that case later, I would have won it.

Around this time, I became interested in the activities of labor organizations and in the economic situation of black people in general. At that time, it was common that practically everyone who wanted a job could get a job. There were industries like U.S. Pipe Shop, Sloss, Birmingham By-Product, the L&N Railroad Company, ACIPCO, McWane, Stockham, and all these places—there was no question about getting a job. But the thing about it, all the jobs available were lower-end and the most difficult of working. Eventually I became active in encouraging young people working at the plants to try to get jobs that weren't available to them.

I worked at L&N for four more years after being denied the apprentice position, until 1950, during which time I served as the local chairman of Local 1044 of the International Brotherhood of Firemen and Oilmen. During this time, they promoted nearly every black man out there. They had to offer all of the laborers promotions to a higher type of job. I felt happy because I felt that I was responsible for those men getting top-rate jobs. Even my father was offered a car man's job, but he wouldn't take it. My brother became a car man. Since I was known as a "hothead," I wasn't promoted, but they couldn't say that about everybody out there, so they had to promote them.

I became aware of some situations in which union contracts discriminated even within the ranks of the union. The idea of "departmental seniority" meant that if I was hired as a laborer in a certain department, I couldn't move out of that department to another. I think it was another way to keep black workers at a minimal level. The union itself devised that method. In other words, black men could have seniority, but if there weren't any jobs in their departments, their seniority had no meaning.[8]

My union was part of the AFL, which had a history of being basically anti-black. I did have some contact with the unions in the CIO. There was a union involving workers at U.S. Pipe and Foundry, I believe it was District 50. The head of District 50 was a man named Moffet in Washington.[9] Rayvon Hinton was working for U.S. Pipe on a job as crane operator. They had given him the opportunity to train, but during this time, he and a white fellow were at odds with one another. The white man struck him, and he struck the white man back. They fired Rayvon, and that's when I became involved. I went to the union headquarters in Washington to deal with that issue and was able to get the government involved in looking at discriminatory practices at U.S. Pipe. I have some letters from Washington about that.

At the time, it was a no-no for a black person to make forward moves that weren't approved by whites. Any white person at that time, especially a police officer, had enough influence that they could attack or threaten a black man with no recourse. Mr. Asbury Howard, a laborer in the Mine, Mill, and Smelter Workers Union and president of the Bessemer Voters' League, was attacked along with his son in the Bessemer City Hall for something he said or did. He had a picture in his office of himself all bloody from where the police struck him.[10]

Our union, the Local 1044, met at the Masonic Temple. I told the men, "If you do your job, I'll defend your rights. But if you're caught asleep, or come to work drunk, or if you're stealing, don't ask me to represent you. I can't defend that." I was more or less a good employee, because I was encouraging people to be good workers. But the company just couldn't control me. I kept a copy of the union contract and a New Testament all the time. I read both of them.

One day, a car man was cutting a piece of waste material in repairing a boxcar, and he had a black helper with him. It was reported to me that this helper was being made to pick up scrap, which was a laborer's duty. I had the privilege of getting off my job to look into problems in the shop. I went up to the area and said, "Mr. Mulvaney, that's scrap material." He said, "Davis, the car man just cut that, and there is a helper right here. Why can't he pick that up and put it in a trash can?" I said, "Because that's laborers' work. That's the agreement." He said, "Davis, you will never make a foreman." He was trying to condition me to accept a position, solving the problem of my activism. He didn't understand that I didn't want to be a foreman—I wanted to be a machinist. After that, they began to get after me.

I was taught at home that all elderly people should be addressed as "Mr." or "Mrs.," so I didn't have a problem with calling my elderly white foreman "Mr. Mulvaney." One day, Mr. Mulvaney said, "Go tell Wade Bradley to send me a fourteen-inch pipe wrench." So I went to the back shop, where I found a white fellow operating a lathe. I asked, "Can you tell me where I can find Wade Bradley?" He looked at me but didn't say a word, and I thought he couldn't hear me, so I said it louder. He grabbed a wrench and said, "You mean Mr. Bradley, don't you?" I said, "You heard me." When he grabbed that wrench, I grabbed a hammer. Now, all of that was just because I was addressing him by his name. That gives you some idea of the conditions at the time.

I was the safety leader for my department. A young white fellow was an apprentice carpenter. He called me Davis, and I called him Cobb. One morning, in the safety meeting, Mr. DeWitt said, "Some of you fellows are getting too familiar with these white men, calling them by their first names. Things have not changed here." When he finished his speech, I said, "Mr. DeWitt, you didn't call the name of the person who had done that, but I refer to Cobb as Cobb, and he refers to me as Davis. You are Mr. DeWitt, because you are my foreman." He didn't say a word.

There is an incident that sticks out in my mind when I think about L&N. I was a tractor operator, and it was customary for me to check the oil in a machine before I started. I checked the oil in the old tractor that morning, found the stick absolutely clean, and discovered that the crankcase was filled with gasoline. If I had started that engine, with the ignition on top, and gasoline fumes in the crankcase, there's no telling what would have happened. I didn't make any noise about it. I had the tractor pulled to the machine shop, drained that gasoline, put oil in, and went about my work. I don't know whether anyone was purposely trying to do me harm.

I found out that the master mechanic, Mr. McWilliams, told an international representative that I was a "troublemaker." I got my committee together to talk about this. I wanted to go to the master mechanic's office, and the men didn't want me to do that. I said, "That is a gross insult to me and every man that I represent. I've only upheld the rules as they are printed." I kept an agreement book and a New Testament in my pocket all the time, and I read both of them.

I decided to write to the director of personnel in Louisville, Kentucky, a man named J. L. Sullivan, and asked him to come to investigate the situation. He asked, "Davis, did the master mechanic curse, or say any bad words to you?" I said, "No, I've never been cursed in my life." He said, "Well, how did the master mechanic insult you?" I said, "It appears that only through curse words can one be insulted." He said, "Well, the company is not going to allow our master mechanic to insult our local chairman, and by the same token, we're not going to allow our local chairman to insult our master mechanic." I said, "Mr. Sullivan, it seems as though you only think that a person is insulted by profane language. If Mr. McWilliams was in the back shop among the labor that I represent, and I called to him saying, 'Hey Mac, come here, I want to see you for a minute,' would I insult him?" Mr. Sullivan never said a word. You see, black people had to be submissive to whites, and I just couldn't handle that.

I did try to respect whites as people. One night, I left my job at about eleven to find a white man lying in the grass near Twenty-seventh Avenue, just before you cross the railroad tracks into Collegeville. He told me that he had been with some friends who had kicked him out of the car and asked me for car fare to the Salvation Army. At the time, car fare for the Tarrant City 22 out of Tarrant was seven cents, so you know how long it has been! I told him that I would take him there. I couldn't find the Salvation Army, so it took us a while, and he must have asked me a dozen times, "Why is it that you stopped to help me? You're black and I'm white." I finally found the Salvation Army on Eleventh Avenue, and the man did not want to leave me. I told him, "I could not pass up on an opportunity to help a man in need." He embraced me, kissed my cheek, and said, "I'll never forget you." I have found that in order to be effective, you have got to love people. We cannot win the battle without love.

I finally lost my job at L&N. I was keeping about three hundred car men busy building boxcars by carrying material to them on my tractor. Well, one day my tractor broke down. Ordinarily, when a tractor was broken, its operator would go to the shop and wait until his tractor was ready before going back to work, but I knew that I couldn't do that. So I kept my work going by using an idle tractor. Mr. Hollingsworth, my immediate foreman, called on the PA system, told me to go to the north end of the shed, and told me to roll wheels.

When Mr. Hollingsworth told me to roll wheels, I knew I could not do it. A boxcar wheel weighs 350 pounds, and the axle weighs 750 pounds. Now, I had a boil under my arm that day, but I didn't stay home from work because I knew that I could still handle my tractor. But to move such heavy wheels, you had to exert quite a bit of effort. I told the foreman, "Mr. Hollingsworth, it's very difficult for me to roll wheels. I came to work because I can handle my tractor, but I've got a boil under my arm." He asked me if I was refusing to work. I said, "I'm not refusing to work. I'm just telling you I can't roll wheels." He said, "You're going to roll wheels." I said, "Well, if you insist that I roll wheels, I prefer punching out." I had the privilege of hitting the clock anytime.

That was the day they had been waiting for. The foreman went to the office, the master mechanic called me in, and I was sent to Dr. McGruder for an examination. I knew my fate was sealed in the envelope he handed to me. I carried it to Dr. McGruder, who examined my arm, sealed the envelope again, and sent me back to the shop. When I got back to the master mechanic's office, he said, "You go down and do anything you want to do." I knew I was going to be fired then.

About three or four months later, the master mechanic came down to the shop and gave me a letter, which I put in my back pocket. He said, "Davis, I want you to read that letter." I said, "I'll read my mail when it's convenient. Right now I'm busy." He was the boss man, and he knew that it was my job to carry this material back and forth. He said, "If you don't mind, read that one now." I took the letter out of my pocket. It said, "You are hereby discharged from service to this company effective immediately." He said, "Do you understand the letter?" I said, "Yes." He said, "Get off the company's premises the quickest way you know how." Now, ten dollars was all the money I had in the world, but I was obedient to him. I knew he wanted me to tell him that I needed my job—which I did—but I walked across the train yard, got off his premises, and went home. It took me three years to win that job back.

The day after I was fired from L&N, I received a postcard from New York from an organization that said it could help me because I was fired illegally. I was afraid that it was a Communist organization. The next day, I carried it to the FBI, which was located down the street from the *Birmingham News*. When I gave the card to an agent, he looked at me and said, "How did your name get on that list?" I said, "I have no idea." He said, "Have a seat over there and see if you can't figure out how your name got on that list. What organization are you a member of?" I said, "I'm a scoutmaster, a member of the labor organization, a mason, and a church member." It was a scary thing. They hurt a lot of people in that process of trying to track down Communists. Paul Robeson was almost destroyed—as a young man, I went to Pizitz to buy one of his records, and the lady said, "We do not have his records." At the time, I didn't know why, but I later found out that he was suspected to be a Communist, so many of his records had been destroyed.

Mr. Hosea Hudson is someone I know who was an avowed Communist. He lived in East Birmingham, in the Greenwood area. At the time, you would wake up in the morning, see little leaflets on your porch, and never know how they got there. Someone was always spreading information around.[11] I once heard Dr. Ballard, a Birmingham physician, say at a church service, "Anytime a black man made any move toward progress, they would brand him as a Communist." In my opinion, the American government was not fearful of communism—they were thinking that communism would advance the cause of black people.

When I lost my job at L&N, I applied at O. C. Hall's car dealership in North Birmingham, because I wanted to be a salesman. I took a test at his office and passed it. He said, "We're going to make a bird dog out of you." In other words, he wanted me to get a sale and then hold it for a real salesman to come around and get the money. I wouldn't accept that.

After trying that, I went to J. Truitt Payne, who sold cars, and asked him if he serviced his used cars. He told me that he sent that work out. I said, "Well, if you have equipment, I could service those cars for you, make a job for myself, and save you some money." He said, "Fellow, I've been on this corner twenty-one years, and it wouldn't do for a car to go a block and stop running." I told him that if I had the equipment, I could tune a car better than anyone in town, or just as well. I had gone to school on the GI Bill to be a mechanic and also attended General Motors Institute in Flint, Michigan. He said, "Come back in two weeks." When I came back in two weeks he told me that he had an opening in the new car department and that he would hire me if I had my tools. At the time, I didn't even own a car, but I had my tools.

When Mr. Payne hired me, he said, "You'll be working for a white fellow. If he calls you a wrong name, it's one or two things you could do. You can tell me about it, or you can pick up a hammer and knock the hell out of him." I said, "Well, if you hire me, I won't make any problems for you."

The gentleman that I worked with at first was named George. It turned out that he and I worked like two peas in a pod, because he found out that I knew mechanics. He had his stall, I had mine, and we prepared new cars for the showroom. When those new cars came off the truck, we checked those cars for rattles or noises and put in the floor mats, radios, and heaters.

After we had been working together for a while, George became ill and had to take off for three or four days. Now, George had been very nice to me, and we had worked well together. I wanted to do whatever I could to help him, so I went to management to ask if men who were sick could receive a salary while they were off. The manager said, "No, Davis, we don't do that. Why do you ask?" I said, "Mr. George is off sick. If you agree to pay him while he's off, I'll work whatever time is necessary to keep these cars moving for the sales department." The manager checked with Mr. Payne, and later in the evening he came out and said, "Davis, we've agreed to pay Mr. George's salary, but you let us know if you need some help out here." Well, I kept those cars moving.

And when George came back, he said, "Davis, they paid me!" I never did tell him that I was responsible for that.

Later, George told me that he was planning to move to Florida for a better job. He said, "I can get you a job in Florida, making more money than you're making here." I told him that I couldn't leave Birmingham. He quit, and they hired a new fellow.

The new fellow came in on his first day wearing white trousers and a white shirt and carrying a cup of coffee in his hand. I had been working on a car that day, and when I returned from road testing it, he said, "Davis, you finish this job here." Then he pointed to the car he had been working on. I did that, because I thought there might have been something else that he had to do. But I found out his game—he wanted me to do all of the work! So I began to slow down on my jobs until he finished his.

One day, a doctor purchased two Chryslers. I had been working on a Chrysler 300, with two four-barrel carburetors—a powerful engine. I was out test-driving it for about fifteen to twenty minutes. When I came back, this new guy was standing in the alley at J. Truitt Payne's shop. He cursed me and asked, "Where have you been?" I jumped out of that car and told him, "None of your damn business. And don't ever ask me where I've been!"

Eventually, I figured out that this guy didn't really know what he was doing. Whenever you would put a radio or heater in a car, there was a template that would let you know where to drill a hole for the antenna. He didn't know what that was there for. You also had a template to tell you where the holes should be drilled for the spotlights. Using the template always helped me to drill my holes in the right place, but he never did it that way.

One day, two orders came into our shop—one for a spotlight to be placed on a car, and another for a car that needed a heater and radio. I figured that the job with the heater and radio would be more difficult, so I worked on that one. Meanwhile, he started drilling on the car that needed the spotlight. Finally he said, "Davis, would you come over here and take a look at this drill?" He had been drilling a long time. Well, the drill came straight through the dash. He knew that he had messed this car up. I went back to my job. Later that evening, the manager asked, "Davis, who that messed up this dash?" I pointed to the fellow. He said, "Davis, why did you take that other job?" I said, "I took the hardest job. I put a heater in, and I put a radio in. I thought that putting the spotlight into that car would be a simple job for him." Well, the manager said, "Davis, be more careful next time." When he said that, I knew it was my time to go.

A few days later, I gave Jack Payne a five-days notice that I would resign. Mr. Payne came to me and said, "Davis, we can't let you go. What's the problem?"

I said, "Mr. Payne, I promised you I wouldn't create a problem for you, and now I see a problem surfacing." Mr. Payne said, "Well, if you're talking about this fellow you work with, today is his last day." I said, "He needs a job just like I need one." And so I quit. I had been there three or four years.

When I left J. Truitt Payne's, I started doing mechanic work around my home. I also worked at the post office for about a year. Finally, an option came open. Mr. Ephraim, who taught me auto mechanics, told me that there was an opening for a mechanic instructor at Dunbar [High School].[12] When I called Mr. Abrams, the principal of Dunbar High School, he asked me to come out there. I told him about the work I had done with Payne, and somehow Miss Nation's name came up. I had worked on her car when her clutch went bad, and from then on, I was her mechanic. She was crazy about me. The principal asked if I thought Miss Nation would recommend me, and when I said yes, he said, "Well, if you know Miss Nation, you're alright." Then I went to the superintendent, who asked me if I would move to Bessemer if they hired me. I said that I would not move from Birmingham, but about five o'clock that evening he called me and told me that if I wanted the job, it was mine.

I taught for about thirty years. When I started out, I had no interest in teaching. I didn't even have college training. Of course, at the time, they didn't care who taught black children. However, my interest and love for children made me proud to have the job, and I really think I made a difference in some of my students' lives.

Sometimes, I think that we lost a lot by integration. I was working in the Bessemer School system at the time, and I know that many of the black teachers were pulled out of black schools and put into the white schools. Around that time, they created another area of education called vocational education and that was a dumping ground for "problem kids." I was proud of vocational education, because I felt confident that a child's selection of a vocation was an asset. However, the system itself saw vocational education as something of a dumping ground for kids.[13]

When I first started working at Dunbar High School, the system wanted to give me the equipment that Bessemer High had used for four or five years.[14] I just wouldn't accept that. The school system had established our program in name only—they didn't intend for my students to become competitive as mechanics. They would let the white students from Bessemer High go to Drennen's [a General Motors dealership] for hands-on work, but they wouldn't let my students. However, I went to Flint, Michigan, for General Motors Institutes during summer vacations, which I paid for out of my own pocket. I wanted to get additional training and materials that I could share with my students. And I discovered that General Motors was very generous to educational programs. Over the years, I was able to teach several young mechanics who now own their own businesses. I tried to give my students moral character about their work as well as strong instruction.

During one summer vacation, I won my case against L&N and was paid for lost time. There had been major cutbacks at L&N, so they were only able to hire me back for vacation vacancies. When a permanent position did open up, it was time for me to go back to work at the school.

I was one of the first teachers appointed to the new Abrams High School[15] in Bessemer. Mr. Abrams had been my principal, the first black boss I had ever had, and I really admired him. He passed away, and a new high school was named in his honor. The new principal, Mr. Branch, was also a black man. An upsetting incident occurred when I was working under Mr. Branch at Abrams.

I served as the school photographer, and one day Mr. Branch instructed me to take pictures of the championship-winning football team on the field at twelve o'clock. Mr. Branch was my principal, and he knew my lunch period ended at twelve. When I returned to my classroom at about 12:03, Mr. S. C. Porch, my immediate supervisor, and the assistant superintendent were in my classroom. Mr. Porch asked, "Where the hell have you been?" I knew he had the right to ask me where I had been, but not in that manner. I said, "Mr. Porch, I've been out getting pictures for the football team as I was instructed by the principal." He said, "I believe you'd better stay in the shop." I said, "It's a simple matter for me to stay in the shop. You go up and tell Mr. Branch you want me to stay in the shop. Surely, if he tells me to be somewhere else the next time you come, you won't find me." At that time, he put his hands on my collar and said, "I mean for you to stay in the shop." I never moved my hand from my side. I looked him in the face. The class was very quiet. I said, "Man, take your filthy hands off me. Take your hands off me right now—do you understand that?" He had not expected that. He dropped his hands and started shaking.

Well, I then left the room and went to Mr. Branch's office, just to relate to him what had happened, not to ask him for any assistance. I said, "Mr. Branch, I was doing what you told me to do. Mr. Porch just handed my collar. I don't play like that." Walter Branch looked at me, walked in his office, closed the door, and never said a word to me about that from then or now.

That day, I realized what a bad situation we as black people were in, when our school officials couldn't defend their own words. Mr. Branch could have said, "Well, I'll straighten this out," but he never said a word. From then on, I became increasingly interested in politics and started writing editorials. Mr. Branch called me one morning and wanted to know, "Davis, what about all this editorial writing?" I said, "What about it?" He said, "Davis, you know what I'm talking about." He said, "Don't say I didn't tell you." He was trying to tell me not to write—but I continued to write.

While I was working at the school system, I had become somewhat involved in the Movement. The Alabama Christian Movement for Human Rights was founded in 1956 when the NAACP was outlawed from operating in Alabama.[16] In my opinion, it was a bad move on behalf of Governor Patterson. If they had just listened to what black people were saying . . . but they took a negative attitude.

Reverend Shuttlesworth, my pastor, was the engineer behind the struggle in Birmingham. I helped to bring Reverend Shuttlesworth to this city. When I worked at L&N, Reverend Shuttlesworth's uncle, Mr. Wells, told me that Reverend Shuttlesworth was in Selma at the First Baptist church and really wanted to come to Birmingham. Well, our pastor, Reverend Laster, had recently died, so the pulpit was vacant. As a member of the church, I could recommend various ministers to the chairman of the pulpit committee, and I recommended that they invite Reverend Shuttlesworth.[17]

I didn't really get involved in the Movement until my church was bombed for the first time, in December of 1956, and that's when a lot of people really got motivated.[18] When they bombed that church the first time, we were cleaning the church up on a Saturday for Sunday-morning church services. I believe from the bottom of my heart that those people who were planting the bombs really weren't trying to hurt anyone. I think they were just trying to terrorize and get us scattered. But they were unsuccessful—it actually pulled us together. It was very similar to the situation in Montgomery during the bus boycott. I guess people had really gotten tired, and we just pulled together.

Every Sunday, they would announce where they would have the Monday-night Movement meeting that week, and you had to be there early to get a seat. At each meeting there were speakers, and good song services. Reverend Shuttlesworth would get up there and share information about what was going on with the Movement. It was something that kept us occupied.

Of course, not all members of the church were really supportive. And not all the pastors of other churches in Birmingham were behind Dr. King and Reverend Shuttlesworth.[19] But my family supported what I was doing. I never had any complaints from my wife, even though my children were really small at that time. When I had duty at the church or any guard duty, I just took that responsibility and got up to go to work the next morning. I couldn't do too much marching in Birmingham, because it took too long to get there from Bessemer. I did march in downtown Bessemer, however.

When I served as a guard, I was usually based at my church. My church is on Twenty-ninth Avenue and Thirty-third Street, which was a dirt road then.

One night, Julius Clark's father and I were on duty from midnight to six in the morning. We had loaded rifles and were instructed to fire and leave if we had to use our guns. That particular night at about three or four o'clock in the morning, I heard a car speeding around Thirty-fourth Street, headed toward the church. I knew that whoever was driving that car didn't know the area—especially the road's steep curve. When the car went across and found he was going into a dead end, he backed up and then went down Twenty-ninth. At that time, Reverend Clark and myself walked out, and we saw this car about three blocks down Twenty-ninth. He was headed west, and another car was headed east. They stopped side by side, just like this. After a while the other car headed to the church, driving slowly. It was a police car. Nothing happened that night, but you could tell the car was up to something, and whoever was driving the car wasn't familiar with the area.

I also helped Stone Johnson to protect Arthur Shores's home on Center Street. One night when I was not on duty there, someone was hurt. Shots were fired by us. I always heard that they came by as if they were going to throw something out of the car, and shots started firing.

Around 1970, the Bessemer Board of Education finally fired me. Later, I won that back and retired. Now, in 1970 I ran for a position as a delegate to the Democratic Convention, and the *Birmingham News* stated that I was the first black person to run for that position. I lost, but I became interested in running for county commissioner after Eddie Gilmore died in 1971. Seventeen candidates, all white, were running for the office, including Tom Gloor. I was a member of the Progressive Democratic Council, the leading black political organization, and I knew that we had quite a few votes at that time. I waited until the last minute on the last day to qualify, but I did it.

At that time, I knew Bob Washington, who was active in the Progressive Democratic Council, and I told him that I was going to qualify for county commissioner. He said, "Bubba, you know if you were a county commissioner, you would be handling millions of dollars. What kind of a large interest you would have! What kind of money you'd count!" I said, "Bob, I've built a home, and that's as far as I've gone. I can make decisions no matter how many dollars are involved, because it's the decisions that count." We left it at that, and I felt that he did not recognize my interest in people. Someone I knew told me that the committee within the Progressives had decided to support me, but on election day they ended up supporting Tom Gloor. If they hadn't, I would have won—the white vote was split seventeen ways.

Around that time, I had an opportunity to go into business and make a good salary, but I would have been doing it for the white man only, and I couldn't do that. Lee Styslinger owned Al Picket Equipment Company. He's a very nice man, and his youngest son and my youngest son are about the same age. I was a caretaker of his property in part of Norwood, near Vanderbilt [Road].

I was interested in starting my own mechanic shop, so I had visited Birmingham Trust [National Bank] to see Mr. Dick about getting a loan for twenty-five hundred dollars. He said, "Why don't you go for five thousand?" I told him that I didn't make it a practice of borrowing money I don't need. I mentioned this to Mr. Styslinger one evening, and he said, "Reuben, let me know how much money you need, how many people you're going to work, how much you're going to pay them, and approximately how long you think it will take for the business to turn a cycle." Two weeks later, I gave him a figure, and he said, "I'll deposit the money in the bank in your name. You write the checks." When I asked how I would pay him back, he said, "You don't pay me back." I was startled. I looked at him and said, "I can't accept your offer." I walked away from that.

The reason that I didn't take his money was because I didn't want to operate his business. I wanted to be my own person. If I had taken his money, I would've been using my influence in the black community to draw in black customers to a white-owned store. I would have been "his man," and I couldn't do that. It would have been like that drive-in in Bessemer that was run by a black man named Mr. James Bend but was owned by a white doctor in Bessemer.

I ran for county commissioner for the second time against Congressman Ben Erdreich. I think I had gotten a lot of people's attention through all of the editorials I had written in the newspapers. I spent less than three hundred dollars on my campaign and received a little more than twenty thousand votes. He spent about forty thousand dollars and got about thirty-five thousand votes. I didn't think that money was actually a factor in the political situation, and I think that's another problem we have. The ballot in America has almost been destroyed. There was no room for decent men in politics at the time I entered.

Eventually I was elected as county commissioner. After the county compromised and set up the districts, Lee Loder and I both ran. William Bell threatened to run. I was at a breakfast one Sunday morning when a fellow asked him, "You're president of the council, so why do you want to be a county commissioner?" I saw a little shimmy in his knee, and I knew then that something was wrong. One Saturday, I was outside cutting my grass and Dr. Gaston was on the phone. He said, "Come by the office, and we'll see about winning this election." The next week, Mayor Arrington and his wife came by. Dr. Arrington said, "Reuben, I came by to tell you that Bell is not going to run." I think that some of the political powers were afraid that I might win without their support, so they came in at the last minute. I had an overwhelming win, with over ninety percent of the black vote and thirty percent of the white vote.

I went into my new position with my head down, because I wanted to be of service to the people of Jefferson County. New offices had recently been built, so I was the first person to use that office space. I asked my pastor to come and dedicate that office to God. My major interests were health care and crime. I knew that crime was not inherited—that if parents were responsible, we could kill crime overnight. Later, I mentioned to the County Commission that we should pass a resolution involving parent accountability for conduct of minor children, but they laughed at that. In terms of health care, I had about fifty people get together to develop a plan for health care in Jefferson County that went into the year 2000. I wanted to emphasize preventive care and to build clinics all over the county in walking distance of children, but their doctors didn't like me for that, so I had to go.

When I was elected, they were about to close Cooper Green [Hospital] any minute, but I got that contract torn with the support of John Katopodis and Jim Gunther. I gave the employees six months notice that they would receive the same pay, but that after that they would have to compete for the job on the county level. Five suits were filed against me because former employees didn't qualify for the job. It wasn't my fault—the County Personnel Board had established the requirements. If the board sent me three names, I was to select one, and that was my responsibility.

In one particular case involving the hospital, I accused the county of conspiracy. The hospital's executive officer asked that a new position be established—supervisor of maternal and infant care. The head nurse in that department, Elizabeth Bonner, was a black female who also happened to be the only nurse in the hospital who had a degree in midwifery. The executive officer wanted a white female to serve in the new position on a temporary basis. I said, "You can't do it like that. If you want the position established, you go to personnel in that department, starting with the head nurse. If all the nurses in the Maternal and Infant Care department refuse to accept the temporary appointment, then and only then can you appoint anyone you like."

About two weeks later, the executive officer called me at home. It was a Friday night. He said that the doctors wanted to talk to me about something important and that they wanted to talk to me right then. When I got to the hospital, about fourteen doctors were in the conference room. "We're concerned about this position in Maternal and Infant Care," one of them said.

"We want a qualified person in that position." I said, "You have one." They said, "She ain't qualified." I said, "Document it. Put your concerns in writing to me." One of these doctors, Dr. Goldberg, asked, "Who is going to deliver these babies?" I responded, "Gentlemen, it seems as if you all have a problem. Pardon me." And I left them.

I think that I was not reelected because I did not have Mayor Arrington's endorsement. I had it when I won, but I did not have it the second time, probably because of the occupational tax. Several men from the coalition told me, "Reuben, this tax will kill Birmingham," and Mayor Arrington said the same thing. I explained to them that the county really needed this money, especially since Cooper Green Hospital was about to be shut down. Mayor Arrington wanted me to delay the vote, but he never told me why.

When I went into the chamber the next morning, that resolution was leading the agenda, and I voted to support it. That evening the mayor came into my office. He said, "Reuben, I have never been so disappointed in my life. You supported that tax." I said, "I never told you I wouldn't." He said, "I can't put up with this," and went on and on about how he couldn't put up with this. Later on, I supported the expansion of the Civic Center with the occupational tax. If the occupational tax hadn't passed, the county wouldn't have had money to put in the Civic Center. My interest was in the people.

I found out that I had misjudged the black people's interest in the political process. I thought that they were reading the newspaper and knew of the struggle that I was having as I tried to keep the hospital going.

As I look back on the Movement, I think that, and I thought then that economic rights should have been the focus of the Movement, rather than blacks' social equality. Of course, the sit-ins and demonstrations did assist blacks in getting clerks' jobs, but I didn't feel there was any major emphasis on economics. I don't think the system would have been as prepared to defend an economic movement as they were to defend a social movement. For example, the first thing that whites hollered was that black men wanted white women, and if the Movement had just focused on jobs, then they couldn't have said that.

From an economic standpoint, I think that the welfare handouts have really retarded our progress—and we're still locked into that now. They are fixing to take that away from us, but it wasn't right from the beginning, because it wasn't designed to help us. During my time in the Bessemer school system, I've seen as many as three, four, and five black girls pregnant in one classroom. I've heard the little girls saying that if they are pregnant, they can get a check if they don't identify a father. It seems that a lot of people have accepted welfare benefits as being essential to their livelihood. The struggle is coming all over again. One advantage I see in the situation right now: it's going to bring us back together, and then we can plot our course from this point on. We are hurting now, far more than we were before the struggle.

I arrived in Washington, D.C., on Amtrak at about 8:30 in the morning during the Million Man March, and it was one of the most exciting days of my life. I saw all these black brothers moving toward that mall, and in my heart I said, "What is this?" The reason that the Million Man March was so significant to me was that this was the first time that black men had shown that kind of strength. If America is saved, it will be saved by the soul of black men, of black people. I feel that once we've completed our work, there will be no need for the NAACP and other Movement organizations because we will have destroyed the strong germ and force of racism. I see the destruction of racism in my lifetime, and I think it is closer than you think, that time when, as Dr. King said, a man will be judged by his character rather than his race.

I went up there basically because I felt there was a need to come together. I had no idea that a million-plus men would show up. But I believe that those men were there because they accept part of the problem, and they wanted to be part of the solution. I wanted to be part of the solution, too. We have had political power, but we blended our political power with white people's dollars. That's a bad combination. That's like taking a sifter trying to clear out the Mississippi, especially when you don't need those dollars. My district is about 70 percent black, and if I get black support, why do I need dollars?

I still hold that America needs statesmen rather than politicians. America needs men that will stand on principle and not look back. The special interests have killed the force of the ballot. That's the reason that the Democratic party has been destroyed and that everybody from the Democratic party is going to the Republican party. That's the trend. White backlash is gaining momentum. It's gaining force.

A lot of people have reasons not to admire or support Minister Farrakhan. The truth is very difficult to accept, and most people have a way of trying to shun the truth. Minister Farrakhan has the personality and knowledge to speak his guts, and some people are going to be offended if they don't think he's saying the right thing. At one time, I was almost skeptical of those fellows that had skinheads and nice black suits and who called the white men "devils." But here is a man who called for millions of black men to come to Washington. By virtue of his call and the overwhelming response, I knew that God was working in that. God can use anybody that He desires, and Minister Farrakhan was a vessel in God's hand. I contend that the minister made that call, but God made the response. There's no way one man could have gotten that kind of response on his own, and I feel as if something big is coming out of this. If America can't see the handiwork of God in this movement, then we are totally lost.

Edited by Braden Phillips-Welborn. BCRI Oral History Project, vol. 13, secs. 4 and 5 (Mar. 20 and Apr. 3, 1996).

Notes

1. A North Birmingham community that is surrounded by railroad tracks and various industrial companies.

2. A middle-class white community within walking distance of Collegeville.

3. A large white high school near downtown Birmingham.

4. For a discussion of pride in the school, see Lynne B. Feldman, *A Sense of Place: Birmingham's Black Middle-Class Community, 1890–1930* (Tuscaloosa: University of Alabama Press, 1999), 127–32.

5. There was a tradition of black children skating in the streets of various communities in Birmingham through the 1960s.

6. In 1942 Congress passed the Soldier Voting Act, which authorized servicemen and -women to vote while overseas or at military bases. It exempted soldiers from all poll taxes. Nevertheless, the act also left the administration of absentee voting in the control of state governments, which were able to limit severely the number of black soldiers and sailors who actually cast ballots. See Alexander Keyssar, *The Right to Vote: The Contested History of Democracy in the United States* (New York: Basic Books, 2000), 246–47.

7. See Bobby M. Wilson, *Race and Place in Birmingham: The Civil Rights and Neighborhood Movements* (New York: Rowman and Littlefield Publishers, 2000), 183.

8. Black dissatisfaction with departmental seniority was also an issue at U.S. Steel. See the Luther McKinstry interview in this volume. See also Judith Stein, *Running Steel, Running America: Race, Economic Policy, and the Decline of Liberalism* (Chapel Hill: University of North Carolina Press, 1998), 159–61.

9. Elwood Moffet was vice president of District 50 until 1962, when he became president. District 50 was expelled from the UMWA in 1963. Maier B. Fox, *United We Stand: The United Mine Workers of America, 1890–1990* (Washington, D.C.: United Mine Workers of America, 1990).

10. See the Asbury Howard Jr. interview in this volume.

11. Hosea Hudson, *Black Worker in the Deep South: A Personal Account by Hosea Hudson* (New York: International Publishers, 1972); Nell I. Painter, *The Narrative of Hosea Hudson: His Life as a Negro Communist in the South* (Cambridge, Mass.: Harvard University Press, 1979).

12. The only black high school in Bessemer, a city in western Jefferson County, thirteen miles from downtown Birmingham.

13. Since the late nineteenth century, industrial or vocational education had been the norm for black schools. See Horace Mann Bond, *Negro Education in Alabama: A Study in Cotton and Steel* (New York: Atheneum, 1969), 214–17, 264–69.

14. Bessemer High was the white school.

15. Abrams High School replaced Dunbar High School.

16. Aldon D. Morris, *The Origins of the Civil Rights Movement* (New York: Free Press, 1984), 68–69.

17. A discussion of how Reverend Shuttlesworth came to Bethel in Collegeville can be found in Andrew M. Manis, *A Fire You Can't Put Out: The Civil Rights Life of Birmingham's Reverend Fred Shuttlesworth* (Tuscaloosa: University of Alabama Press, 1999), 68–69.

18. Ibid., 106–15.

19. See BCRI's Oral History Project interviews, Fred Shuttlesworth, vol. 23, John Porter, vol. 27, and Henry Goodgame Sr., vol. 20.

Jerome "Buddy" Cooper

Born January 15, 1913, in Brookwood, Tuscaloosa County, Alabama. Graduate of Phillips High School in Birmingham, Harvard College, and Harvard Law School. Served as law clerk for Supreme Court Justice Hugo Black and attorney for the United Steelworkers of America (USWA). *"Bull Connor arrested a whole bunch of kids. The bond was raised to something like twenty-five hundred dollars, and for all of these kids, it was going to cost about $250,000. The president [Kennedy] asked the Steelworkers, the AFL-CIO, and Auto Workers to put up that money. He thinks the interest of the country requires it, and I think it does. They mechanically transferred the money, by telegraph or something."*

Labor's Attorney

I consider my parents to have been Alabamians, but neither of them was born here. My mother was born in Poland and brought to Birmingham when she was three months old. When she died in her early nineties, we considered her to have been an early settler of Birmingham. My father was a little older than my mother. He was born in Lithuania and came to this area when he was thirteen years old.

My father was a merchant. He, his brother, and his brother-in-law, Kellerman, operated a general store in Brookwood and another one in Surles. Before I was born, my father and his brother opened one of the first department stores in downtown Birmingham. It was called Cooper Brothers and was located on Second Avenue between Nineteenth and Twentieth Streets. The building was later occupied by Burger Phillips and has since been remodeled. In 1907, when the store had not been operating for very long, my uncle [my father's partner] became ill, went to Johns Hopkins [hospital], began to experience severe depression, and closed the store. He didn't come back until 1919. At that time, my grandparents were living in Birmingham's North Side at Eighth Avenue and Fifteenth or Sixteenth Street, just a few blocks from where the institute is now. That house was standing until just a few years ago.

I was born in a village called Brookwood, in Tuscaloosa County. Brookwood was the site of some major coal mines, but it was also an agricultural area. I remember a coal miner telling me one time that when he testified before the United States Congress on legislation to help coal miners, he raised some questions about farming. One opposing senator said, "Well, you're a coal miner, so you wouldn't know anything about farming, would you?" And that man said, "Coal miners made so little working in the mines, we had to farm in order not to starve."

We moved from Brookwood to Birmingham in 1919, and I began attending South Highland Grammar School that year. I grew up at 1601 Fifteenth Avenue South, which was right at the foot of Vulcan[1] in the South Side.

In Brookwood, we had an elderly black nurse. She came with us when we moved to Birmingham. My sister and I were both between six and eight years old at this time, and her children had already married. I think her children stayed in Brookwood.

I remember that she sometimes would take us for a picnic lunch on the South Side. My mother would fix a big basket of food, and then the nurse would take my sister and me on the Tidewater line out to Avondale Park, where we would spend the day. They had an elephant there named Miss Fancy, a few little animals, and a fish pond. Then we would retrace our steps and ride the streetcar home. On the streetcar, our nurse always sat with us in the white section.[2] Once or twice, the white motorman made comments, and she told him where to go. We were her children, and she was going to sit wherever we sat. There was never a big scene about it or anything.

One of the first memories that I have of being taught about race was when my father responded to something I said on one of our Sunday walks. I don't remember how the subject came up, but I was quoting something that I had heard someone else say. This person had used the word "nigger." Well, my father said to me, "Nice people don't use that word." I asked what I should say, and he said, "You say 'colored people.'" Now I understand that it has assumed another form. I understand that some black people don't care whether it's "colored" or "black," but other people are very sensitive about it. I never forgot what he said: "Nice people don't." And he never did use that word, that I can recall.

There were no black people at Phillips High School, but there was an incident involving my own race that occurred while I was there. I have always been sort of a frustrated politician, and I'm glad that I was frustrated in most instances. I ran for the secretary of the student body, which numbered about fifteen hundred to two thousand at that time. It was a large school, and the political campaign was one of the big events of the year. One day, one of my campaigners came up to me and said, "Buddy, so-and-so has put out the word that you're Jewish." I said, "Well, I am." He said, "You are?" But I won anyway. I beat a very prominent, very fine lady from a socially distinguished family in Birmingham.

I never objected to someone referring to me as being Jewish. I'm a backslid Jew philosophically, but my reaction depends on the circumstances. If someone said to me, "You Jew," I might dislike that. I might have taken them on. I do recall having a couple of scrapes. But if someone just said, "I understand you're Jewish," then I would think, "Well, I am."

I graduated from Phillips High School in the spring of 1929 and started at Harvard College that fall. It was a little awkward at times—I was a lost ball in high weeds, really. I was sixteen years old and had never been out of Alabama, except once when we went over the state line to Chattanooga. But my father had a dedication to education and learning. He had gone to parochial and Hebrew school as a little boy, but that was all. Miss Claribell Send, who taught me Latin at Phillips High School, got me interested in Harvard. When my father heard about Harvard and what it stood for, he was insistent, so I went. It was pretty difficult to make the transition that first year.

I went to Harvard in the fall of 1929, which was the year that the stock market crashed. At that point, my older sister was beginning her third year in college. Up until then, my family had been quite well off, but the crash led to the depreciation of real estate, which was where my father's funds were. My father had to go back to working twelve-hour days in a small retail store on Second Avenue. My mother also went to work for about ten dollars a week. We had driven big, fine cars, but during that time we rode the streetcars.

I went to school for the first year or two without financial difficulty. Incidentally, I had gotten a scholarship when I registered as a freshman, but I hadn't sought one. My father asked me what it was, and I told him that I thought it was some program to maintain national distribution in the student body. He told me that we didn't need that, so I ought to give it back so that some other boy might be able to attend.

Two years later, by the end of my sophomore year, I told the dean that I couldn't return because we were penniless. He said, "Well, there are many scholarships available, so you'll just have to make scholarship grades. We don't want anybody to have to lose out here just because he is financially unable to attend." So I buckled down and was fortunate enough to get a scholarship. I lived in Cambridge from September to June. I wasn't even able to return home for Christmas. It cost money.

When I graduated from Harvard in 1933, I couldn't get a job. The whole country had gone flat because of the Depression. I tried to help my father in his store, since he no longer had a secretary. I remember that I did a lot of reading in the store until my father reminded me that it was not a library and that I needed to "work the stock" even if there were no customers.

In the fall of 1933 I went back to Harvard for law school. I made the grades to get my scholarship. I wasn't a football player. I have always had a strange reaction to these stories about scholarship holders in college these days, who are hardly scholars. I think they ought to just call them paid athletes.

After I finished law school, Harvard Law School Dean Roscoe Pound recommended me for an appointment as law clerk to Judge David J. Davis, the United States district judge for the Northern District of Alabama. It was really a secretarial position—we didn't call them "law clerks" then. Judge Davis was the only federal judge in the whole of North Alabama then, and I worked with him for almost a year. He was a grand man, a wonderful fellow. When I started with Judge Davis, he had just taken the place of a judge who had been sick for a whole year, so we both worked day and night on all of the cases that had piled up.

As a young man, Judge Davis had ridden in a covered wagon from Wedowee, Alabama, to Oklahoma. His parents homesteaded there and did pretty well for a year or two. They had a bad crop or something and came back to North Alabama. Well, Davis then went to Exeter, or one of those New England secondary schools, and then directly to Yale Law School. I don't think he even went to four years of undergraduate college. He had a scholarship at Yale Law School and wrote for the law journal. He handled some very important things during his time as a district judge, like writing an opinion and judgment sustaining the Social Security Act. That situation started in a lawsuit here in the Northern District of Alabama.[3]

Judge Davis and Supreme Court Justice Hugo Black had been law partners. When Justice Black was appointed, Judge Davis called me into his office and said Justice Black wanted me to be his law clerk. It was not unusual for the law clerk of an appeals judge or a district judge to be elevated. But my heart stopped beating when I heard that, and I said, "I'll have to ask my father." Judge Davis laughed and said into the phone, "He wants to talk to his daddy first."

So I ran over to my daddy's store, told him about this wonderful call, and asked what he thought I should do. He thought for a minute and said, "Well, let me tell you something, J. A. You go back and tell Judge Davis that you won't take that job if it will, in any way, inconvenience him. Tell him that you want to do whatever is in his best interest first." My father knew that Judge Davis had all that work stacked up because the previous judge had been so ill. Looking back on it, that was pretty remarkable advice. I went back and followed my father's advice. Judge Davis laughed and said, "I've got a hundred applications for your position."

I remember very sharply the first day when I met Justice Black in Washington, D.C. He was a very warm, genial man, and, of course, he was one of my heroes. I confess to an honest bias about him.

Justice Black was one of the great miracles of my lifetime. He was born in the frontier of Alabama, in a slave culture where opportunities for blacks were terribly limited. Now, how did it happen that this person born into that atmosphere, in that culture, had within him somehow the seeds of this international vision of all men being able to walk erect and live in freedom? How did that come about? It didn't happen to his brother. It didn't happen to his neighbor next-door. It just happened. I can't explain it. Now, all of the historians and the psychologists have got all kinds of reasons, but I can't explain it.

Black was a member of the Ku Klux Klan, and many people see that as a problem. It was difficult, if not impossible, for anyone to be elected in those times without Klan support—whether they were running for positions as judges, senators, or governor. It was a political necessity. I don't try to defend the Klan in any way—it's contrary to all of my inner instincts. One thing that I am grateful for is that no one ever intimated that Hugo Black ever participated in the Klan atrocities, any of the terrible things that the Klan did. He went to their meetings, made speeches, and got their votes when he could. He used to like to say, "I didn't get their endorsement, but I got their votes." A man from Jasper was actually the official Klan endorsee in 1926 when Black was first elected to the Senate.

After two and a half years, I came back to Birmingham as the acting regional attorney for the Wage/Hour division of the U.S. Department of Labor. The minimum wage law, the Wage/Hour Bill, had just become law, and I was one of that bunch of "Communists" who were trying to get the minimum wage in this area up to twenty-five cents from ten cents. Yeah, we sure were destroying the country and all of its underpinnings! During this time, I was getting to know a lot of the people who were looking at labor and race in the city.

Phil Murray was president of the Steelworkers and the CIO that was dedicated to the principles that the CIO and the United Mine Workers had professed: representation of all people without discrimination of any kind based on race, creed, or national origin. Phil Murray and John Ramsey got a group together of about thirty union officers and ministers.[4] One was Reverend [J. L.] Ware, a young black man who was later on the Community Affairs Committee and who was a militant in a decent, persuasive sort of way.[5] Anyway, this group had luncheon meetings in a private area at the Redmont Hotel, where we had apparently found a sympathetic manager who would allow for integrated meetings even though they were illegal. The group was a race and labor fellowship, and it was one of the stepping-stones that Murray had envisioned.

After we met a couple of times at the Redmont, someone said, "We call ourselves a religion and labor fellowship, but we never meet in a religious setting—only at this hotel. Why don't we meet in a place that has some connection with religion?" We all agreed that would be a good thing to do. Two or three of the people at the meetings said, "Gosh, I would like to do it at my church, but I have to be honest about it. I think it would cause all kinds of commotion." I said, "I know I can't get permission at my temple. I know that's disgraceful, but I can't do it. I'm not much influence on anything there, anyway."

Finally, a lovely young Episcopal minister named Dr. [William Henry] Marmion offered to allow us to use St. Mary's on Highland Episcopal church. Now that's an old, established, fashionable church that a lot of socially prominent people attend. He said, "We'll have our next meeting at my church." Well, that sounded good. It was revolutionary. We met in the side building there and sat at tables. The white ladies of the sisterhood served us. The air was electric. They walked in like automatons, and they were polite but they never said a word. I guess that Dr. Marmion said grace.

This group was about half black and half white, and we dealt with complaints in the mills and the mines. We talked about what we could do to improve the seniority situation. It was easier to discuss the mine workers, because they never had the variety of jobs that we had in the steel mills. John Ramsey would talk about spreading the feeling of brotherhood. I can't remember any of the real agendas.

I enlisted in the military two days after Pearl Harbor, December 9, 1941. I went into the army as a private after passing my physical by bribing a sergeant who knew that I couldn't pass the eye test. I only stayed in the army a short time, because I had dependents, and they hadn't provided for that. But later I served for a long time in the navy. I was married at the time, with one child and another on the way. In a way, it was a cruel thing that I did to my wife and kids, but I had decided that I didn't want to live in a world run by Adolph Hitler.

Just about all of the unions in the building trades were segregated at this time. All of the AFL. The CIO was sort of on the threshold in bringing black organizers in.

Now, by 1946 and 1947, the Steelworkers had basically been organized. The minorities—blacks and the women who had gotten in during the war, when there was a manpower shortage—were in the union and were receiving benefits. They got the same insurance, vacations, and rates of pay for a given job. The problem was that the top jobs were almost universally white jobs.

There were actually separate lines of promotion, so it was the policy of the Steelworkers to merge those lines of promotion. We didn't really get it going too well until President Truman issued an executive order that prohibited contracts with employers who discriminated on the basis of race, religion, and so forth.[6] That gave us some legal status to begin merging, and we did.

Bill Mitch was the father of the man who was my partner for forty years, and he came here as a union man. He was one of John L. Lewis's arms, and his job was to organize the coal mines. He organized all kinds of people [men, women, Communists, white and black] in the Mine Workers union. He really built the foundation for what came about in the CIO later on. I'm not too sure about my history, but I think that in the early strikes in the coal mines in the 1920s the employers brought in strikebreakers, mostly black field-workers. They made only fifty cents a day, while the regular employees made two dollars a day. Mr. Mitch was a brave man, and he told them that there wasn't going to be any Ku Klux Klan in the Mine Workers—that the Constitution forbade it.[7]

Howard Strevel was a younger Bill Mitch. He was sent here to answer the complaints that many blacks were making about seniority still being discriminatory. Howard started working on that—merging the lines of promotion. He was threatened on the phone, and so was I. People would call at night and say, "We know where you are, and we're coming out there tonight." That's not a very pleasant experience. But Strevel was a great big fellow. He didn't scare easily.

I got to know Asbury Howard when the Mine Mill Union was a big union and an important part of the CIO. He was one of the original organizers for Mine Mill in the 1930s. [Maurice] Travis, the president of Mine Mill, was beaten up during that campaign.[8]

Asbury Howard was on the Board of Directors when warfare broke out between the Steelworkers and the Smelter Workers. They had a big fight, and Maurice Travis lost an eye. After the election was over, he filed a lawsuit against the Steelworkers for the damages that he suffered in that fight. We represented the Steelworkers, Travis represented the Smelter Workers, and I negotiated a settlement. I told the Steelworkers, "We can't defend that sort of thing. The man's been hurt, he shouldn't have been, and he should be paid." They paid him.[9]

Asbury came to see me at that time, and I don't know if Travis was with him. I think that Cliff Durr was representing them, that fellow who later became an assistant general counsel of the Steelworkers and who had been on the labor board years before.[10] The three of them came to me to discuss settlement of that case. I remember that Asbury didn't have much to say, but at that time he was probably negotiating to get himself on the staff of the Steelworkers.[11]

There was an effort by the Steelworkers to get the former Mine Mill officialdom and their followers to join the Steelworkers. Many people did that. Asbury Howard eventually became an official with the Steelworkers. I remember at that meeting, Asbury was quiet, but he shook hands with me and handed me a piece of paper that said, "I want to talk to you." I don't recall whether we ever talked again.

Asbury was later attacked on the sidewalk outside the Bessemer Courthouse where the registrars were sitting. Asbury was leading a small group of five to seven blacks to register to vote. Evidently they tried to go in and were told that they could not, and the cops just beat them. They even beat Asbury's son.[12]

In 1956 the NAACP was outlawed from operating here in Alabama. As a result of that, the Alabama Christian Movement for Human Rights was organized by Fred Shuttlesworth. Between 1956 and 1963, the Alabama Christian Movement was involved in a number of different efforts to change the status quo. In 1957, Fred and his wife attempted to enroll their children in Phillips High School. There's a picture of Mr. Shuttlesworth leading his daughter, holding her hand as she went up the stairs at Phillips High School. On each side of the steps, there were these jeering fellows with sticks. I don't know if they had baseball bats or something. That picture reminded me of a picture that appeared in the *New York Times* in about 1940, before we got into the war. The photograph showed a young Jewish couple, a husband and wife, leading their little girl somewhere. And on each side were mobs of people, storm troopers and ordinary civilians, just laughing and having fun as they saw this little child frightened to death. And I thought of how universal this hatred is.[13]

I'm not turf-tending here today, because, as Mr. Colonel [Johnson] likes to say, I consider myself only a foot soldier in all of this. While Martin Luther King and his group were meeting here in 1963, these crowds of school kids kind of swept through downtown, through the stores. I was working downtown, and I don't remember too much about that.[14]

Howard Strevel was in the midst of combining lines of promotion out at Fairfield when he and Mr. [Reuben] Farr, the district director [of the USWA], looked out the window and saw this great group of kids coming up the street. Mr. Farr said, "We're halfway through this, but do you think we ought to slow up a little while?" And Howard said, "Hell, Mr. Farr, we're up to our ears in it now. Let's just go on ahead and finish it." So while there was this great conflict with the merchants, we were trying hard to get our job done where it really counted.

Bull Connor arrested a whole bunch of kids. I don't remember—it could have been several hundred. I don't remember the numbers, but the jail was full, and they had them corralled at Fair Park or someplace.

I got a phone call at about eleven or twelve at night. It was the general counsel of the Steelworkers union, David Feller. Arthur Goldberg had then gone to be secretary of labor. Davy said, "Buddy, President Kennedy has had Bobby contact Walter Reuther [president of the United Autoworkers] and Dave McDonald [president of the USWA] to put up the bond to get these kids out of jail in Birmingham." It used to cost a minimal amount, just a few dollars, to appeal a case from the city court to the circuit court. They had passed some sort of ordinance to raise the cost to appeal the kind of charge these kids had been given [nuisance, interference with passage, illegal congregating, etc.]. The bond was raised to something like twenty-five hundred dollars, and for all of these kids it was going to cost about $250,000.

The president asked the Steelworkers, the AFL-CIO, and Auto Workers to put up that money. And I said, "Davy, I don't know whether we legally can do this. This is trust money that the unions own. Surely if a group of union members get arrested because they are doing something as members of the Klan, we are not going to put up money for them." He said, "Well, maybe not, but the president wants this done." I said, "Well, then, we'll do it." I had to clear it with Mr. Farr, the director, and Howard Strevel. I called them in the middle of the night, got them up, gave them this outline, and said, "We've got to do it. The president wants us. He thinks the interest of the country requires it, and I think it does. Of course, all three of us know that when word gets out, we'll be looking for a job." They said, "We know that, but if the president says that this is what is required, then this is what we'll do." I said, "I'll pass the word." I called Davy back and told him that it would be done. They mechanically transferred the money, by telegraph or something.

There were only three people who knew where the money was. A fellow named Smith, a young lawyer who was representing the downtown merchants, knew. So did the president of Birmingham Trust National Bank, who later went from here to Montgomery. The banker was going to open some kind of special account to segregate this money in before paying it to the court registry. I took the wire up to this Smith boy's office and said, "The money is here. We three—you, me, and this banker—are the only people who know about this or how it's being handled. And we are the ones who will catch hell for it, so welcome." I didn't hear anything about that for a good while.

Smith or somebody took the money to the city court registry, put it on deposit with them, and managed to free all of those kids. I had to tell Mr. Farr and Howard this. Feller had said that Martin Luther King had said that if the kids weren't out by a certain time, the demonstrations would start all over again. So it was something that had to be done immediately. And it was a decent thing to do. I'm very glad to have been a small part of it. I won't say that I wasn't nervous.

At times, the Chamber of Commerce, Newt Gingrich, and others have put out literature describing the wildness and unreasonable attitudes of the labor unions. In at least that one incident, if the unions didn't save Birmingham, they at least preserved it more quickly than it otherwise would have been preserved. Not only did they put their jobs on the line, they put their well-being on the line. They put their family on the line. I remember when the segregationists shot through Howard Strevel's house. His wife and kid were in there. My wife and kid were sleeping in our back room when a man called and told me that they were on the way to bomb our house. That's a very unhealthy feeling.

The unions were involved in the situation when Vivian Malone was trying to register at the University of Alabama, and Wallace had said he was going to stand in the door to prevent it. The attorney general and federal government had dispatched a body of troops down there. General Henry Graham showed up, and Wallace postured out there a minute or two in the doorway.[15]

Before that happened, the secretary of the AFL-CIO, Ace Trammel, called along with Whizzer White, who later became some kind of attorney general and then went on to the Supreme Court, to find out if we could get some white union people to mingle with the crowd and keep the Klan or anybody who got out of line quiet. They wanted for nothing to happen, and they wanted us to find some big boys who were committed to our philosophy.

Ace Trammel, who was a pretty big boy in those days, said he would do it. He got a couple of fellows from the United Rubber Workers local union in Tuscaloosa to help him. That particular union had a lot of Klan influence on it, unfortunately. But these three or four guys were out in the mob, and their assignment, as I understand it, was to quiet down anyone who was getting too loud. And nothing did happen. General Graham marched up to the governor, gave him a smart salute, and said, "Step aside, Governor." And he stepped aside. I can't remember too well whether I was there, or whether I heard this and talked about it so many times that I think I was there. But anyway, she did register. Wallace backed down, and the troops didn't have to do anything.

Wallace was a good deal smarter than Bull Connor. In many respects, Bull Connor was a rather stupid fellow, while Wallace was a bright guy. The tragedy is that his brightness, intellect, and capacity to control people were not directed in the right directions. He made the wrong choices. I think it's one of the great tragedies of our lifetimes. I think that people would have done what he said if he had just come out and said, "Look, folks, the Supreme Court has acted, we are law-abiding people, and I'm your governor. I'm telling you it's tough. I know it's a difficult thing to do." It would have made a big difference—he was so popular.

Similarly, integration would have gone like a charm if Eisenhower as president had come out and said, "The Supreme Court has acted, so let's not have any trouble, and let's get the schools integrated as we build the country and our communities." Instead, he went around grumbling and growling about what the Supreme Court was doing. Then, when he had to do something, he acted the way a general acts and sent in the troops. So instead of having a solution, we had thirty years of warfare. Those are two tragic situations, because those two men had power—control over other people's minds.

I don't think Bull Connor had the same kind of power and control. I remember hearing Mervyn Sterne, who was a good man in many respects but was a white man who wanted to control the white leadership, say, "Bull is a crude sort of fellow, but he's honest." To me, that's absurd. What was there to be honest about? He was an honest racist who believed that he was the master.

I have resented the fact that no one has ever publicized how the three labor unions in Birmingham got the kids out of jail, enabled the negotiations to go on, and gave Martin Luther King an honorable basis for talking further. In a real sense, I think that the unions contributed to saving Birmingham. As I told Mike Calvert at Operation New Birmingham [ONB], "Now, on this breakfast program [Unity Breakfast, organized in memory of Dr. Martin Luther King Jr.], it's fine to talk about the merchants who negotiated this thing. I'm all for them. They didn't put up any money, but they negotiated. The people who put up the money ought to be recognized."

I joined Operation New Birmingham on a commitment from the business manager of the *Birmingham News,* Vincent Townsend. I told Vincent, "I have a lot of friends in the Chamber of Commerce. They are fine people who do a lot of good things. But they are so politically opposed to me that I can't be a member of that." He said that ONB was not going to be like that and promised that it would be separate from the chamber. On that commitment, I became a member of ONB and set up the Community Affairs Committee [CAC] along with Albert Smith. Cecil Bauer and the president of one of the schools were involved in the CAC, and the two of them really got us off the ground. Vincent Townsend deserves a lot of credit as well. When he was coming up, he was a scraper who stepped on a lot of people's backs, but when he got up there, he wanted to use his power to aid this community in becoming a better place.

Edited by Braden Phillips-Welborn. BCRI Oral History Project, vol. 10, sec. 1 (Sept. 20, 1995).

Notes

1. A fifty-six-foot-tall statue of the Roman god of fire situated on Red Mountain overlooking Birmingham.

2. By law, white passengers sat in the front, and black passengers were required to sit in rear seats, behind a movable barrier.

3. *Steward Machine Co. v. Davis,* 301 U.S. 548 (1937).

4. John Ramsay was a southern union official who remained devoted to the Highlander School and the Southern Regional Council even after the CIO had turned away from them in 1946. See John Egerton, *Speak Now against the Day: The Generation before the Civil Rights Movement in the South* (New York: Alfred A. Knopf, 1994), 447–48.

5. Reverend Ware was pastor of the Trinity Baptist church, president of the Birmingham Baptist Ministers' Conference, and briefly, in December 1952, president of the Birmingham NAACP. Wilson O. Fallin, *The African American Church in Birmingham, Alabama, 1815–1963* (New York: Garland Press, 1997), 132–33, 135, 137, 146, 157.

6. A report entitled "To Secure These Rights" was issued by a committee appointed by Truman in 1946. The committee recommended "the elimination of segregation, based on race, color, creed, or national origin, from American life." It was President Kennedy who issued Executive Order 10925 on March 6, 1961, banning future federal procurement contracts with companies that discriminated.

7. On mine workers' unions before 1940 and the role of Mitch, see the introduction to this volume.

8. Maurice E. Travis was briefly president of Mine Mill, 1946–47, then resigned from that post and became secretary-treasurer. Gary M. Fink, ed., *Biographical Dictionary of American Labor* (Westport, Conn.: Greenwood Press, 1974), 556–57.

9. Horace Huntley, "The Rise and Fall of Mine Mill in Alabama: The Status Quo against Interracial Unionism, 1933–1949," in *The Journal of the Birmingham Historical Society: An Anthology Honoring Marvin Yeomans Whiting,* ed. James L. Baggett (Birmingham, Ala.: Birmingham Historical Society, 2000), 205–6.

10. Clifford Durr was a stalwart of the Southern Conference on Human Welfare and husband of Virginia Durr. See Egerton, *Speak Now against the Day,* 180–81, 620–21.

11. Asbury Howard did become an international representative of the United Steelworkers, but only after Mine Mill had merged with the USWA in 1967. Fink, ed., *Biographical Dictionary,* 303.

12. For a very different version of this attack, see the Asbury Howard Jr. interview in this volume.

13. See Andrew M. Manis, *A Fire You Can't Put Out: The Civil Rights Life of Birmingham's Reverend Fred Shuttlesworth* (Tuscaloosa: University of Alabama Press, 1999), 147–52.

14. See David J. Garrow, *Bearing the Cross: Martin Luther King Jr. and the Southern Christian Leadership Conference* (New York: William Morrow and Co., 1986), 236–60.

15. Deputy Attorney General Nicholas Katzenbach escorted Vivian Malone and James Hood the morning of June 11, 1963. Later that day the students were escorted by the federalized Alabama National Guard commanding general, Henry Graham. See ibid., 268–69; Diane McWhorter, *Carry Me Home: Birmingham, Alabama; The Climactic Battle of the Civil Rights Revolution* (New York: Simon and Schuster, 2001), 460–62.

David P. Earle

Born July 26, 1906, in Meridian, Mississippi. Family moved to Birmingham in 1912. Worked as miner, delivery boy, and presser in the dry cleaning industry. Helped organize workers in the dry cleaning business before leaving Birmingham for New York. Worked in the dry cleaning industry, served in the army, worked in the postal service, retired, and returned to live in Birmingham. Deceased, December 2000. *"If you were a presser at a cleaners, you could get a job anywhere. I did it all. I pressed and I sewed and I dry cleaned and I spotted. That's what I did for most of my life. When I went to New York, I was pressing two suits for fifteen cents."*

Solidarities and Accomplishments: From Iron Mines to the Dry Cleaning Business

I was born in 1906 in Meridian, Mississippi. I came to Birmingham when I was six, in 1912. Riley School up there now is the fifth building they built. It was called Tarrant Grammar School. It was named after a fellow who lived on Hickory Avenue, Henry Tarrant. That was the first school that I attended. I had a good time going to school. I do remember that up to the third grade, we had to take a whole page and learn it without the book. We had to recite "The Village Blacksmith." Some of the fellows had to learn it—well, all of us would have to learn it, but one of the fellows would have to recite it.

My father was an insurance man for Union Mutual Aid Insurance Company. The company moved him from Meridian [to] here. I don't know how long he was here before we came. W. B. Driver was the district manager. They were in the Pythian Temple.

I had one brother and four sisters. I'm the second child. I got one sister older than me. We were all two years apart, except the two that were born in Birmingham. I had a brother and sister born in Birmingham. Four of us came from Meridian. It was one boy and three girls. My mother was a teacher. She taught at TCI [Tennessee Coal and Iron] School in Wenonah, in the camp. The first school she got when she came to Birmingham was in Rosedale, and she taught at Rosedale one or two years. But the advantage then of teachers working for TCI, the county gave them so much, and then they got so much from the company. That was one of the advantages of working for TCI. At that time TCI schools—in TCI they had the ore mines, the coal mines, and the furnaces. Well, then, all the mining camps like Ishkooda and Wenonah . . . had schools there, but they were supposed to be for the miners' children and the people that lived in the camp because they cut the miners sixty-five cents every fifteen days for schooling. Everybody that worked in the mines paid, if you had children or you didn't have children. You see, at that time it looked like if anything you took out of people's salaries so they didn't see it, they didn't care. All the miners had to pay sixty-five cents for school and sixty-five cents for carbide. Carbide was something that looked like little rocks and it made a gas. You put water at the top in this little thing and carbide in the bottom. That was your light for down in the mine because it was dark down there.

In Riley, back when the mines were running, it was very few women in Riley that worked. Women stayed at home, and all the men wanted were food when he got home. That caused more fights than anything: not having the food ready. But he took care of his house, and he took care of his children. The world is just so much different today. People got more material things now than we had back then, but we had plenty to eat because we could raise hogs and chickens. When I was there, Riley was in the county. And at that time the county didn't have a high school.[1]

I went to the ninth grade. You know the church, like Miles, you know the CME church down here on Sixth Avenue, they had a school out in Mason City, Central Alabama Institute. It was run by the CME, Methodist. Riley went to the seventh grade. My last year in school was at TCI, because my mother was able to work me in there some kind of way, because you weren't supposed to go if you didn't live in the camp. But I did the seventh grade over at Wenonah. It's burned down now. We had a big school down there where we used to give dances, and they had an auditorium and everything down there.

TCI schools were better than any schools in the United States because we had a toothbrush drill, you had to go out there and exercise, and they taught home economics. You could get lunches at that time for three cents. You could get some soup and crackers and little things. And they taught the girls how to sew, cook, and housekeep. That building was separate from the school, but it was just right up the hill from the school. And every Christmas, every child that went to a TCI school got a box of candy, and they had a big Christmas tree. And also they could go to the hospital. In most of the schools they taught gardening. The children had little plots. That was one of my mother's classes. She taught that, but she also had to teach books too. And a white man would come by every now and then. You never knew when he was coming and give you this quick test like you're trying to pass a postal exam or something like that. You'd know the answer, but they just give you so many minutes to do it in. They would come around every now and then and give you those kinds of tests.

They had a regular education system. The superintendent was a man named Mr. Blackwell. He was white. All of the teachers were black. Most of the mining camps had a few houses there for whites. But on Red Mountain, there was only one completely white camp. That was number eleven camp. That was in Ishkooda. The mines . . . Ishkooda was number fourteen, thirteen, twelve, and eleven. And Wenonah was number ten, nine, eight, and seven. I don't remember the numbers down in Muscoda. Wenonah was the largest of those camps, and each one of them had schools. They even had two schools in Wenonah. They had the one where my mother taught, and then they had a school down at the number seven mine that went to the fifth grade. After they finished the fifth grade, they would have to come up where we were.

The company had churches. They had two churches—Galilee. There's a Galilee church now, but the company had one on their grounds. The church was right across from the school. Almost all the houses in Wenonah were four rooms, at least. And up in there, when they built that new camp up there some of them were five rooms.

I went from Wenonah to Central Alabama Institute in Mason City. My father passed in 1925. After that I just took over the family and sent two sisters through college. One finished Spelman, and one of them finished Alabama State. I started work when I was twelve years old at Burger Philips. It was just Burger then. At that time the store was located on Second Avenue between Twentieth and Twenty-first Streets. And then I worked at Pizitz. You see, back then all the stores, the grocery stores and drug stores, had deliveries. You know, they rode bicycles. I went to work when I was twelve years—in 1918 during the influenza epidemic during World War I. There wasn't a summer when I was going to school that I didn't work.

Every year I went to school, I was able to find some kind of job. In fact, most boys did, because all these drug and grocery stores had two or three bicycle delivery boys. When I was working at Burger's they had two motorcycles and a truck for deliveries. The motorcycles delivered in town, and the trucks went west one day and east one day. Free delivery. At that time it was just Burger's. But it was more Philips's than it was Burger's. It was three Philips brothers.

Louis Philips, Isaac, and I can't think of the other one's name. But it was three Philips brothers and only one Burger. Old man Burger never married. But after I left they named it Burger Philips, and they moved it down, I think it was on Third Avenue.

[Next] I worked at Pizitz. I was doing the same thing. A "special delivery boy," they called it. I worked at the trolley car shop down on Third Avenue and Eleventh Street. I worked there at night, washing windows on the trolley cars. Back then, they wouldn't let you work if you were school age, after September. You had to go back to school. That's why I can't understand today. We could not come downtown during school hours. It was a fellow that had a cork leg named Geechy. He was the truant officer, I guess that's what they call it now, but if he caught you out in the street—at that time over there where all the city stuff is now, it was just one jail over there, and they called it South Side Jail. And that's where he would take you. He never did get me, because I went to school. I never had no problem with the law.

She [my mother] went to college. They called it Meridian Academy. That was equal at that time to a college. A few years after we were here, my father stopped working with the insurance company and went to work for Windham Brothers.[2] My father did the carpentry work on the Masonic Temple. He quit the insurance company and started carpentry. He worked for Windham Construction Company, and he worked for Windham all over. Windham used to have jobs from Tuskegee to Tupelo, Mississippi. He was a contractor. There were two brothers, B. L. and T. C. B. L. didn't have any children; T. C. did.

I went in the mines in 1924. I worked in number nine, ore mine. And when I went in the ore mines, it was only four white men in the mines. One was the foreman, but they called him the "bank boss." And the other come around—you had a number in the mine. My number in the mine was 4908. A badge I had to wear. But I had two. And it had that number on there. Well, that's what you had to leave on the top when you went down in the mines. But when I went in the mines, wasn't no white men in there at that time. They started to coming in there when they put the machinery in there. They had put what they called "drags" in there. That was something that would, after they blew the rocks, they would have to pull it to where they could load it on the cars. When you go down in the mines, it's room to walk like this, and the thing that is pulling the ore out is in the middle. But they work off the side. They would go so far as they could as long as they could get ore.

I was a mule boy. I was too young to be a mucker. I was seventeen when I went in the mine. I went in the mine that year after school closed. My people didn't want me to go in the mines. But all the other boys, all my friends was in there. The mucker loaded the rock, put it in the car. But they got rid of him when they put the drags in there. He would have to be there around the drag. The drags were like these lifts you see now, a shovel-like thing, and it would pull the whole . . . they had track, you know, and as they went back they would lay tracks, and cars would go in and bring the ore to where they had the slope. They had a big thing, which then pulled the ore out. The mules pulled the empty cars up, and the way the mines were, the cart would come back by itself.

The mules stayed down there. They had a big stall down there. I worked in number ten, number eight, and nine. If something would go wrong, they would move us. Just like so many people don't know, but in the ore mines the blacks did all the work. They did the drilling, and all the foremen were practically black. I know Willie Myatt. He was a foreman in the mine. His wife was a classmate of mine. His wife Lucille, we were in Wenonah together in the seventh grade.

All the foremen in the mine were black. Ty Rhodes, Orzell Billingsley, not the lawyer, but his father. Orzell Sr., he was a big man over in number eight. When I went in the mines, it was two white foremen in there. All the rest of them were black. Morris Hagley, when I first went in the mine, he was the mine foreman after you got down in the mine, he had a six-man crew. He had six men to work under him. He had the mule boy and the drag runner, and he had two muckers. But all they had to do was go up and see that the drag made the right connections, but all the foremen were black. In the other mines, like the Woodward Mine and Sloss Mine, they had black contractors. The company would give them so much money, and they would have to buy the powder and other supplies and pay the men, and what was left was theirs. Willie Myatt's father-in-law, he was a big man down at Sloss. Bessemer Sloss had two mines down there. You see, it was nineteen ore mines over there. And the Republic had Spaulding and the Ishkooda and Clinton mine, that wasn't nothing. And then Woodward had Songo.

I came out in '26. That wasn't for me. I went in dry cleaning. You see, dry cleaning used to be a big thing here. Back then there was no synthetic material. All you had was cotton, silk, wool, and linen. Well, that meant your suit was wool, and you couldn't put that in the wash. Of course, people didn't have no washing machines. But your suit was wool, so you have to have dry cleaning. So they used to have big price wars here. It was five real big dry cleaners here—Utopia, Sunshine, Tom Jones, those were the big boys. A lot of black people had dry cleaning at that time. The Pippen Brothers dry cleaning, their shop was right across from Sixteenth Street church. Flozell and Maxwell Pittman, now they're dead. Maxwell's daughter married McNair, the commissioner. You see, the Pippens lived well, because in the old days they didn't have public transportation. If you been here all your life, you know when it was Avenue F. Well, the people in Titusville didn't have no transportation. So people used to run jitneys over there. That's what the Pippens did.

That's the way they had to travel, in jitneys. That's what they called them. But they weren't nothing but somebody with a car. Their father also had a little store out there in Cleveland or Mason City, right on the line there. Well, they had to have them then, because they didn't have no transportation. The trolleys didn't run over in that part. I worked for a little shop right down on Eleventh Street. Right down there now where I-65 is.

We used to do most of the Cobb trolley-car uniforms and the foundry uniforms. Because every time they'd had a big fire, we would have a whole lot of work. That's the man I worked for. That's who he catered to.

Back then a lot of the black people thought it was better to educate the girl so she wouldn't have to work in the white folks' kitchen. And that's the way they did back then. That was the thinking of a lot of black men at that time.

My Involvement with the Labor Movement

I helped organized the Laundry Workers union. You see it used to be ten big laundries here. It was the Mystic, Peerless, the Empire, Ideal, and Imperial wash for white people only. Birmingham Linen Supply that was considered laundry, but they mostly rented their stuff to hotels. See, back then you didn't have any paper napkins. All they could use was linen. By them having to use linen they had to be laundered, because people didn't have washing machines and things like they got now.

Well, I always want to stick my neck out for some reason. And four of us from Riley—Philip Wilkerson, Andrew Bailey, and Fred Baker—we took money out of our pocket and bought little flyers to announce when and where the meeting would be. You see, at that time, the Jehovah's Witnesses had a hall down on Sixteenth Street and Second Avenue, and that's where we rented the hall for the meeting. At that time I wasn't working but three days a week. But we would go there in the afternoon when the people would be getting off in the laundries and let them know. At that time the trolley-car men had a union. The white conductor and motormen, they were already union. It wasn't but two of us working there, and he kind of leaned toward the union. Well, like I said, most of his [laundry] business was from the trolley-car men.

He didn't know what I was doing. I wasn't one of those people who have to ask a white person or tell a white person everything I do. He didn't know I was doing it. There's one fellow, he dared us to come on his property to talk to him. We had a big breakthrough, because at that time, most of the people working in the laundry were women. We organized the union in '34. You know, when Roosevelt said everybody could organize.[3] Well, that's when we . . . 'cause you saw they were working those women for $4.50 a week. That's what the pay was, with no limit on hours. Because Monday, Tuesday, and Wednesdays, some of them had to work until seven or eight o'clock. They had to work until they got finished. The first minimum wage was sixteen cents an hour. We had a hard time trying to explain to some women that it would be better to work for sixteen cents a hour, and if you had to work over forty hours you would get overtime. Some of them couldn't see that. They said the man was good to them. Well, a lot of those people, because the boss would lend them some money, he was good to them. And he wasn't making nothing to start with. But the man lend him some money before payday, he was good to them. We never did get all of them no way, but we got enough to close the places. Our local was 109, and the drivers were with us, because you know all of them had drivers. Well, old man Steele, he had a driver to go around and pick up. We closed everything, every laundry and dry cleaner, down in Birmingham for two years. Not, you know, when the contract. . . . But, you know, they got to the union.

When they found out what I was doing, I was, as they say back then, "a smart nigger." I was blacklisted, so I went to New York. Wasn't nothing else here for me to do.

At the time, it's hard for me to explain it to you what dry cleaning was back then. If you were a presser at a cleaner, you could get a job anywhere. I did it all. I pressed and I sewed and I dry cleaned and I spotted. That's what I did for most of my life.

Well, when I went to New York I was pressing two suits for fifteen cents. The man wasn't charging the company but a quarter. That's what it was to clean a suit here. They used to have price wars here. You could get a suit cleaned for twenty-five cents.

In 1929 the Pullman Company came down here and took a lot of fellows to New York. The group I grew up with in Riley, all of us were like brothers. If I had it, you had it. And so anywhere one of us was, in the group I grew up with, anywhere, California, New York, and they'd help you. But in '29, when they came and got the Pullman Porters, if you knew one of the Pullman Porters, you knew you had somewhere to stay and eat if you got there. All you had to do was find a job. And even here. Let's see, I know we got five boys jobs at Pizitz. Riley boys just stuck together. They helped me when I got there. And as far as I can remember, that's the way they were. That's the reason I can't understand the way people are today.

I got married in New York. My wife was from here in Riley. A presser, at that time, could find a job anywhere. I didn't stay in New York City but six months, and then I went up to Middletown, which is in Orange County [New York]. I stayed in Middletown until I went in the service. I went in the service in '43 from Middletown.

I left Middletown and come to White Plans to dry clean. I stayed in White Plains about twenty-five years. I came back to Birmingham in '89. Most of the other boys are dead that I grew up with. I didn't drink. I didn't stay out at night. My mama had a curfew. We had to be home at 11:30. We didn't ever break curfew. I know my father put a niece out. She come to the house after 11:30, and she couldn't get in.

When I moved back [to Birmingham], a lot of people told me I'd get lost. But I told you, I worked at Burger's two years. I worked at Pizitz delivering. I had to know the city, because I had . . . when I went to the stores, to Pizitz and Burger's both, they still had mules. They had trucks and everything, but they had mules. One Christmas Eve the motorcycle broke down, and I had to go get the mule and go deliver the packages on the North Side at night. We didn't have flashlights then, you had a lantern. Well, that's what I had in the wagon for light. And every time I would hit a bump, those lanterns would go out, and I just let it stay out. I wasn't seeing nothing with it no way. So I just let it stay out and went on and did my work. I had twelve stops that night.

I studied *Ancient History* by West, and it had a lot of quotations in there. The one I can remember best, and of course this was during the time of the Persian Empire, a historian wrote that:

> An ill fascination that hastens ills of prey
> Where wealth accumulate and men decay.[4]

It had a lot of different quotations all through it like that.

We didn't have no money, but we always had enough to eat. Because when I was living in Riley, it was still in the county, and we could have hogs and chickens. And back then, we could go in the woods and pick blackberries, muscadines, and in our yard we had from May to September, got ripe tomatoes to September. We had plums and pears. We used to get a lot. By my mother teaching gardening, she used to get a lot of samples from different places.

You see, when I was young, baseball was the thing. Baseball was everywhere. Wenonah had a team. ACIPCO had a team. Baseball was the big thing back then because all these plants, ACIPCO and Stockham, the Pipe Shop in Bessemer, everybody. . . .

I tried to play, but I couldn't. So I just wasn't cut out. My father tried to make a baseball player out of me. He'd get me the things, but I just wasn't cut out for baseball. We played at Riley, we played down there on the ditch.

This was when we were going to school, and then Riley had a team once. You know they didn't play in no league, but they played places like East Thomas, Fairfield, Ensley. But a lot of boys were able to make it to the majors of the Negro Leagues. Birmingham had some Black Barons. The Black Barons all I can read about is in the forties, but it was a Black Baron team before then. It was a fellow named Joe Rush Domer. He had a bootblack stand and a pool hall and hotel down there on Eighteenth Street. His daughter sold papers like the *Amsterdam News* and the *Pittsburgh Courier.*

In the old days it was a blind black fellow here, Monroe Kennedy. He brought the bands here, like Duke Ellington, Cab Calloway. He brought them . . . at that time, the Masonic Temple was in its glory. They'd bring them in to the Masonic Temple.

In the old days we had these classes where you worked. You know, like if your father worked for the railroad, give you dirt under your feet. At one time they had two barbershops here. The black men cut on the white man's hair. One was on First Avenue between Nineteenth and Twentieth, and one was on Nineteenth Street there, near Fourth Avenue. At that time, the city hall was there. They cut only the white men's hair. Some of their children looked down on you as scum. They considered themselves in a different class.

Well, there was a fellow living out there on Fourth Avenue named Bester Steele. He was the senior fireman on the L&N, but you know they never would let the black firemen get in the union. They could have seniority, but not through the union. You couldn't join the union. When they put some kind of automatic coal thing on the Hummingbird, they took him off. He took the case to court and won. He lived on Fourth Avenue North. He was a fireman, and his father was there, I guess you'd call it a switch engine, the one that made up the trains in the yard. His father worked at the L&N.[5]

They were the upper crust. That's the way the children looked at it. The children whose parents worked in the mills and the mines . . . they were low classes. If you were working for the railroad, and a place like that barbershop, and what else was a high-up. The teachers and preachers were, too. Because mostly, at that time all the black doctors had an office in the Pythian Temple and Masonic Temple. My wife worked for Dr. Bryant and Dr. Taggert. Dr. Bryant was a medical doctor, and Dr. Taggert was a dentist. He was in the Masonic Temple. Dr. Bryant was in the Pythian Temple. Dr. Anderson was a dentist, and he worked for both of them. They had the offices together. The Penny Savings Bank went down about 1915 or '16.[6] It went down early. I was small.

I left Birmingham in 1936, and I came back in 1989. It look like to me that some things were changed. I don't know how to say it, but in Riley coming up, I played with white children when I was young enough to play. Of course, their people didn't want them to do it. They called them away from us. But the children didn't have nobody else to play with, so they played with us. It wasn't but one or two [white] families out there. Down on the corner, right there at the trolley track there was a white family or some foreign family. I don't know what they were, but they were white. They even went to the black churches, and the Ku Klux Klan came out there and kept beating them. The Klan ran them away from out there.

They didn't go to school, but they would go to church, and the children would play with us. I know we made those boys go in the store and steal candy, because we had wagons. We took two wheelbarrow wheels and two baby buggy wheels and made a wagon. Take a piece of two by four and make a wagon, and we rode down the hill. And we made them steal candy for us—that was our pay for using our wagons.

There was a fellow here named Willie Shields, he lived down in Powderly. The man had a brain almost as good as Einstein. But he had so much faith that white people wouldn't do him no harm. Now, in the old days before plastic was invented, they put paper bags over clothes. And the paper bag, they had to pull it up on a pulley and then pull it down on the suit. Well, he invented a sack, and one of the cleaners here, one of the big cleaners . . . was it Cliff Ellis? I think it was, but anyway, the first one he invented, the guy just give him thirty-five hundred dollars for the patent. Well, now, if he gave him thirty-five hundred dollars for it, what did he make off of it? He invented the machine for using the bag. They would have to pull the bag up and then pull it down over the suit.

He lived in Powderly on Brookhaven Avenue, I think. But I went to his house a lot. He was older than I was. Every big dry cleaning plant here, he installed it. He was that smart. He knew how to connect all these different pipes up, but he also was a good . . . he invented a lot of things. He lived good, but he had enough patents and ideas to have been a rich man, but he give them away. One of the machines, one of the cleaners here gave him thirty-five hundred dollars for the patent. When I left here, he had invented some kind of thing. He used a sewing machine motor, and it was an improvement over the other one. He had let three cleaners have it. Allison in Bessemer, that's still down there. And one of the guys, it was Avenue Z, then. He let him have it. I have forgotten who had the other one. But I cussed him out that he let them have it before he got the patent on it. And I told him, I said, "Shields, somebody else could come down and get a patent on the thing before you started letting people have it." But he was just a man that thought white folks wouldn't do him any harm.

He was also a magician. He could let you saw him in half, you know, put you in the thing. He had an old box that he would put you in and saw you in half. But he wouldn't talk to you about that. But he could do that. And his father at that time had a saw shop. His father had a place down on Fifteenth Street and Third Avenue. He sharpened saws and knifes. I might could figure or remember where it was, but I know it was in that area. I don't know exactly where it was. A lot of people never heard of Willie Shields.

Edited by Horace Huntley. BCRI Oral History Project, vol. 13, sec. 2 (Mar. 6, 1995).

Notes

1. Riley is located in Southwest Birmingham between Powderly and Travellick. Hillman is a neighboring community. The names of these communities and others in the area reflect their labor backgrounds.

2. One of the most successful black construction companies in the Southeast. In addition to many private homes, they built the Masonic and Pythian Temples and the Sixteenth Street and Sixth Avenue Baptist churches. See Birmingham Historical Society, *True Tales of Birmingham* (Birmingham, Ala.: Birmingham Historical Society, 1992); Lynne B. Feldman, *A Sense of Place: Birmingham's Black Middle-Class Community, 1890–1930* (Tuscaloosa: University of Alabama Press, 1999).

3. He refers to the National Industrial Recovery Act. See Irving Bernstein, *Turbulent Years: A History of the American Worker, 1933–1941* (New York: Houghton Mifflin, 1971), 27–36.

4. There is a clear similarity between these words as remembered by Earle and the eighteenth-century poet and social critic Oliver Goldsmith's account of the destruction of the English peasantry by early capitalist farming, "The Deserted Village."

5. The case was *Bester Williams Steele v. The Louisville and Nashville Company, the Brotherhood of Railway Firemen, et al.*, 65 Sup. Ct. 228 (1944). For discussions of the case, see the introduction to this volume; Eric Arnesen *Brotherhoods of Color: Black Railroad Workers and the Struggle for Equality* (Cambridge, Mass.: Harvard University Press, 2001), 205–9; William H. Harris, *The Harder We Run: Black Workers since the Civil War* (New York: Oxford University Press, 1982).

6. W. R. Pettiford founded the Alabama Penny Savings Bank in 1895.

George Price

Born April 9, 1921, in Eutaw, Greene County, Alabama. Member of the NAACP; director of voter registration for the ACMHR; committee member, recording secretary, and vice president of the International Union of Mine, Mill, and Smelter Workers, Local 836; and vice president of USWA Local 6612. *"[The union] made all the difference in the world. Without the union, they would run off anybody they want to and do what they wanted to do. They probably would pay different rates or wages for different people. Blacks would always be underpaid, but the union made it so where blacks received what whites received doing the same type of work. If it had not been for the union, then other [white] workers might have an advantage over you."*

The Union, the Movement, and the Vote

I was born in Greene County, Alabama, and at the age of three months old I was brought to Birmingham. I grew up in the Avondale and Woodlawn section of Birmingham. My aunt raised me, and my parents remained in Eutaw until their deaths. I attended Thomas School in Avondale, and from there I went to Lincoln School. I attended high school at Parker. I was a freshman at Talladega College, but due to the lack of money, I had to come out of school at about three months. So I couldn't go back to school then until I went into the armed forces of the United States of America. And when I got out of the armed forces, I used my GI Bill a few years later to go back to school to complete my education. I attended Tuskegee Institute. In college I majored in general education and business.

After college I went to work for Connors Steel as an iron inspector for a short period of time. After that, I left and went to New York to better my condition. After I had been in New York eighteen or nineteen months, my aunt that I lived with in Birmingham took sick. They called me, and I came from New

York to see about her. I spent maybe two weeks here, and I went back to my job in New York. I was there maybe a week and a half before I was called back to see about her again. When I came back, she was so sick, I put her in the hospital, and I just stayed until she died. I remained in Birmingham then and went to work for General Houseware Corporation, and I remained there until I retired. I was a welder for them.

I first became acquainted with the labor union when I worked at Connors Steel and when I was with Dupont; I was with a labor union, too. I've always, wherever I worked, if there was a labor union available, I always joined. With the Mine, Mill, and Smelter Workers I went from a shop steward to vice president in the labor union. I was a shop steward for maybe six months and from there to a committeeman and from a committeeman to vice president over a period of years. And I was elected vice president at least three different times. This was during the 1950s. Asbury Howard[1] and me were good friends, and we negotiated contracts and filed with the grievance committee, fighting cases for men and trying to see that people get their fair share of rights when men were fired from their jobs. Asbury Howard and I worked together for a number of years doing this.

During the time that I worked for the company, it was very rude to the workers. We always had some up-road that we always had to fight for, and we had to call Asbury Howard in, being the vice president of Mill, Mine, and Smelter Workers, in most cases. Then we had a problem during contract negotiations trying to get increases in benefits, and the company wasn't too liberal about doing that. We got such raises as five cents and seven cents and a dime, and maybe the most I've ever saw there was fifteen cents on the hour. The union made all the difference in the world. Without the union, they would run off anybody they want to and do what they wanted to do. They probably would pay different rates or wages for different people. When I mean different people, blacks would always be underpaid, but the union made it so where blacks received what whites received doing the same type of work. So the union also made a difference in seniority, whereas if you had seniority over another person, whether they were white or black, the union saw to it that you got what was just for you by applying the seniority as it was supposed to be applied. If it had not been for the union, then other workers might have an advantage over you.[2]

During this time, I lived on the edge of Norwood on Tenth Avenue North. Most of the people in that community were ordinary working people. There wasn't anybody that I know that earned what I would consider a decent salary or made enough money to live in the type of community that they should have been able to live in. They worked in that area, and there were other areas that they worked in beside there.

There was no relationship at that time with the Birmingham Police Department, because the Birmingham Police Department was lily-white. There weren't any blacks in the police department, and the police weren't too nice to black people, period, in that area. I was stopped going to work several times by the police, just coming to work, and they searched me and wanted to know where I came from and know where I was going. So when they didn't find no gun, they decided to let me go on home. And there was times that I come out the plant to my car, and the police passed on the street, and if they see you getting in the car, they would turn around, stop, and question you, and you just got off from work. We had to go to the company and talk to the company concerning how rude the police were towards the workers when they got off at night.

You see, at one time I was working from three to eleven, and when you get off at eleven o'clock and take a bath, it's 11:30. You get to your car, it's about twenty minutes to twelve, so the police was on a rampage at that time, and they weren't too nice to black people at all. The company would call the police department, and they would talk to Jamie Moore, who was chief of police at that time, and they said that the police wouldn't bother us anymore. So they lightened up. They weren't quite as bad as they had been. They had been following fellows all the way to the gate on the eleven-to-seven shift. Whenever they got off at night, there was a row of houses where black people stayed, just beyond the plant and down a dead-end street. Usually when you come out of the gate, the police were there to intimidate the black workers.

I first got involved in the civil rights movement when I was in the armed forces. I had a battery commander who was a captain. He was a lawyer in civilian life, and he was a captain in the armed forces. And he looked over the payroll and found that we were drawing maybe nine or ten dollars a month, and he felt that that was too much money. He felt we didn't need that much money, so he called a formation and asked did anybody want to join the NAACP. The officer thought ten dollars a month was a lot because we were overseas, and when you get overseas in the armed forces, some of the things that you have to buy in the United States of America, such as soap, tooth powder, and the things that a person needs, the government gives them to you. So you really don't have a lot to spend the money for, unless you're in a place where you can go to town where the ladies are, and we weren't right where the ladies were, we were out in the jungles, so he decided that we were drawing too much money. That caused me to get involved in it. It was about twenty that joined the NAACP at that time. He said it was two dollars to join the NAACP, and when he got through explaining, a fellow by the name of Willie J. Whitings walked out of the line, and I walked out, and he said, "All you want to join the NAACP, go to my office, and I'll write you up and give you a card." So he wrote us up and gave us a card to become a member of the NAACP. That happened in 1944, overseas. He felt like we'd give two dollars of that to the NAACP because they were fighting the fight back in the United States of America. They had some race riots in Georgia and Detroit and around, and the NAACP was fighting because people were being put in jail unjustified.

When I got back out of the service, there was a NAACP chapter in Titusville,[3] headed by Reverend T. L. Lane. I joined that chapter and started working with that chapter. I got out of the service in 1947. I was active in the NAACP from 1947 until 1956. We went to meetings, and we had a situation in Birmingham where a policeman's wife got in a [dispute about a] parking place [with] a black [man] that worked at ACIPCO, by the name of Parker.[4] I guess she told her husband, and the police arrested Parker over a parking space. They arrested Parker and put him in jail, and sometime during that night or the next night they went to jail and beat Parker up in jail. And the NAACP got on to that particular case, and I became directly involved. At the same time, there were some houses being bombed on Center Street, all the way up from maybe Eleventh Avenue up to the top of the Center Street hill there, three or four houses had been bombed, and then the NAACP was all the legal organization that we had in this town at that particular time to fight for the victims.[5] Perpetrators bombed them because they didn't want black people to live in that community. The community was white until blacks began to move in, and black homes were being bombed.

When the NAACP was outlawed in '56, John Patterson was the attorney general of the State of Alabama, and then the leaders got together and organized the Alabama Christian Movement for Human Rights. We met at Smith and Gaston Funeral Home, and we discussed it, and we discussed it again. We got a charter, and we set a meeting to be at Sardis Baptist church on June 5, 1956, and the Alabama Christian Movement for Human Rights was born. The organization had not been set up, and the officers had to be appointed and elected, and after the officers were appointed and elected, then we got a chance to go. It was about three meetings before we got all the officers appointed.

A typical mass meeting was as many people that probably could get into a church at that particular time. We discussed the problems of black people, what we had to do, because it was crucial in this town at that particular time. It was hardly possible for black people to vote. It was hardly possible for black people to live in certain communities without their houses being bombed. It was hardly possible for black people to have a nice automobile up and down the street without being intimidated by the policemen. And at the same time Bethel Baptist church was bombed, and later on, after Bethel Baptist church was bombed, Sixteenth Street church was bombed as we went along.

There was a very few people registered to vote at that particular time, and it was so hard for people to become registered until we had set up a way to teach them, and we had a questionnaire of about maybe fifty or forty-five questions. Probably took a college graduate to pass to be registered. And so many people were being turned down, not all of them on education, because they didn't ask legal questions. We had all the answers to the legal questions, but they asked questions that you probably wouldn't know. For instance, they asked women, "When was your first child born?" and then they asked her when did she get married. Then they asked women, "You sure all them children your husband's children?" And they turn them around on more questions. And we kept records on those that they turned down, and we, over a period of maybe three years, we'd had something like forty thousand folks turned down by the Board of Registrars. I have been credited with registering over seventeen thousand people to vote during the Alabama Christian Movement period.

At all meetings, Birmingham police were present. Their purpose was to watch and to see and to hear what was going on. We welcomed them. We thought they shouldn't have been there. A lot of times we made statements as to whether they should have been somewhere else trying to catch some crook, 'cause we were Christian people trying to get our rights and freedom, but they didn't pay any attention. They were at the meeting on time every Monday night. Nobody did anything to them. They enjoyed it so they got where they laughed, but they realized that they were in the wrong place, and they were in the wrong place watching God's people.

I was never arrested. I stayed out for a purpose. Being a board member, we had to look out for others. I would have been arrested like all the rest of them, but I was out for a purpose, to help get others out of jail. I helped to raise funds for the Movement, but I didn't do much speaking for raising funds, but for the event of the civil rights movement, I spoke all the time. I spoke at the mass meetings every Monday night for years. When I first got started, I got a little kick from my family. They said a few things to me that I didn't think too much of, because they didn't quite understand what was going on and what was involved. So I tried to explain to my family, but they didn't accept all I said. They saw they weren't going to stop me, so they quit talking to me about it. So I just kept on. So finally, they started coming in one by one. I finally got them all into the Movement.

I can remember different incidents when the Movement was challenged.

The Shuttlesworth children were on a bus coming to Birmingham, and they were pulled off the bus in Gadsden, Alabama, and put in jail, and we knew that it was a possibility it wouldn't be safe for one or two people to go to Gadsden to try to get the children out. So we had a little convoy, five or six cars, and I was driving a car that belonged to Mr. Colonel Stone Johnson, and we went to Gadsden. I had the papers, bonds to get the children out of jail, but when I got to Gadsden, Alabama, it was denied for me to get the children out of jail. So I couldn't get the children out of jail because they wouldn't accept the bonds. They turned the bonds down, even though they were signed by responsible people and people in authority. But the officials in Gadsden wouldn't accept this. So we had to come back to Birmingham without the children and go back at another time to get the children. The children were arrested because they refused to give up their seats to whites on the bus. They were young; they ran from maybe from thirteen to about seventeen years old. Another group went back, and they released them, but they had to do some work and had to get some lawyers in order to get them out of jail. They had to get a bondsman from Gadsden instead of Birmingham.[6]

I was a member of New Hope Baptist church during the civil rights movement. Quite a few members at our church were involved, and my pastor, Reverend Herman Stone, was also, and his wife. Sure, there were a lot of pastors that were not involved. My pastor was brilliant. He was from Atlanta, Georgia, and part of his talk was registering and voting. So there was no problem to get Reverend involved. I heard him say some things that I respect him really high for. He'd take the money out of his own pocket and had a clinic at New Hope Baptist church for the members and other people to come in and learn how to go down and register and vote. At that particular time, we had some members in New Hope church was in age, something like fifty, sixty years old, and they went down to vote, and we had a poll tax in the city of Birmingham, and they had to pay poll tax from the age they were, twenty-one up to fifty-six or sixty or seventy years of age. Some of them paid thirty and forty dollars back poll tax before they could vote in that church. And the chairman of the Deacon Board was an elderly man, pretty close to seventy years old, and he paid his poll tax, and they charged him poll taxes from twenty-one years to seventy years before he had the privilege to vote. And there were more than him. Deacon Cliff Watkins, after Mr. Ben Grisby passed on, Deacon Cliff Watkins became the chairman of the deacon board. When he became the chairman of the deacon board, he went down and registered and had to pay a lot of money. Mr. C. C. Jones was a deacon at New Hope and had been there a long time. I understand he paid thirty-some dollars, and on goes the story. Whereas the Board of Registrars make you pay all that back tax before they let blacks vote.[7]

Riding the buses in the city of Birmingham was a hard task. I was downtown one day not too long after the Supreme Court handed down the decision that the buses were integrated. You know, in the segregated days, you rode the bus in the back of the bus, and it made no difference how crowded the bus was with blacks, they didn't let but so many blacks ride. They put a board there, and the blacks could not ride up front. They had to stand in the back. But then, after the Supreme Court ruled on the bus, I was downtown and caught the bus, and when I caught the bus, I sat in the white section. Didn't many people sit down behind me, but when I got where I was supposed to get off, the bus driver didn't let me off, so we went another block. So I got out and took my pencil and paper and took the number of the bus and his number. He was kind of nasty about it. It wasn't a law then. We had to go and negotiate the buses because bus drivers were still doing the same thing as they were doing in the segregation days. We had to go to Tennessee and get some white students from a school in Tennessee and bring them to Birmingham and put [them] in the back of the bus in order to make it totally integrated.

The bus drivers didn't become nice until the Alabama Christian Movement board meeting met with the bus company and the City of Birmingham, and the city attorney told the bus company what the bus drivers were doing. So the bus company said that they would tell the bus drivers to just drive the bus, don't mess with the passengers. Then the stuff began to let up, but before then, they were not actually harassing, but they were making it inconvenient for the passengers. And even in the segregated days, it was terrible. It was almost unbearable in the segregated days, where sometimes if the bus was crowded, you had to go into the back door of the bus. Blacks couldn't even go in the front door and stand up in front of the board. Of course you didn't have the privilege to sit down, even though there were seats available. The bus driver was just too nasty to move the board, so you had to stand up until you got where you were going.[8]

I can remember an incident when Reverend Shuttlesworth tried to enroll his children at Phillips High School, and they beat him up. Reverend Phifer was, at that time, the second vice president of the Alabama Christian Movement for Human Rights, so he drove Reverend Shuttlesworth to Phillips High School. We had to plan it, but I had to work, and I couldn't get off. If I could have gotten off, I would have been there. I got off that afternoon, and they had taken Reverend Shuttlesworth home because he was beaten up. The perpetrators were around with rocks and cans in their hands, and there were people from my family and friends that I know were there to testify to what the perpetrators did when Reverend Shuttlesworth got out of the car. They crowded around and beat him up. They stabbed Reverend Shuttlesworth's wife also and said all kinds of nasty words. The language was bad that the perpetrators used because they used the word "nigger," and there was no such thing as a nigger, that's just what they wanted to use to disgrace black people. It's ironic that today Phillips High School is 99.9 percent black.

In '62, Miles College students got involved in a selective buying campaign. They came to the Movement. We had a young people's division in the Movement. So Miles College students organized a buying campaign by going down in the city to buy different products at different places. At that particular time, there were places in the stores that blacks . . . were segregated. I bought the better-quality shoes not because I was able to buy them but because I didn't want to be segregated. The stores that sold the lesser-quality shoes had a special place for you to sit down. They'd take you back into the store where nobody would be, unless it'd be one or two blacks. All the whites would be up front where you could buy a pair of shoes at a reasonable price. But where you had to pay right smart of money for the shoes, then they weren't so segregated. You could sit down wherever anybody else sat. That caused me to pay a little bit more money for my shoes, because I didn't want to go back there. And two or three stores I went into, they'd carry you back in the back to sit you down to try on a pair of shoes, and I didn't like that. Regal Shoe Store, Flagg Brothers Shoe Store, and Bob Young's Shoe Store all had those policies. Odum, Bowers, and White allowed you to go in and sit wherever you wanted.[9]

During the demonstrations in April and May, we marched to the city jail on Sunday, and they would have the hose pipes and water, and [we] prayed, and some of the preachers said they just wanted to go up to the jail to pray, and they refused to let us go. So some started walking off, and all of us walked off, and we went on to the jail. But the fire department was out there with hose pipes to keep us from going to the jail, just to pray. We had a lot of children, and vicious German police dogs, and the hose pipes were strong that they turned on any number of people. There were probably a thousand children. They knocked children down in the street and, at the same time, sicked the dogs on the people, and the children had to fight the dogs off. But they didn't have anything to fight the dogs with. But, at the same time, people were somewhat devastated because of the fire hoses and because of the dogs. The police did not do anything to keep the dogs off the people, nor did the fire department turn the water off. It was a tragic situation in Birmingham at that time. This did not stop people from becoming involved; instead, it increased people getting involved. Instead of driving people from the Movement, people came more and more and more.

Dr. King and I were good friends, and he sent for me to come to Montgomery, Alabama. I am the person that came up with the ten reasons why black people should vote. He called Reverend Shuttlesworth and told him to bring me to Montgomery—he wanted to talk with me. So Reverend Shuttlesworth and Reverend Gardner and Charles Billips and Mrs. Lola Hendricks and myself went to Montgomery to Dr. Martin Luther King's establishment. He had an office there. We discussed the ten reasons why black people should vote. Dr. King became a good friend of mine during the civil rights struggle. We discussed a lot of things, and even during the demonstrations here in Birmingham, we sat down at the old Smith and Gaston building maybe until twelve, one, and two o'clock in the morning deciding what to do for Birmingham, because we had three thousand people in jail, and we had run out of money, and so we got fifty thousand dollars from the SCLC. Reverend Ralph David Abernathy was the treasurer, and he give us a check for fifty thousand dollars to help us get some of the people out of jail, but that wasn't a drop in the bucket. We couldn't get the people out of jail with fifty thousand dollars because the bonds were two thousand dollars for children, so we had to go to Atlanta and get a federal judge to hand down a decree and order they turn the children loose and let them go back to school. So we put a lawyer on the plane and sent him to Atlanta and filed the case in Atlanta with the Fifth Circuit Appeals Court. Judge Gwynn was the federal judge at that particular time, and [he] ordered [them] to put the children back in school. That's how we got them out of jail, most of them.[10]

I don't think I would change anything much from what actually happened. It was a day-to-day thing. What came up today, you deal with today. During that struggle, we had to take people to the Board of Registrars, and they'd be turned down and couldn't vote and couldn't register, and we had to set up clinics throughout the city to teach our people how to register. And after teaching them how to register, when they registered, come back to the clinic and teach them how to vote, because during that period of time, I remember that in general elections you have maybe, at that time, a hundred or 135 people running for thirty offices or twenty-five offices, and you had to pick over a hundred-and-something people to choose twenty-five people. And if you vote, pull the lever by the wrong person's name, the vote wouldn't count, and you used machines then, and a lot of people weren't so familiar with machines. They allowed you three minutes in the machine, and I've been in the line many times when there were other members of other races being in the machines ten and fifteen minutes, nobody say nothing. But when blacks were in the machine over three minutes, somebody was telling them they were spending too much time, and I have spoke myself to the poll people at the polling place in the precinct, "Give them a little bit more time, you're a little unfair," and sometimes they would, and sometimes they wouldn't. In a major election, the building would be full of people, and on the outside, you'd have maybe two or three lines around the corner. So the polls would have to be opened to nine and ten o'clock to get all the folks over. They closed the doors at seven o'clock, and if all is not in the building at seven o'clock, the rest don't get a chance to register. That has happened to black folks as well as whites, mostly blacks.

When South Africans went to the ballot in the early 1990s they were voting with a ballot you push in a hole, just mark it with a pencil in South Africa and push it in a box. But in Birmingham, Alabama, you had a machine sitting over there that had been programmed with people's names on it, and you had to look on that machine and find the person's name that you was looking for and pull the lever by that name, which took much more time to do it. And you had to read real fast. You could hardly make any mistakes, 'cause if you made any mistakes, then the ballot wouldn't count. So you would lose that ballot. We'd lose some ballots during that time. That was somewhat unfair to a lot of voters and especially to blacks.

Edited by Desiree Fisher. BCRI Oral History Project, vol. 4, sec. 2 (Mar. 24, 1995).

Notes

1. Howard was the international representative and vice president of the International Union of Mine, Mill, and Smelter Workers. He was also president of the Bessemer branch of the NAACP and the Bessemer Voters' League.

2. On the union before the 1950s, see Horace Huntley, "Iron Ore Miners and Mine Mill in Alabama, 1933–1952" (Ph.D. dissertation, University of Pittsburgh, 1976).

3. An intercity community southwest of downtown Birmingham.

4. He is probably referring to Charles Patrick. See Andrew Manis, *A Fire You Can't Put Out: The Civil Rights Life of Birmingham's Reverend Fred Shuttlesworth* (Tuscaloosa: University of Alabama Press, 1999), 81.

5. That area is referred to as Dynamite Hill. Glenn T. Eskew, *But for Birmingham: The Local and National Movements in the Civil Rights Struggle* (Chapel Hill: University of North Carolina Press, 1997), 68–69.

6. This episode is described in detail in Manis, *Fire You Can't Put Out,* 246–52.

7. The poll tax is discussed in Linda Reed, *Simple Decency and Common Sense: The Southern Conference Movement, 1938–1963* (Bloomington: University of Indiana Press, 1991), 70–73.

8. Conflicts on buses are discussed in Robin D. G. Kelley, *Race Rebels: Culture, Politics, and the Black Working Class* (New York: Free Press, 1994), 55–77.

9. See Diane McWhorter, *Carry Me Home: Birmingham, Alabama; The Climactic Battle of the Civil Rights Revolution* (New York: Simon and Schuster, 2001), 255–56; BCRI Oral History Project interviews with Frank Dukes (vol. 6, sec. 1), Joe Dickson (vol. 14, sec. 1), Jonathon McPherson (vol. 46, sec. 4).

10. Much of the bail money was donated by labor organizations, including the National Maritime Union, the United Auto Workers, and the USWA. See McWhorter, *Carry Me Home*, 418–20. See also the interview with Jerome "Buddy" Cooper in this volume.

Eula McGill

Born May 15, 1911, in Resaca, Georgia. Worked as a spinner in cotton mills. Organizer and business agent for the Amalgamated Clothing Workers of America for more than fifty years. Organized locals and led strikes in Alabama, Mississippi, Florida, Kentucky, Tennessee, and the Carolinas. Inducted into the Alabama Organized Labor Hall of Fame. *"Do you know when I retired I had 100 percent in every shop, except one? I had twenty-three thousand members in North Alabama. Everyone was 100 percent except one. Because I made the union interesting for them. I visited the business agent[s], and once a month I was in each shop myself."*

"I Didn't Go Nowhere but Up after That."

I was born on May 15, 1911, in a little country town called Resaca. My father worked in the ore mines in a little town called Sugar Valley, Georgia, near there, but he could walk from our house to the mine. The company wasn't a very big operation. My family rented from a man named Mr. Nance, and it was a big spring there. It was called Nance's Spring, and it furnished water. The last battle of the Civil War was fought just above Nance's Spring. I went by there a lot of times. It was usually when I was working and traveling. I constantly went by, and it is still a beautiful place. I had a cousin that lived right across the road from there. I want to tell you that my father's people were from East Tennessee, and they fought with the federal troops. A lot of people from North Georgia fought, and they had a regiment from Alabama. A lot of people don't know that. That went from Winston County.

Anyway, I was born there, and the mine worked out when I was between six and seven years old. They got out all the ore that they economically could get out. So we moved to Gadsden [in eastern Alabama] where my father went to work in the steel plant, Gulf State Street Steel, in the carpenter division. He was a carpenter by trade. My mother worked inside the home with me and my sister, who was seven years older. My sister quit school and went to work in the cotton mill. I loved school, and the reason I quit, my father was laid off his job. Back then you had no laws, and when papa got forty, that was the end of a man's working life in what they called public work. He had lost his job, and I had to quit school and go to work in the cotton mill so we could eat. I told them I was age fourteen.[1] They didn't check back then very careful, anyhow. By the way, that child labor law was passed in 1911, the year I was born.

We went up to the mill, and they hired us. They put us on the payroll when they thought you had trained sufficiently. In my case, I worked six weeks before they put me on the payroll. My first paycheck for fifty-six hours was $3.10, and they took a dime out for ice water and a penny out of each dollar. In that case, three cents for the company doctor, whether you used him or not, you had to pay. They just took it. We never had any ice water, by the way. They just took that out and kept it.

I worked there about two years and then married at sixteen. All the young girls back then, they thought they were going to be old maids if they didn't get married. Anyway, it was unfortunate. Anyway, it didn't work out. My daddy had gotten a job at Alabama Power, and so we lived near a town called Wetumpka [in south central Alabama]. Papa worked Jordan Dam, and he worked until that dam was finished. We stayed there briefly. That is where my child was born. We then came to Birmingham. My sister had married and lived in Ensley. Her husband worked in construction, where he was a plasterer. And we moved in the house with them until we could do better. I went to work in a cotton mill out on Vanderbilt Road. And going from Ensley Highlands that far on the streetcar from Ensley Highlands, it took me two hours to go to work and two hours to come back. I worked twelve-hour shifts until the Wages and Hour Law got cut to forty.[2] It would take me that long to go back and forth because I had to transfer in town and catch a Norwood car and ride to the end of the line and then walk four blocks on to the mill. We organized the union there, and I told someone one day, I said when I turn twenty-one, I couldn't wait until I got eligible to vote. I borrowed $1.50 to pay my poll tax. I paid my poll tax and voted for Roosevelt, and I joined the labor union, and I didn't go nowhere but up after that. We had bad working conditions. The mill it was just . . . it was what we called a "hobo mill." Because the conditions were so bad, people just worked there to get a few pennies to go somewhere else. I was a spinner and not suited for the job because I was too tall. I became a union member and a representative, and I had a lot of influence over the bosses to try to suit the person to the job. If you didn't like the job, don't let her work on it because it hurts him and her too. If she is happy on the job . . . and when I first became a union representative, the companies felt like if they give into a person, they would be abdicating their authority. Some of the things that were first started organizing . . ., of course, we didn't have a very good union. But as time went on, I am happy to say that some of the things that happened to me in the mill that I wanted changed, I got them changed. The local agreements in the shops down here, later on they become part of our national agreement.[3] One was sick leave. I would get so tired of the boss when a girl would be off, he would hire her back like a new hand and start her over. She would say, "No, I was off sick." "No you weren't, and blah, blah, blah." I said, "We spent so much money and time arguing about it, so let's make an agreement." So we got sick leave signed. The company signed sick leave, and they signed three copies. The workers signed it, and the plant manager signed it, and the union business agent signed it. The company had a copy, the worker had a copy, and the union officer had a copy. That way I didn't have to argue. I spent time on something else instead of arguing over some foolish thing.

Another thing about transferring from one job to another: If a job became open, and a girl wanted to transfer, oh, no, no, no, no, and I got that agreed to on a local agreement, and it became a part of the national agreement later on. Oh, waiting time. A girl would be without work. It was piecework, you see, and the operators would be without work, and they would just sit there. They weren't making any money; the company wasn't making any money either. So I got waiting time instituted. That was to make management see they had work, not to give them pay for not working. I convinced the management it was for their benefit to pay waiting time, so their local management would see that people had worked, to help management. See, I always approached anything that I took about the workers to show management where it helped them. Because they could care less about the worker. I am proud to say of all the managements that I dealt with over the years, which is forty-some-odd years, I only had one manager that would just not agree with me regardless. He just, I think he was just defiant. I hate to say this, but he was from Mississippi, and he managed a shop out from Florence. A good company. We had it under contract for years. Every time . . . and I had a chair-lady of the shop, a black woman, very intelligent, very smart, had a good education. He would not deal with her. He wouldn't settle nothing with me, and he wouldn't agree with me. The workforce was mixed. We got that before all those other things. Arrow and Breman had a few black people. I represented that company over there in Georgia.

By the way, my union never had a segregated meeting. The union I was a member of was the Amalgamated Clothing Workers of America [ACWA]. Sidney Hillman was the organizer, and to a lot of people he is very well known.[4] He was very active and a big friend of Roosevelt. He believed that not only should the union protect the workers and help them on the job, but outside the job and in the community. We had the first health and welfare benefits paid for by the employer. We had the first public housing, workers' cooperative housing, partners in Chicago and New York and Philadelphia. We couldn't have them south because we were too scattered. I wanted to try one time to get one started in Atlanta, but people were too scattered that way and didn't have a bit of transportation. It was called Amalgamated Housing, a big apartment building for the workers, and we owned and operated our banks. The workers owned the banks. That's another thing you don't see now. We got our first banks in 1929.[5] Amalgamated Bank of Chicago and an Amalgamated Bank of New York, and they are in existence today, except the Chicago Bank. We sold it and put it in our insurance fund to start our insurance fund. We were the first ones to have employee-paid insurance.

I became involved in the unions because my father was a union man, being a carpenter. I went to my first union meeting when I was seven years old. I was on my first picket line when I was seven years old with a friend of my mother's in Rainbow City, which is part of Gadsden now. There is a big mill there, Dwight Mill. My father's cousin was general superintendent. That was the first mill I went to work in. He would come through the mill, and he would look at me, because he would come visit us when my grandmother would come. Because she was his aunt, and he would come to see Aunt Nan, he called her. The Agricolas was one of the founders of Gadsden. They donated this land to build this plant. I forget now what year they built it in, but I went to Gadsden to the celebration. I can't remember right now. I know I went to work there in 1927. I think it was. But the Agricolas donated that land with the stipulation that it had to operate thirty years without closing down as much as thirty days, or the land would revert back to Agricolas. That was to keep them from coming fly-by-night and operating spasmodically. I was happily working when the thirty years was up. They shut down for thirty days to retool the plant. I went back to work, and I was making seven dollars a week when I was there.

When I came back to work they had a new system called the Bedaux system, which was a stretch-out. Bob Priestman invented this so-called engineering process, it was called the Bedaux system, which we called the stretch-out, to give us more looms to run and more looms to run and stretched us out and gave us more room to work.[6] When my secondhand, who was my immediate supervisor, came around, you wouldn't believe what they was paying me. Unless you asked you wouldn't know you got a paycheck. Because I was always braising, you know, I always said what I thought. Now that is one thing I did all my life. I asked, I can't think of his name now, but I asked him, "What's this job paying?" He said, "$3.10," and I walked out. I walked out, not knowing where my next job was coming from. My daddy didn't have a job; I just walked out and had this child that was less than a year old. My husband in the meantime had gotten in trouble and had been arrested. I went on home, and I told papa what had happened, and he said, "You did the right thing."

Well, I came to Birmingham and stayed with my sister in Ensley Highland and started working in that mill here, which was a lousy mill, dirty and nasty. I was not yet a union official because everybody that talked about a union got fired or got blacklisted. The craft unions like the printers and the machinists and the highly skilled workers and the craft workers, they were skilled, and they could withhold their labor, and it was cheaper for the company to recognize them than to lose the money while they were on strike. I was in the AFL; that was the only union. People had so much confidence in Roosevelt and the politicians at that time, and we had some wonderful politicians in Alabama back then.

They had so much confidence that, by gosh, the people just came out on the strike and walked out. It was a spontaneous thing. And we had to run our own strike; we had no representatives. My sister had an automobile, and we helped organize the Women's Trade Union League and assisted unions, and my sister was in it. During the 1934 strike northern companies owned Huntsville and Prattville, Alabama, and they got recognition during the '34 strike. They got recognition, and I think the Prattsville Company is still operating.

My immediate supervisor was a nice man and a good fellow. When I went to Washington to the Women's Trade Union meeting, they took me along. They sent me to a labor school. I went on the weekends when I was working in the mill. I was in the Women's Trade Union then. It is the oldest women's organization in the country, formed in the late 1800s.[7] It was formed in Chicago. And 10 percent of the membership would be professional women, and we had a lot of society women who wanted to help women workers. Now, they could open doors for us that we couldn't open. They could talk to judges, get us out of jail when we were in jail, because they had good connections. So we had a league here. Molly Dowd, who was on the national board, came here from Huntsville and worked at Loveman's department store. She formed a league here, and I was a member of it. So whenever we went to Washington in 1936 for the national convention of the Women's Trade Union League, Mrs. Roosevelt had delegations from Huntsville and Birmingham as her guests that week in the White House. And she belonged to the one in New York and the New York delegation. We stayed the week in the White House. Well it broke in the newspaper, and when I came back from that convention, the old owner come up from Mississippi and fired me himself. That's how I lost my job.

The next month we had the Southern Conference of Human Welfare here.

And Mrs. Roosevelt came here for it.[8] And I did not tell her I had gotten fired. I just thought she would just think I had left; I didn't tell her about it. But every time she come anywhere in the South she notify me. It went on for years and years and years. I know she came here one time to speak to the Business Professional Women's Club, and they were charging the people to come. She was speaking at the Boutwell Auditorium, it was called then. She sent me a word through her secretary, Melvina Thompson, to come to a reception that they were giving for her at the Tutwiler Hotel, and I had to walk to town, because I was fired and didn't have any carfare. I walked to town. I was living then with a girl up on Twelfth Avenue North, and she went to work for the WPA, and I was too proud.

There were two labor lawyers here, John Busby and Johnny Carlton, who lost their jobs in 1919 in the railroad strike, and then they didn't get their jobs back, so they studied law and became lawyers. They were the first labor lawyers I ever knew. I wound up at their office, and a lot of times he [John Busby] would take me to lunch. I worked in organizing German tailors there in Birmingham. All the department stores had tailors that repaired men's suits, and Mr. Muir had a tailor shop, and he made suits across from the Tutwiler. He was the one that introduced me to the Amalgamated Clothing Workers. Then I helped organize the ore miners in Bessemer called the Mine, Mill, and Smelter Workers. They all eventually became part of the Steelworkers;[9] of course, the mines worked out, you know, like the ore did.

I was at the mine in Bessemer. I hate to see them ore mines go down. I have a warm spot for Bessemer. [When I was twenty-three years old and on the staff,] we had such a good women's auxiliary down there, down by that theater where it used to be a union hall. When they were out of work, we would go to these stores and get handouts to feed the strikers. You see, there were no strike benefits, and they had no money back then. They had no money to pay the basic strike benefits, so we had to make up, and we would go around the little communities and make up for money from the local, pass a hat, and that way we would use the money to pay utility bills, and they would see a doctor, and what we could gather up from stores. We would go to the stores, and we would get clothes and jewelry. When people went on strike, they would help gather up to help them economically while they were on strike, because we didn't have no money to pay strike benefits.

[I came back to Alabama in the 1950s.] I came over briefly to help with Leeds, and then we had a lot of shops move here in Alabama that had already recognized us. Arrow came, Cotler came, and a lot of companies put shops here in Alabama. They already recognized the union. And we had all our contracts signed that any new shops opened, if we organized them, they had to recognize us, and then we didn't have to go through elections. We had it in all our contracts that even if a new shop opened up, and they weren't union, that if we signed the majority up they would recognize us without an election, but we would have card checks, to be recognized at the labor board. If you were not certified with the labor board, you don't have a standing in a strike, but you can have a card check without going through election. So we have somebody, an impartial person, come in and check the cards against the people's signature to verify that they signed the card. That's called a card check, and that's the way we got most of the shops. But we got a lot in Alabama.

We had a girl over here . . . the only person that I think we had on our staff that just did not do the job. And the person [who] was the director at the time, the only time I have ever known this to happen: he was going with her. That's why he put her on the staff. I found that out, and I talked to him about that. He was a good friend. I said, "You know what, I don't believe. . . ." There was one thing that I did not agree with is men organizing and going with the workers in the shop. And I found out he was going with her. I told him, I said, "Hey, you shouldn't do that." But anyhow, him and me worked well together, and we were good buddies and all that, and he was a damn good organizer, but he was no good at nothing else. He was an organizer, and that was the end of it, because he couldn't say no to people. And when you are business agent, sometimes the workers aren't always right, they are wrong sometimes, and you have to straighten it out. Gladys Dickason[10] has always sent me with him everywhere because he couldn't help but lie. He would get up and just tell some of the fairest tales you wanted to hear. He was a good person, though. Anyway, so she [the director's girlfriend] came over here. Gladys put her in charge of the North Alabama area.

Gladys got sick and had to retire early, and Charlie English took over. He was her assistant, so he stepped up into the job. His grandfather was one of my oldest friends. He ran our newspaper, and Charlie English, his grandfather, oh, a fine old gentleman. He was old back then. He was a wonderful speaker. Oh God, you would have just been thrilled to hear him speak. Anyway, Charlie took over, so I was in Atlanta having a good time. I love Atlanta. I love Atlanta. I was organizing, and I had a good thing going. I had shops organized down South. I went down in South Georgia and got a good thing going there. And the Teamsters were helping. I got along good with the Teamsters, because the Teamsters would organize, and the company would try to take their work somewhere else, they would tell me where it was. A lot of people don't know that things were like that. They wouldn't cross our picket line. They would honor our picket line. We had in our contract that the supervisor can't do the production work except with the consent of the union, when it is necessary.

They don't have that in their contracts. That's one weakness of the Teamsters. Their bosses can drive their trucks. I don't know why they don't have that. But anyway, the boss would get in the truck, and the driver would get out at the picket line, and the boss would go across the picket line, but when that truck driver got back in there he would fire it up, it was hot cargo. Anyway, the Teamsters worked very well. I have always loved the Teamster Union. Now the only thing is wrong, and I think with the Teamsters, is each locality runs their own business. Our union, the national executive board has the last say. That's not true with the Teamsters; each district runs his own business and can make its own rules.

Most time they were good people. I loved working with them. We had a good one here in Birmingham for a while. But the last time I went over there where the warehouses were, I thought they had some nonunion agitators all the time. I didn't get any cooperation, so I don't think they are very strong around Birmingham. You will never make me think . . . I knew Jimmy Hoffa and Josephine because I was close with the Teamsters. One of my best friends, his wife, today is one of my best friends in Thomaston, Georgia. He was a driver. But I tell you, they were fine people. Of course, he is Atlanta. I got acquainted with Jimmy Hoffa and Josephine. He would come there and meet us in Atlanta. Tony Zilledge, who was on the staff of the Teamsters Union, was a good friend of Andrew Young in Atlanta. That's how I met Andrew, through Tony Zilledge. We had a good relationship with Andrew through Tony. Tony worked, and we got Andrew elected to Congress. Carter made us so mad when he got in as president: he put him on the United Nations, and that made me so mad. As hard as we worked to get him into Congress, where he could do something. Andrew resigned. He couldn't say no, the president had appointed him. He thought he was doing him a favor, but he put him where he was ineffective.

We never had a segregated union. In the days when it was against the law to meet together, we used black churches and the Salvation Army. We never had a segregated union meeting in the South. Now, sometimes they automatically would separate themselves in the hall, they automatically would do it, nobody would say anything. They just automatically do it, but they didn't have to. But we never, no, no, no, we never . . . we met somewhere where we could meet together. We used this black Masonic hall for our dances and things, so we were never separated.

I came back to Birmingham when Charlie Lucas, our subdirector, asked me to come back. He was the vice president of the union. His headquarters was in New York, but he was a southern director, in charge of the South. He had the last say about what went on and directing the staff. I said, "I will work anywhere you want me to, but I had hoped I could finish my time as an organizer because I really love organizing, and I am having such a good time down here, but I will go anywhere you want." So he sent me back. I had never saw such a mess. There were grievances piled up that hadn't been settled, and we took [them] up. I worked seven days a week, night and day, for a year, taking care of back grievances and settling back grievances, and I set up an education department down here in the South, and an education committee, and I set up a plan. In this right-to-work state I didn't have but one [union] shop. Some of them just barely had the majority in them. I could lose a contract. Well, she hadn't done her job. I called the business agents together and set up a plan to sign all the members. Each union steward will have union cards and insurance cards. When a person is hired and put on the job, that union steward, the first day she goes on the job will take her a union card and the insurance and have her sign both of them at the same time. That way the boss will not have time to get to them before we do. Do you know when I retired I had 100 percent in every shop except one? I had a 100 percent membership. I had twenty-three thousand members in North Alabama. Everyone was a 100 percent union except one, because I made the union interesting for them. I visited the business agents, and once a month I was in each shop myself. I was at a shop in Centerville. One girl wouldn't join, and I didn't know why she wouldn't join. I had 100 percent in every shop. I retired in 1982 in Birmingham. Yes. I had to come back and build a union. We had nothing here. Every summer I had a labor school. I got UAB CLEAR [the University of Alabama at Birmingham, Center for Labor Education and Research]. I had weekend classes. They didn't have to come, but I attempted it.

We had to fight for our civil rights. So many people think civil rights are just black rights. Civil rights are everybody rights. They are human rights. I very seldom use the word "civil rights." They think its only black. I say "human rights" because that is what it is. We are becoming more and more . . . we are getting a lot of Spanish. They are having problems up there. You see, them people don't know no better. They don't respect anybody else. I was raised among all kinds of people. But the turn of the century, in the 1900s, the steel mills went to France and Italy and Germany over there, and especially Italy and Poland, and brought back a lot of workers, thought they could be docile in order to cheat them, and they fooled them. So in the steel towns I was raised among all kinds of nationalities. One of my best friends was Clara Troncoli. They moved to Birmingham later. Before Papa died he met up with her on the street one day. He said, "I saw Clara Troncoli." Mainly the people who lived around us were Polish, Italians, and the black section started right across the street. And we played together all the time. My mother's best friend was a black woman, Barbara. She would come in and sit down and eat with us just like it was nothing. My people had no prejudices. I think everybody has a certain amount of prejudice about everything, but as far as race is concerned, people stood on their own as human beings. That is the way I was raised.

You see, Tuxedo Junction was just below where we lived. Erskine Hawkins [the great jazz musician who came from here] popularized Tuxedo Junction. We would walk over here, and the nightclubs down there, oh, had the most wonderful black folks, [and they] were dressed [to kill]. Oh, you should have seen them. And we couldn't go in, of course, but we would go and sit outside and listen to the music. And we would walk on the hill from over here, and when they revived Tuxedo Junction again, you know, and begin to have those days, I didn't miss a one of them.

When I was growing up there were kids in our school that wouldn't hold an Italian kid's hands when we would play games. It was funny. There were no blacks, and most of the Italian children went to the Catholic school in Gadsden. They had to pay to go because the kids mistreated them. The teachers were helpless to do anything about it, but I was always nice to them because I was raised among them. Most of the kids were raised by folks working in cotton mills, and I reckon they were just prejudiced against everybody. Once social change begins, it cannot be reversed. You can't uneducate the person who has learned to read. You cannot humiliate the person who feels pride. You cannot oppress the people who are not afraid anymore. Now that is [the way it seems] to me, and we are all one class of human race.

I have read Darwin's theory of evolution. I have read a lot of books. I learned to read before I went to school. I would read everything I would get ahold of. We couldn't afford to buy books. I would get ahold of a book wherever I could get it. Do you know I learned about highways before they had numbers on them, and I started traveling? I learned all of the maps on the side. I would get that number of the road. And on the map I would count so many roads, and then I know that's where highway so-and-so. That's the way I would find the roads, by looking at that map and counting how many roads down. I learned that the highways, the even numbers are East and West and odd numbers are North and South, that's it, U.S. highways. I couldn't have gone nowhere without a map. I would write it down on a piece of paper and look at the map and write it down, take so-and-so, to so-and-so, and turn left.

My mother couldn't read or write. She never had any schooling. Papa had a good education. I don't know why he didn't teach her to read or write. I know why I didn't: she was too proud. You know what? You would never know it. If she could have read, ain't no telling what she would have done. Nobody knew she couldn't read or write. If somebody gives her something to read, she would say, "I don't have my glasses, would you mind reading that for me?" We had a play at school, and we needed something called excelsior. I said, "Mama, we need something to go on our stage, and the teacher called it excelsior. Do you know what that is?" "Why, of course," she said. "It's what they packed dishes in. You get dishes, that wood shaving was in them big boxes they packed dishes in, before you had the other things." I said, "Mama is smart. She know something the teacher doesn't." My mother was an environmentalist. She said, "You got to take care of the earth, they ain't making more earth." She didn't want no salt on the ground, no grease on the ground; she wouldn't use any poison on her vegetable gardens. She cared nothing about flowers. She would plant sunflowers, but some reason or another sunflowers were good for a garden. She would go out and look at her beans. She would turn every leaf. She would kill the eggs before they hatch, and her own potatoes she would kill the eggs before they hatched out. She wouldn't have to use no poison. She wouldn't use no poison, wouldn't use nothing. You know, farmers used to come around and sell that manure, and that is what she used to raise her vegetables. They would come around in a little wagon, usually a one-horse wagon with a load of compost, they called it, and people would buy it because they would plant the gardens. Mama always had something growing.

My sister was a good cook, because she got married and kept house. I never did that. Later on she went to work to the NYA [National Youth Administration]. I told you that Rosa Parks was in that school she ran down there. [My sister went to] the NYA schools to teach, so black women wouldn't have to do domestic work. Rosa Parks was in there. And later on, when Leroy Stratford put that shop down, she went to work as a member of our union. She went to Highlander Folk School[11]—it was over the mountain—to learn about the unions.

Back in the thirties I went to Highlander. I went there not as a student, I went just to think. I couldn't take off and go to school. Hell, I got my education. I knew more than Miles [Horton] did. Miles and me were good friends, and his wife, Zelfield. Miles was a wonderful person. Highlander was a beautiful place. Do you know the labor unions forsook it? Our union didn't, we still used it, and a lot of CIO unions, but the AFL called it Communist. They [the AFL] didn't do anything outside of looking at their membership, but they didn't believe in any political action until we started and they caught on, copied us. But they didn't believe in educating the workers. They never had no school or nothing. When I worked out here in the plant I didn't have a contract, but [I was] a union member, and we could have a delegate to the central labor body, and I was elected delegate to the labor body, and it wasn't but one other woman, and she was in the . . . I don't know, maybe one of the newspapers.

They would say, "Sit down, you don't know what you talking about." Well, you know what? Everybody that was an officer of that union had a job at the courthouse.

We walked out and formed the CIO. We didn't leave many people in there.

Yeah, you see, the Amalgamated Clothing Workers wasn't taken in the AFL until 1932.[12] They were independent from the beginning. Everybody wouldn't let them come in because they were that old United Garment Workers. We had the trade organized 98 percent in 1939. Men's clothing was organized. There was only one shop that wasn't union. It was old Slow Bill down here in Columbus, Georgia. All the other shops were union shops because, you see, they were predominantly situated in the North, and most people were ethnic people. And by nature they stuck together. How the Amalgamated was formed was this way. Hart, Schaffner, and Marx had the union, the United Garment Workers, and Frank Rosenblum and some of the old timers got themselves somewhere and elected to attend the United Garment Workers convention that had to be held in Nashville, Tennessee. When they got here they cooked up some kind of idea and wouldn't recognize his delegates. They claimed their credentials weren't in order, and they weren't seated. Well, that made a bunch of the other people mad. They called him, and he advised them to get together and form a group together to go back and try to do something and they didn't, so that's when Amalgamated was formed in Nashville, Tennessee, for this group of workers who were not recognized in the United Garment Workers convention.

They [the United Garment Workers–AFL] never had more than forty thousand union members. They didn't organize in anything but work clothes. They used the building trade to force the company into recognizing them, and they were making their money selling the label. They sold their union label. We give our label away. But they sold the union label, and that is how they made their money, selling the label, and they didn't do anything for the people, that's the truth, because they were really a company union. As long as they could sell their label to make money they didn't need the members. When we walked out and formed the Amalgamated I wasn't there, 'cause that was in 1914. I was working, but Mr. Moore, that tailor you had told me about, he is the one that told me all this history about. That's where I learned it from, him. Of course, then I had studied labor history.

Everywhere we would go to start an organizing campaign, they would start an argument. They would come in and talk to the boss and say, "Oh, sign the contract with us." In fact, then we started organizing convict labor. We won an election in one shop. The election was in Lexington, Tennessee, because all railroad men lived there. Then the company, I happened to be in a Nashville hotel one night, and I saw the United Garment Workers members, and they had signed a back-door agreement. That's why a law was passed, so you couldn't do that. They signed a back-door agreement for every one of those shops except the one that we won the election in.

Edited and abridged by Horace Huntley and David Montgomery. BCRI Oral History Project, not indexed (July 26, 2000).

Notes

1. For child labor, see Philip Taft, *Organizing Dixie: Alabama Workers in the Industrial Era,* rev. and ed. Gary Fink (Westport, Conn.: Greenwood Press, 1981).

2. See Jonathan Grossman, "Fair Labor Standards Act of 1938: Maximum Struggle for a Minimum Wage," in *Monthly Labor Review* 101 (June 1978): 22–30. McGill may be referring to the reduction of hours under the NRA Cotton Textile Code in December 1933. Janet Irons, *Testing the New Deal: The General Textile Strike of 1934 in the American South* (Urbana: University of Illinois Press, 2000), 97–98.

3. Janet Irons points out that the United Textile Workers survived the 1934 strike in much better condition in Alabama than elsewhere in the South, with more union members there in 1936 than the other three major textile states put together. Irons, *Testing the New Deal,* 162–63.

4. McGill had been active between 1933 and 1935 in the United Textile Workers–AFL. Ibid., 70, 100.

5. The ACWA established its bank in Chicago in 1922 and its New York bank in 1923. Selig Perlman and Philip Taft, *History of Labor in the United States,* vol. 4 (New York: Macmillan, 1935), 575.

6. On the Bedaux system, see David Montgomery, *Fall of the House of Labor: The Workplace, the State, and American Labor Activism, 1865–1925* (New York: Cambridge University Press, 1987), 440–41.

7. The National Women's Trade Union League was founded in 1903. For its history, see Elizabeth Anne Payne, *Reform, Labor, and Feminism: Margaret Dreier Robbins and the National Women's Trade Union League* (Urbana: University of Illinois Press, 1988).

8. The SCHW convention in Birmingham was in November 1938. See the introduction to this volume.

9. For a discussion of the struggle between the Steelworkers and Mine Mill, see Horace Huntley, "The Rise and Fall of Mine Mill in Alabama: The Status Quo against Interracial Unionism, 1933–1949," in *The Journal of the Birmingham Historical Society: An Anthology Honoring Marvin Yeomans Whiting,* ed. James L. Baggett (Birmingham, Ala.: Birmingham Historical Society, 2000), 197–208.

10. Head of the research department of the ACWA and faculty member at Bryn Mawr College.

11. Founded by Myles Horton in 1932 at Monteagle, Tennessee, to train union organizers. Used as a civil- and human-rights educational retreat from the 1950s to the present. See Myles Horton, *The Long Haul: An Autobiography* (New York: Teachers College Press, 1990).

12. The previously independent ACWA affiliated with the AFL in October 1933 after the difficult negotiations with the United Garment Workers that McGill discusses. See Irving Bernstein, *Turbulent Years: A History of the American Worker, 1933–1941* (Boston: Houghton Mifflin, 1971), 90–91.

Mattie Collins Haywood

Born November 23, 1919, near Linden in Marengo County, Alabama. One of thirteen children; grew up on a farm. Moved to Birmingham in 1939 and worked as a domestic worker. Member of the ACMHR. President of the Finley Avenue Civic League. Worked in voter registration in the 1950s. *"I have worked in private homes, and you just see how you are treated sometime. You always that colored girl, and you got to go to the back. And I don't care how much they grin in your face, you still a colored person, you hear me."*

"You Always That Colored Girl"

I was born in Marengo County. I had twelve brothers and sisters, and I was second-oldest. Most times, during farming season, my mama worked on the farm. But her time mostly was with the children. Whenever the babies would get up some size, then she would go out to the farm and work. But she still had to see about the house and all the children. My grandfather ran a milk dairy in Marengo County. He owned a plantation, and we had a herd of cows and a milk dairy. So we had to help them too. We worked all summer. We had to milk them and get the milk ready for the milkman. We had to milk the cows. We didn't have these modern things to use to milk cows. We had to milk with our hands. And then we would get the milk all strained up and fixed up to put in the big milk cans to put out on the street for the milkman to pick up before day the next morning.

That's what we lived off of. We didn't have any store to get any milk from. We lived off our cow milk and the butter. And we churned our milk. We had to let the milk set up and clabber, and then we took our churn and churned milk and got butter. It wasn't so hard because we didn't know anything else to do but go to school and then work in the field and see about the cows and chickens. That was our living. People were much healthier then. They didn't have to worry about all this stuff you are doing now. You see me, I'm going to live to get a hundred. I'm rough off the farm and loved it then. But now I hate it. I look back, I hated working for nothing. We had to make a living that way, and you didn't get paid like you get a check every month, every week, or every other week. We got paid once a year unless we worked with somebody else's farm.

You got paid once a year because we had to farm. You had to sell your cotton, and if you made enough of cotton to sell, then you did that, too. Don't go way back there, I get mad every time I think about I didn't get no paydays.

School was pretty good. I can just say it wasn't good for blacks, because we didn't have nowhere to go but to church. We didn't have schools like we have now. The only people that had schools were the whites. And if it wasn't but ten [whites] living in your neighborhood you could play around with them, but when they left the neighborhood they were very much different because they had a school to go to. Now, when we moved from down where we were living down in Marengo County and moved to a place called Springhill, Alabama, then we went to a school. I left the fifth grade and got into junior high, and that's the last school I went to, because I wanted to get off the farm. When my sister come for me, I was glad to go.

My older sister was living in a place called Forestdale, Alabama.[1] She wanted me to come and stay awhile. She had gotten sick and needed somebody to work in her place, so I was glad to go, and she came for me. Mother didn't want me to go, but she said, "Mattie, you go on, but I want you to come on back." But I didn't go back. It was a better city than where I was, because at least you were right at a little shopping area [rather than] with one store with all the things you buy for your farm. It was a very good experience. We had church every other Sunday.

Down home, if we milked a cow, and a neighbor didn't have a cow or no milk, we would share milk and butter. If they killed a hog or something like that, it was shared. You see, we were kind of like a family. Nobody had to do without, because they had what we had. We didn't have to do without because we had what they had.

I was in the tenth grade when I came to live with my sister, and I never went back to school, because when I left I went to work. And by my working in her place, I got a chance to get five dollars a week salary. That was a heap of money for a seventeen-year-old girl. A girl used to having no money, and that was good money.

We would make dresses. We weren't buying dresses ready-made, because most of the parents would make the children clothes, and we would take some of the money and buy some material and get a pattern and make a dress to wear.

When I came to Birmingham in 1939, Birmingham wasn't nothing but a smoke stack. Nothing but TCI [Tennessee Coal and Iron], nothing but smog. You go out there in all that soot, and in a few minutes you could wipe that soot out your nose and get it all on your clothes. It was just that terrible. You see, after the years change, then people knew that this was a health hazard, so then they started to cutting that out. And that's some of the things that caused the closing of TCI. It was one of the greatest steel companies in the state of Alabama. They had a lot of fellows employed, and it messed up a lot of folk when they closed it down. Those men would send children to college and buy homes, and so many things that ordinarily they would not have been able to do.

People that worked there didn't have to have education. That's what bothered me about the plant closing. You didn't have to have finished any grade, and all you had to have was a good mind to work and a strong body. He didn't have to have any sense about writing his name, just put an X down. So now, they've worked there all that time, and not old enough to retire, and the plant shut down.

A lot of people had bought homes, and they lost those homes. They weren't really old enough to retire and couldn't get any Social Security. That was the sad part about it.

My husband went in the army in 1943, the same year I joined New Pilgrim Baptist church. We didn't have any children then. All my children were born in the hospital and went to public school in Birmingham. All of them graduated from public school, and all of them were baptized by Reverend N. H. Smith. I joined under Reverend Perry. He came just two Sundays a month because he lived in Memphis, Tennessee. Reverend Smith wasn't in Birmingham then.

I have worked in private homes, and you just see how you are treated some time. You always that colored girl, and you got to go to the back. And I don't care how much they grin in your face, you still a colored person, you hear me. So I would have to work because that's the way I could always get a job. Naturally, they were hiring, paying you about four dollars a week. Domestic work was all black women could do. Even if they got to the twelfth grade, they still couldn't get nothing but a maid in a hospital or work domestic work.

They treated you pretty good as long as you stayed in your place. But I didn't have any problem out of them because I always like to work at houses where children were, because I loved children. White or black. And even when I used to put in an ad for a job, when I first came to Birmingham, I would want one where they had some children. You could write an ad in the newspaper, it was about fifteen cents. I would get to run an ad that I would like to have a job where there were children. They needed someone to keep their children, so I would get the job. But when they made me mad, I would walk off the job.

I asked one boss, Mrs. Porter, about going to church. I said, "Now, my mother raised me up in church, I'm a born-again Christian, and I just cannot work every Sunday." I said, "You're going to have to give me at least one Sunday a month to go to church." So she went in there and talked to her husband, and he said, "Mattie, we can't hardly let you go on Sunday, we need you here to fix the dinner." I said, "Well, I asked you for two Sundays a month to go to church, because I've been working Sunday after Sunday." And she said, "I'm sorry." Now, guess what I was making a week? Four dollars a week for seven days. I didn't say anything. I walked off.

I walked off another job where I worked for an old Jew, with his rich self. He didn't have nothing but money. I was even renting one of his houses, and he wanted to work me for seven days from seven to seven, for $2.50. He wanted to tell me how to serve the food: "You supposed to serve on this side." And I just set the plate down on the table and walked out. I don't take no mess, because you see, I been pushed around too much when I was growing up.

Under Reverend Smith, my church was involved in the movement. I was so glad to get in that movement. And when I got in that demonstration, when I learned about that, I was glad to get in there. My husband said, "Mattie, don't go." He said, "I'm working up here, and this man will find out that you're in that demonstration, he would fire me." I said, "Well, if he fire you off that job, God has got another one for you." He said, "Well, just don't you get in there."

I think it was in 1953 or '54. I met Shuttlesworth, and he said he wants us to go back to our neighborhoods and set up a Civic League and get the people to vote. Nobody was voting. Everybody was scared. They didn't get real scared until Shuttlesworth's house got bombed. And then they said, "Don't talk to me about voting. I will lose my job." I couldn't get my teachers to go vote. They were scared. So that's what bothered me. I thought everybody had a right to vote if they wanted to, but I found out they did not have that right. It took me a long time to get registered. You had to know how many representatives, how people were sent from different districts. I hadn't studied up on things like that. We weren't taught politics when we were coming up. That wasn't even taught in the schools. We had to pay the poll tax. I was glad we got in there because we cut out the poll tax. I paid poll taxes a long time before I could register because I couldn't keep up with everything on the list, you know, how many representatives you got in Montgomery or Washington. A lot of people couldn't do it. The educated folks could not do it. But no white men had that problem. They let the white folks walk in there, sign their name, and go in and vote.

I had to go back and work on the teachers, because you wanted them to be as brave as you are, but those people were scared, until after we broke down the barrier of poll taxes and got it fixed so they wouldn't get out of their job. Miss Lucinda Robey was the only strong person that stood up for what she believed in. She was a principal of a school. She got stuck with that movement and registered to vote, and that's where it started with her.

My son and all the children were getting out of school, and they went up to Atlantic Mills and got arrested. When John didn't come home that night, I got up and called Lola Hendricks[2] and I said, "John didn't come home last night, what happened?" She said, "Well, did he demonstrate?" I said, "Yes, he did." She said, "Well, he's in jail." So he was very proud to be there because they had so many of them there, they couldn't do nothing but put them out there and make a fool out the white folks. Bessemer told them, "Don't send no more down here, we don't have any more room for them. We don't have food. We can't feed them." We just made a big fool out of them. Honey, I just loved it. We would be in meetings all day and sometimes half the night.

After, Fred had King to come in, because the black preachers got scared too, so they turned on Fred.[3] So Fred was kind of like out there with the street folks, like common people like me and others. So it looked like things were going to go down, and that's what the white man thought. And when Fred called King, that's when the ball got to rolling back again. I tell everybody Fred is my man regardless, because he stood a lot in Birmingham. We had the Ku Klux to fight here. We dealt with the water fountains, with voter education, get off the poll tax, and jobs and things for people. So we had many things to fight in Birmingham. Birmingham was evil. It was so evil until those fellows would just as soon come into your yard and house at night when you're in bed and throw something like a big blaze in your yard. It was just terrible here.

They just didn't want the black man to talk to the white girl. As long as you don't say nothing to that white girl. Charlie could play with you and me as much as he wanted, and his wife don't say a word. But if he messed with that white girl, he was already dead because they are going to take him out into the woods and lynch him.[4]

You get on the bus, pay your money, and sit in your seat. Fred had already given us a lecture before we left the meeting. He said, "Now, when you get on the bus, just get there and sit down because you got blacks going to say, 'What they sitting up there for?'" Every time you moved the board, "Hey." The bus man looking out the mirror up there. "Hey, put that board back up there." The board was a dividing line. Blacks on this side, whites on this side. At the water fountain it was a dividing line. The bathroom was a dividing line.

We had a lot to do, and we worked hard, and I was one of the persons that was so glad to be with the people to work hard and do some changing. And now they are trying to put us back because our young people are not taking too much interest in anything. Love and respect yourself. You can't look at what somebody else is doing and do it.

Edited and abridged by Horace Huntley. BCRI Oral History Project, vol. 12, sec. 7 (Mar. 1, 1996).

Notes

1. A northwest suburb of Birmingham.
2. Recording secretary of the ACMHR.
3. Fred Shuttlesworth and Martin Luther King Jr.
4. See A. Leon Higginbotham Jr., *Shades of Freedom: Racial Politics and Presumptions of the American Legal Process* (New York: Oxford University Press, 1996).

Jimmie Louis Warren

Born March 30, 1942, in Marion, Perry County, Alabama. One of twelve children who grew up in the Black Belt of Alabama. Moved to Birmingham in 1959. Worked with the SNCC and the ACMHR. Was a machine operator at U.S. Pipe in North Birmingham. *"[T]he Christian Movement kind of gave me an insight on how to handle myself out there on the job, as I had this little training from Talladega and Atlanta from SNCC about how to move up when things come open. You got to be able to accept the opportunity to be prepared. And so that's how I started out. I almost got run off. They tried to run me off out there, but they weren't able to do so. I had to get on them, file complaints. I even filed complaints against the union because when I got involved in it, I went to the union hall and I discovered that the union was segregated. . . . 'Now, I'm trying to straighten out U.S. Pipe, and here I'm paying my union dues, and I'm not free at the union hall.'"*

"The Christian Movement Gave Me an Insight on How to Handle Myself Out There on the Job"

I was born in Marion, Alabama, in a county called Perry County, in 1942. About twenty miles from Selma, Alabama. I have six sisters and six brothers. I'm the seventh child.

They [my parents] didn't have very much [education]. I don't know how many years they went to school because my mother died in '48. I was six years old when she died. She was a person who stayed at home and tended to the family. My father was a farmer. He was something like a sharecropper. We all worked on the farm. My daddy was the leader of the farm, but he didn't own the farm. We wasn't a group of people that was slave-like, it's just that we were living on the place that belong to a white man, and they called it sharecropping.

The sharecropping was something like half and half. My daddy would furnish the labor, and the white man, who was the owner of the property, he furnished the land. And so, since my father furnished the labor, the owner of the property would get half, and my father would get half. [We raised] cotton, corn, and that's the only thing he [the landowner] got half of. [We also planted] peas, greens, okra, you name it. Any type of vegetable. Watermelons, peanuts, potatoes, white potatoes, and on and on. That's all for the family. The sharecropper only got half of the corn and half of the cotton.

I remember [living and working on a farm]. As matter of fact, that's something that's hard to erase, because I can think more back then than what I can at the present time, because being on the farm, it was nice really. As a kid I learned how to live and to provide for myself on the farm, and we had to grow mostly everything that we would eat. So I was something like a shepherd. I had to tend to the cattle, hogs, and what have you. We had everything when it comes to livestock to survive on. That's one thing that the sharecropper did own—we owned our own beef and pork and what have you.

[We were] living on this particular, what I call a plantation. And it's called the Mayday Place. After my mother died in '48, my father moved up further toward what you call Five Points. What you called the Starter Place. John W. Sullen [was the owner].

My elementary [school] that I went to was Providence. Only blacks could go there at that time. We had to walk to school, and all the people that lived around, because whites was in the same community, but whites went to separate schools. They also had a bus to ride; we walked to school.

Blacks didn't start school until they were seven years old. I was six years old when my mother died, so I started school the following year. I think at that time you started school in May, if I'm not mistaken. No, I think it was September, because May is the time we usually be coming out of school. From May up to around August, or a little earlier, I would say about mid-June, my father would lay by. That means that the crop is being taken care of and is being cultivated. And so we worked from that time to time to go to school. When it was time for us to go to school in August or September, we would go and register and sign up for school. And then, after the cotton began to bulb and crack open, then we had to get out of school and go to the field and pick the cotton, because you had to get the cotton up and out of the field at a certain time, before the winter came in.

When I finished the sixth grade, they had built what they called the Keith High School. And they had another elementary school next to it. And from there you would go from sixth grade until about the eighth grade. But I never did attend that particular elementary school because I attended the one down at Five Points, which is Providence.

[In high school] I played baseball. There were no baseball teams as such until you went to Keith High School. And there was a basketball team. But when I was coming up I didn't get a chance to play on the basketball team, because I left there when I was about seventeen, and all this began to unfold about basketball. I was a pitcher in baseball, and also a catcher. At the time, we didn't have basketball or football. There was no football, period, at Keith High School when I left from down there.

I had got tired of working, sharecropping. I told my daddy I didn't want to work sharecropping anymore, because that particular year, prior to my coming to Birmingham, my daddy made fifty bales of cotton, and we had what you call at the end of the year a settlement. The white man would come and pay my daddy off, out of all the cotton we had picked and harvested. At the end of the year he would give him a certain amount. It was supposed to be half of what he had made, and the white man did all the settling. He had a truck that would pick up the cotton and carry it to the gin house, and they would process it. Each week my daddy would get a check, and this helped carry us through. But at the end of the year it's what they called half and half. You receive a check each week for the work that he would do. And so at the end of the year, what I call settlement. And then all the people that own the place would come in there once a year, after we had harvested everything at the end of the year. So they would call them in one by one and called my daddy. Of course, my mother was no longer living at that time, so I, and I think one of my brothers or sister, went in with him to sit down with the white man for him to tell us what we had done this year. And so he went through the little things and said, "Well, Mr. Warren, you got a nice crop, a fine group of people, you did good work." And he said, "Here's your part."

When he gave him the check he said it was sixteen hundred dollars, and at that time, when I left, I told my daddy, "Is this all? Sixteen hundred dollars behind fifty bales of cotton?" I know at the time that when we went out to pick cotton, we was paid something like three dollars a hundred pounds. You had to pick a hundred pounds. So we had what you called, after they processed the cotton, you got seeds in it, and it takes the seeds when you go to the gin house. They separate the seed from the cotton. And a bale of cotton weigh anywhere from four hundred pounds up. So all of our bale didn't fall lower than four hundred, because if it fell lower than four hundred, that's what you would call a light bale, and it's cheap.

And so my eyes had began to come open. I had a little schooling. And the little bit I did know, I told my dad, I said, "Behind fifty bales of cotton, I think this isn't enough. You're being cheated." And I said, "Only sixteen hundred dollars out of fifty bales of cotton, and we don't know how much it cost a bale, we don't have a receipt about how much he got per bale." And I said, "I'm just not going to work anymore in the field." So I left and stopped working for my daddy along with the white man and worked for another man, which is a black man. He owned his own land. I drove a tractor. If I'm not mistaken, at that time it was something like $2.50 a day. I think [I worked for him] about six months, and I didn't like it. I thought the money was too little, so I left, and me and another friend of mine, it was during the summer, I went to Selma to a candy factory there. I wasn't able to get on, so I met up on another man that worked as a carpenter. He tore down houses. He was a black man, and I worked with him. He paid me pretty good.

I just went there [to Selma] to work. I wasn't living in Selma. Every morning I would catch the bus and go to Selma and work with him. In the afternoon, when I got off, I would go about fifteen miles from there to Orrville. And from Orrville down to Five Points was about five miles. So, when I got off work I would [hitchhike] from Selma to Orrville. Most times I would get a ride. I did it about six months. So, I know if I got to Orrville there was a white lady that lived down below us, she would get off around five or six o'clock, and I'd go to where she worked at in Orrville. She worked at this depot, and I would ride home with her. But most times I got a ride from when I was on the highway walking. People were very good about picking you up. [The white woman's] name was Mrs. Wilson. She was living down not too far from us. She had a place. She was living with her auntie or her grandmother. She was old. She was a secretary at the depot in Orrville. Everybody know everybody and got along just fine. She would pick me up and drop me off because she had to pass by my daddy's house to get to her house, so she would drop me off. We used to go and pick the pecans for her, and she would pay us and give us part of the pecans.

We had a little run-in before I left Orrville, with a white man about another friend of mine. He was the type of white folk, if you didn't do like he want you to do, then he would try to beat you up. And so this particular white man, he went to beat him up [with a wrench], and so [my friend] took the wrench from the white man, so he had to leave from down there, and we took him to Selma, and he caught the bus to Gary, Indiana.

The problem was that there was some type of conflict with the work. He was living with his grandmother at the time. There were some more boys. And like I said, when it come to a time you have a run-in, you argue with the white man, he thought he had the privilege to beat you. But none of us, except my oldest brother, was jumped on by the white man. My brother was living in Birmingham, and the white man accused him of coming down and taking some of the people away one by one, which was some of my brothers-in-laws. After that, hard feelings developed between the white man, Mr. Sullivan, and my daddy. Things just began to unravel. We had never had nothing like that happen before, all while we was coming up. We thought it was wrong for him to do that. So we take it to the . . . the young man's name was Chester. His daddy lived in Gary, Indiana, so he [Chester] left there, and he never did come back. He moved from Gary back to New York, and that's where he died several years ago. He [the white man] was so outdone because he never had this to happen to him, and so he got mad, went home, and we assumed he went to get his gun. He came back, and my daddy owned an automobile, so we rushed him to Selma, put him on his path. His grandmother who he lived with told us to get him out from down there. So we carried him to Selma, put him on the bus, and he went to Gary, Indiana.

[That] set my tone with white folk, period. You know, prior to my coming to Birmingham, after I stopped working with my father on the farm, I started to driving a tractor also for this white man. He was paying three dollars a day, and I would plow and lay some corn. I had the tractor in a gear that I shouldn't have had it in, and it run faster so I could get through plowing the corn quicker. And I cut up a lot of corn. So he came out to see how I was doing and looked at the corn and told me that the corn was cut and I was running too fast. So I got down there, and he told me to get off and uncover it. He said every bit of it. I told him I wasn't going to uncover nothing. And so I left the tractor parked there and ran home. I sat on my daddy's porch where I was living at, and he told my daddy what I had did, and that's one reason I didn't work for him no more. That's when I went to the black man and started driving a tractor, Mr. Harris. That's how that happened. He told my daddy, he said, "Your boy getting smart, and he don't want to do what I tell him to do." And so I didn't have enough sense to realize that when you cause a problem, you be quiet, but I couldn't stop there, so I had to take a stand, so I left and came to Birmingham. He [Daddy] didn't say anything.

I had three brothers older than me. By this time they all had left. All three of them had come to Birmingham. I had one to leave Birmingham; the next oldest one went to Cincinnati, Ohio. There he was killed in 1956. I had came to Birmingham prior to my coming in '58 and stayed with my oldest brother a while during the summer. I liked it, although I had other relatives living in Birmingham and Bessemer. I had about four uncles [who] lived in Bessemer, which were my mother's brothers.

I came to Birmingham [to stay] in '59. I always wanted to be a boxer. I wanted to fight, so I came to Birmingham and joined the YMCA. I can't 'call the instructor that was there, but I boxed a lot at the YMCA on the South Side. Mr. Mark, I think his name was. But anyway, I was supposed to go to Montgomery for the Golden Glove, but I got tired, and I went to the [Alabama] Christian Movement [for Human Rights], so I didn't get a chance to.

When I came to Birmingham, I had a sister and a brother living in Birmingham. Well, I had two brothers. My third-oldest brother and my oldest sister were living together. My brother and my sister were working at the chicken house, what you call Marshall Durbin Chicken House. It was produce. And I came up to visit, really, and then I did want to stay, but they weren't too much about me staying. They wanted me to go back and help my daddy. I told them I wasn't going back because I didn't want to. So I went to apply for a job, me and another guy that I know. His name was Robert. So we went to Birmingham Paper Company, and we filled out an application and got hired the same day. I was a stock handler. They later merged with St. Regis Paper Company, which makes school supplies. I was stocking paper inside the warehouse. It was located on Fifth Avenue South and Twentieth Street. Right there where the old Bonanza [restaurant] used to be there. They tore it down and built a federal building there, an income tax place. I worked there about a good, I would say maybe two years. I got hired in '59, April. I came, then when I got my job, I came back down to see them all, so I had two younger sisters that were down there, and I helped them to make it through high school. I supported them.

And I worked there until 1961. It was almost two and a half years. I got involved with the Christian Movement while I was working there.

At that time I was living in North Birmingham on Tenth Avenue. There used to be a Buffalo Rock soda place there on Twenty-sixth Street. That's where my sister was living. At that time my sister moved out in North Birmingham, so I had put in an application when I was living there on Tenth Avenue. We moved out there in North Birmingham right across from U.S. Pipe shopping center. There was a store across from where I was living. The fellow that owned it was Italian. His name was Tony. So when I filled out the application over there, I gave him the telephone number at the Birmingham Paper Company so he could call and reach me. So I received a call to come to go for a physical examination. Tony had a guy that worked for him, and he sent him over there and told me I had a telephone call. I had been praying that the Lord would bless me with a job. And so when that phone call came in, I went on and answered it, and that's who it was. So they asked me when could I come and go to get a physical examination. I worked there about two and a half years. I got tied up in the Christian Movement, and the news broke that I was involved, and they knew about it, and they picked around until they fired me.

I got involved in it [the Movement] because [of] the march and Dr. King and Shuttlesworth. First of all, I was knowing about Shuttlesworth before I came to Birmingham, because a lot of marches were going on during that time, and Shuttlesworth first tried to enter Phillips High School with his children. And so this made me interested, because I always had a hunger and thirst for being set free, and I always thought something was wrong—that why should we be treated the way we was treated because of the color of our skin?

The first [mass meeting] I attended was at New Pilgrim Baptist church. And this was when Dr. King came, and he spoke there. It was so crowded I never did get in. And so during the Christian Movement they used to meet on Monday night. They used to meet right here at Sixteenth Street Baptist church. That was their headquarters, and that's where they mostly met at, and that's how I started out.[1]

It impressed me a whole lot because Dr. King was a man who . . . I never heard a man speak so eloquently. He was a dynamic speaker. It was just something. I didn't know nothing about being a speaker. It was just something that was in this man that when he spoke, everybody listened. His speech sank deep into me. And I used to go to church down in my hometown, and all the preachers would preach about it, John 3:16, "God so loved the world. . . ." They were showing me how to serve God but wasn't showing me how to pull myself up out of the miry clay and to make a better life for myself.

I don't think anybody invited me, because it was in me when I came to Birmingham to try to better my condition. So when I came, I learned about it listening to the radio. At that time, Shelley the Playboy and Willie McKinstry was some of the main disc jockeys at that time. And so I began to attend the Monday night meetings, and then I followed up, and I got hooked up, and I couldn't turn it loose.

[I went to an Alabama and Georgia Tech game in 1961.] Me and another friend of mine named Wilson Brown. I think now he lives in Atlanta. There was some friend of his, which was white, asked him if he wanted to go to a ball game. At that time they would integrate certain things. So he said yes, and he got two tickets. We had met one another at a Christian Movement [meeting], so he asked me would I go. I said, "Sure, why not?" And so we went to this ball game on Saturday. We sat there until the game was over with. While we were in the game there were some whites in the crowd saying, "We got two niggers in here." So we just sat still because we had been instructed to not take offense, to be nonviolent, and not to fight back.

So we sat there until the game was over. So the game was over, and we began to go out, and they attacked us. So I ran on out the gate toward Graymont [Avenue], and Wilson went another way, and I ran to the police. The police car was sitting there, and the police stopped me. They told me to get in the car. I got in the car. When I got in, one of the white men stuck his fist through the window and hit me in the face. And so the police got me and brought me on downtown to the city jail. And they came in and questioned me to see if I could identify any of them. I told them, "No." I didn't know who it was. They knew who it was because they were the ones who stopped it. [We were] the only two [blacks] that were there, myself and Wilson Brown. At that time they were supposed to be integrating and a lot of things, and blacks would not exercise the privilege they did have. So the only blacks that were there were those that had on white coats [concessions workers].

When I got to work on Monday, I was the talk of the town. They had got the news when I got to work that morning. All [of] the guys were telling me, "Man, we heard all on the radio how you been out to Legion Field." Most of the white folks watch TV and listen to the radio, because that was Alabama playing. And when I got to work I could see how they looked at me. My supervisor, when I walked in, gave me a cold shoulder. So it wasn't long before I was terminated. We had a union rep, but it wasn't any good. I was fired simply because they accused me of laying around on the job. I had never had no problem on the job. They framed me.

A mass meeting was very inspirational to me. It was something to motivate you. It was the type of meeting that would educate you, tell you what rights you had and what the law stood for, that you had a right. And then, once you received those rights, you exercised them. This helped to motivate me more. Then I began to act upon the laws passed, and I began to say that I had the privilege to do these things, so I tried it out.

After they passed the law that you had the right to sit anywhere on the bus, you don't have to sit on the back no more, I was coming from work. At this particular time I was working at Birmingham Paper Company. That evening I got off work at three o'clock. I got on the bus, and it was a seat vacant beside this white fellow. It was so crowded that people were standing on the bus. All the rest of the black folk was sitting in the back or standing up. It always had been vacant seats when you come to white folks, because more blacks really rode the bus. And at this particular stop this white lady got off the bus. Where she had been sitting beside this white gentleman, I sat down beside him. Nobody would sit in the seat, so I sat beside him. He grabbed me and said no nigger was going to sit by him. He was in Alabama, and ain't nobody's nigger going to sit by him. So he grabbed me, and I stayed in the seat. He tried to push me out of the seat, and I held on to the seat. We were instructed not to fight back.

[The driver] stopped the bus, got off, and made a phone call, right there on Twenty-sixth Street and about Twentieth Avenue in North Birmingham. He stopped at a telephone booth and called the police. The police came there—there were two of them. He said, "There he is, sitting back there." So the police came on the bus and asked me to come off the bus, so I came off the bus. They searched me and asked the white fellow, "Is this the one?" He said, "Yes." He asked me what did I do. I told him, "I sat down beside him. I had a right to." He said, "Okay. Get in the police car." They arrested me, taking me in, and locked me up.

I could see the faces of some of them [black passengers], how happy they were. They said to stand up and be a man. Nobody else had enough nerve to sit beside a white person on the bus. They were all for me. I remember there was a person on the bus that I knew, and she came to trial to testify on my behalf. While I was in the car, the police took me to city hall, which was downtown. Then they transferred me in one of those trucks, and he told me, he said, "He's one of Shuttlesworth's demonstrators." I said, "That's right." So they carried me over on the South Side. Warren Bail Company bailed me out.

I went to trial, and the judge found me guilty and gave me 180 days. [My lawyer] appealed my case, and so I got out on bail, and that Monday night I went to the meeting, Christian Movement meeting, out here in East Birmingham. I don't remember the name of the church, but it was a big Baptist church out in East Birmingham. I told what had happened. W. L. Williams was the lawyer at that time when I got arrested. When my trial came up he represented me. We appealed it to the state court, and they found me not guilty and got the 180 days off. I had to pay a fine, about 180 dollars in court costs.

I was only arrested one time. That was the incident on the bus. So after I got fired and I was free again to get around, Wilson Brown and I went to Atlanta to the SNCC organization.

SNCC was not a well-known power organization such as SCLC, noted for training folks how to demonstrate and protect yourself at all times and not strike back. Though we went to Atlanta for some classes at Morehouse College, Wilson and I, and [we] also went to Talladega College. They had some classes there. And believe it or not, this is the first time I had ever been on a college campus. To tell you the truth, there was a college in Selma called Selma University, and I didn't even know it was there until I came to Birmingham. We weren't really taught about things like this. The first college I went to was Talladega College. When I got there I just lit up because I never seen so many black folks at an institution, and it would be for black people, and I just fell in love with it. And I was never ever able to go to college, no more than trade school, barber college.

Because I had got fired, we, me and Wilson, went to Morehouse, and we met this white girl from Chicago. She was part of the SNCC organization, and she wanted to come back to Birmingham with us. There was another young lady with her, I can't think of her name. This was in '61. And there was another black girl, she went out to Miles College. We decided we would bring the white girl back, and we didn't think we would get in trouble. But the police trailed us all the way from the time we left Atlanta. When we got into Marietta, Georgia, and we stopped at the bus station to get something to eat, this is where they saw us. And they trailed us all the way back home. They would stop us and gave us tickets. So we pulled over and turned around and called Atlanta and SNCC and told them what happened. We got an escort out of Marietta. We looked at it as if we weren't intending to get out of Marietta, Georgia. SNCC sent somebody down, and they trailed us out of Marietta, Georgia.

She [the white girl] came all the way back to Birmingham. She stayed here. I don't know who she stayed with, but I think the Christian Movement put her up, because that Monday, when we came to the meeting, we got somewhat chewed out about bringing this white girl all the way back from Atlanta, riding with us.

If I'm not mistaken, I think the Christian Movement put her up, because we went down to Gaston Lounge, and there we met some of the Movement people, I can't think of his name, but he was the guy that went to jail with Shuttlesworth, the preacher. At that time Shuttlesworth wasn't there. So he passed it on to Shuttlesworth and everything, and they got together and put her up at the motel.

After that I married in '62, I married my wife that I got now, and at that particular time I was drawing unemployment. I would get something like twenty-seven dollars a week. I married my wife while I was drawing unemployment. And then I said to myself, I told Wilson, "You know what? I'm getting out of this. It's just not for me. I've lost one job." So my brother was working at U.S. Pipe, my oldest brother. So he got me on at U.S. Pipe. I got hired out there in '62, December the seventeenth.

It [the Movement] was in my heart. I left for awhile, and I got out there, and I stayed out there until about the last of '63. Then I found myself. I nearly quit going to the Movement meetings, and then I found myself attacking the people out there—fistfighting because of the discrimination they had out there. And then I met a fellow called Willie Hicks out there and Jack Daniel and Henry Ruckers.

We went out to the Dobbs House Restaurant at the airport one Sunday afternoon, myself, Jim Hendricks,[2] and Willie Hicks and Jack Daniel. There had never been a sit-in out there. . . . They refused to serve [us] at first. Then they told us they were closing, so I said, "Closing? How you closing, and these white people come in here and you're waiting on them?" And so they finally decided they would wait on us, and we all got a ham sandwich and a Coke, and they charged us ten dollars apiece for a ham sandwich. So we sat there and ate and paid for it. Jim said he wasn't going to eat his—he was going to take it home, keep it, and put it in the freezer, and he did. We ate ours. From there on, they closed the cafeteria and wouldn't let nobody else come in. Then they told us they were closed and we would have to leave, so we left. We were not arrested, because about that time they had passed a law saying we had the right to go in and be seated.

When I went to Dobbs, I was working at U.S. Pipe. I had gotten hired. But I knew Jim Hendricks before I started working at U.S. Pipe. But I didn't know Willie Hicks and Jack Daniel because, you see, the Movement, we all were encouraged to go down to the Hendricks Brothers and patronize and buy food and eat down there. That's how I learned about the Hendricks Brothers, because they were part of the Christian Movement. And so when I got hired out at U.S. Pipe, one of the brothers was working out at night in the gym, and all this stuff begin to blow. So they finally found somebody that would have enough guts to challenge the people out there at U.S. Pipe. And so I always was involved in filing grievances on the job. They came up to me somehow and asked me, and I already had a little experience prior to coming out there, so we got together. Willie Hicks, Jim Hendricks, Jack Daniel, and myself.

When I got hired at U.S. Pipe, I started out as a common laborer. So I began to . . . they had what you called a bid process, you bid on jobs. We have separate boards from the black and white. Have to bid on what they called colored jobs. They had one side for the whites, you know you couldn't cross over. And so later on we got together, and I said, "Well now, I think we entitled to bid on the job we want to bid on, and the laws are changing." So we decided we'd bid on them. Some of them got them, some of them didn't. And then those that we did get, white folks didn't bid on them, so they had to give it to us. So they found out ways to disqualify some of us. I never disqualified on one. All they need to say is, "You weren't doing the job." But simply having a union out there, they couldn't fire us because if you did your job, you had thirty days to do the job, and if you couldn't come to their standard they would disqualify you and put you on another job or either lay you off until a job come up and you could come back out there and bid on one.

And so the Christian Movement kind of gave me an insight on how to handle myself out there on the job, as I had this little training from Talladega and Atlanta from SNCC about how to move up when things come open. You got to be able to accept the opportunity to be prepared. And so that's how I started out. I almost got run off. They tried to run me off out there, but they weren't able to do so. I had to get on them, file complaints. I even filed complaints against the union because when I got involved in it, I went to the union hall and I discovered that the union was segregated.

It was the Molder's Union. It used to be the Molders and Allied Workers Union, but they merged, and it became GMP.[3] And so the president of the union was nothing but a Ku Klux, and he rode around with Ku Klux signs, and after I got there and went to a union meeting, I saw they had separate rest rooms in the union hall, and I looked at all that. I said, "Now, I'm trying to straighten out U.S. Pipe, and here I'm paying my union dues, and I'm not free at the union hall." So what I did was, we got back together, Hicks and I and Jack Daniel and Jim Hendricks. I said, "We're sitting in at the union hall, where all the blacks was on one side, and all the whites were on one side." So we, instead of sitting on the so-called black side, we would sit on the opposite side where the whites would sit. So they didn't say nothing. [Most blacks still] just sat on the other side. They didn't say anything either, but it motivated them. You see, you always got to have a leader. And so after we broke that down, they began to integrate. So that was a lot of talk. And so finally they accepted it, and I told them, "You all are going to have to move the signs you got up here." And so they did. This is the union we filed a charge against. And so it still got the two water fountains. They are there today. And in the restrooms they had a "colored" and a "white" restroom, they still got the same two restrooms. We all use all the restrooms.

After my eyes became open, then I began to attend union meetings and find what it's all about. Then I ran for office, but I didn't make it. They always did have two blacks on committee, hand-picked. And so they didn't have but two. You couldn't have but two. They had seven committees, and only two could be on them. We voted, but you had what you called a nomination. And so they always would nominate what I called a rubber-stamp black. We didn't nominate them, so they always won out simply because all the white folks going to vote for those two.

You had more whites in the union, but there weren't more whites at the place where I was working. At that time, when I was there, they had seven hundred employees, and four hundred of them were black.

[Blacks] belong to the union. Blacks have a way . . . some of them are still stigmatized. They think things just are going to get better. I found out if you want to know what goes on in a house, you got to get on the inside. On the outside looking in, you can't be of much service. And I proved to them what they can do, if you come together. So we started to have meetings outside the union hall, just blacks at the YMCA on the South Side. I was the head of it, me and Hicks. We had a secretary and treasurer, president, and things like that. And so we would get blacks to come and educate them about what they can do. Some of them even thought I was wrong. They gave me bad vibes, saying I was going to lose my job, "You are going to cause us to lose our jobs." Now I said, "Well, I said anything not worth fighting for is not worth having." And so I had made up my mind then, I told the Lord, I said, "Lord, you know I said I wouldn't get involved anymore, but here I am. I guess I must have been wrong. You didn't pay me any attention in the first place."

It was just a matter of time that I would have my foot in the door. And so I got my foot in the door. Of course, I had to file a lot of complaints before I got in the door, because there wasn't an EEOC branch in Birmingham at that time. And we are responsible for the EEOC branch here. I, myself, the guys that work at U.S. Pipe that was on this committee we formed, and also ACIPCO Pipe Shop and U.S. Steel, and Stockham Valve, we had people from each plant. We all got together to have a meeting at the YMCA on Sunday afternoon, how we would come about stretching ourselves where we work at. Then we filed so many complaints then they had to put a branch here. That's how it came about. The first one that was put here was on Eighth Avenue, 2121 Building.

They called me "agitator," and they called me a Black Muslim. I told them, "Well, I'm not a Muslim, but I am black, and I have nothing against Black Muslims, as such, but I don't belong to the organization. But I am black, and I attended some of the Muslim meetings at that time." You see, you were stamped when you get involved in certain things—they would mark you. And so they tried. They did everything. They put the Ku Klux sign on our job trying to discourage us, but they couldn't.

After that, we filed a complaint on U.S. Pipe to integrate all facilities, the job, the restroom, bathhouse, and everything out there. So we had a big cafeteria out there, it was built in 1948. So they had blacks on one side, whites on the other side. Blacks would go in one door, whites in the other door. The whites had white plates, we had green plates. The whites had white coffee cups, we had green coffee cups. And so they wouldn't even let us eat out of the same dishes. They had segregation in there. They had a partition, so we boycotted. The law was passed, and we are going to have to tear it down. So we stayed out of the cafeteria, and they couldn't operate. We stayed out of the cafeteria, and then the president of the pipe shop came out and talked to me and Hicks. I'll never forget him, Mr. Jack McGill. After that he came to the YMCA Fourth Avenue when they were building and cut the ribbon. He asked me what was the matter, and I told him, "Well, the law is passed. We have a right to equal facility, and we are not going to go ahead and spend our money anymore. And all of these signs have got to come down." And so we boycotted and closed the cafeteria. They couldn't operate because more blacks was there, we loved to eat, you know. U.S. Pipe owned it, but they had contract people come in to run the cafeteria. So they said they couldn't operate, and it closed down. They finally took our petition on everything, and we started to go back in. When we started going back in, then the whites stopped going in. It stayed like that for years. We integrated the bath, and the whites quit taking a bath and went home dirty. We integrated everything.

Whites would drift back, some of them. Some of them would still go home. Then I became, in the beholder's eye, I was a hero. I didn't go around patting myself on the back, but I realized what I had accomplished, and when some said I couldn't do it, and even some of the union official blacks got mad at us and told us, "You're destroying things. What you're doing, you're taking our jobs." And we said, "How we taking your job? You don't got no job. You not even guaranteed a job. You're here today and gone tomorrow." That's the way we looked at it. And things began to open up. We began to bid on jobs, and blacks began to come in. They started bidding on these jobs and started getting the jobs, but they were still being harassed. And so we told them, "Well, we don't have a black supervisor." On and on. One thing led to another one. And so we filed a charge on them and told them that there was no black supervisor, and there's no black in salary, there're no blacks in the office, so we hired the first black person in personnel—a black woman named Jeanette Parker—and that's how that came about. And we hired the first black man, they promoted him, his name was Glenn. He became the first black supervisor. He was working in the storeroom, but he never could get promoted, so he got promoted to supervisor. And we began to step up.

You know, I often tell the people, and then they began to say, "Well, things just ain't going to change." I said, "Well, that's the way the children of Israel felt until God sent Moses to Egypt and said, 'Let my people go.'" And now all you got to do is take everything you got and put it on your shoulder and walk out. I said, "It's no longer that old saying, 'You black, get back.'" I said, "Now, you got an opportunity, the law has been changed, now we got to exercise our right." I said, "Some of them might not make it, some of them might get killed, but we're willing to take the chance." And we survived out here today. Today I'm still here at fifty-four years of age. When I went there I was twenty years old. So I seen a whole lot of heartaches and pain, but it was worth that. I got able to move up. I had an opportunity to be a supervisor. I didn't want it, because I thought that he tried to use me for a rubber stamp, trying to shut my mouth, and I'm still fighting. I'm the type of person, I can't see myself being a supervisor at the time because I couldn't accept some of the things that they would have the supervisor go through. And, then again, I know being a supervisor, there's a lot of things you can change, but I didn't want that position. I'm kind of like Moses; I'd rather be with my people than to live in the king's house.

Edited by Horace Huntley. BCRI Oral History Project, vol. 16, sec. 4 (May 17, 1996).

Notes

1. There is a perception that Sixteenth Street Baptist church was the headquarters for the Movement, but it was not. In fact, it did not allow Movement meetings to be held there until Reverend John Cross became pastor in 1962.

2. Elias Hendricks's brother; Lola Hendricks is his sister-in-law.

3. Glass, Molders, Pottery, Plastics, and Allied Workers International Union.

Asbury Howard Jr.

Born in 1930 in Bessemer, Alabama. His father was vice president of Mine, Mill, and Smelter Workers Union and the USWA. His uncle was Will Hall, better known as John L. Lewis because he was a "tough miner" who represented the UMWA. Worked in the auto industry in Detroit and the postal system in Bessemer. He was a staunch supporter of the Bessemer Voters' League. *"I became a youth director of the Bessemer Voters' League. Very few of my friends and relatives were involved. They were proud, but they were scared. They supported us and brought us food down on the picket line. They called me crazy because I would do things that others wouldn't dare do. The police even thought I was crazy. So I played it to the hilt. They said, 'Don't say nothing to him. Don't bother him, he's crazy.' When the police arrested a black man, they were known for whipping up on them. I told them on an occasion when they arrested me, 'I'm not taking no whipping.' I told them, 'Don't you hit me.' I used to see police come in one direction, and I would be going the other, and I would turn around and let them chase me. I didn't realize how dangerous it was."*

Police Harassment of Blacks Fighting for the Vote

My father was from Autaugaville. He was born and raised in Autaugaville. My mother was born in a little town outside of Mobile. I was born in Bessemer, 1930, in a little community known as Muscoda. It is a mining town. I was born there and got my basic education there. I went there from the first grade and graduated there in the twelfth grade. Mine was the last graduating class from that high school. I had one sister, and her name is Cleopatra Cox. She's fifty-seven years old and now lives in Central Park. I'm the big brother.

My daddy, I think he completed the ninth grade, and my mother, perhaps the tenth grade. Neither of them graduated from high school. My mother was a housewife. My dad started in the ore mines in that little community, there in Bessemer. He became the secretary of the union and later, international representative for the Mine, Mill, and Smelter Workers Union. He would eventually be elected as international vice president of Mine Mill in the 1940s.[1] He was so dedicated, and he wasn't afraid of anything. One incident, when the National Guards had surrounded the community, and they were firing on the community, and they had broken into homes, looking for weapons and various things. Our house was the warehouse for all of the weapons, and I was just a little boy. I found my uncle and told him that Daddy had some guns and to get over there. Everybody just grabbed me and told me to shut up.

Well, I was a daddy's boy. Whatever Daddy did, I was always around. My mother and sister knew nothing about his other life. They only knew him as a father and a husband, but he didn't involve his family, as such. I was with him on all of the occasions that dealt with civil rights. He was jailed several times. I remember one instance where he was in one area during the strikes, and they were attacked by a bunch of whites, and they had a shoot-out. He wounded one of the whites, and finally the authorities came and told them to surrender their weapons. He told them if they surrendered theirs first, then they would surrender. After they surrendered theirs, then he walked up to the chief and turned his over. He shot one man in the hip.

I finished high school in Muscoda, and then I went to Morehouse College. I wanted to go to Fisk. My daddy knew some people that went to Morehouse. So he took me down, before I finished high school, to look at and get a feel for the campus. That was 1946. I was sixteen years old, and my daddy said, "Well, you go to Morehouse, or you get a job." I didn't have any problem going to Morehouse then. I graduated in 1950.

I was drafted into the army and served in Korea. After I was discharged I came back home for a short time and worked for Johnson Publishing Company as their local representative selling *Ebony* and *Jet* magazines. Then I moved to Detroit for three or four years. I came home on a visit and got in trouble. My daddy and I were attacked in Bessemer. We defended ourselves and were arrested. I got out of jail on bond and couldn't go back to Detroit. So I got involved in the civil rights movement.

Well, Daddy and I were attacked. Dad had a fine painting that he bought in Kansas City of a black with his hands chained, and it was saying, "You can't eat here, you can't play here, you can't worship here," and various things we couldn't do. This painting was on a painter's easel, and the chief of police just happened to see it. This was probably on Tuesday, and they didn't charge him until that Friday. He was charged with incitement to riot. After his trial, we were attacked by a mob of white men. Black men were not allowed to attend the trial. I was allowed to attend after being questioned by a policeman. After he learned that I was the son, he said, "Oh, come on in." It was a planned attack. There were thirty-five to forty persons who were already in the courtroom. They were not local whites. He [his father] was on the stairs. I saw the attack begin, and I shouted, "Look out!" For that, the police arrested me for disorderly conduct and striking a police officer, but they couldn't prove that, so they could only charge me with disorderly conduct and resisting arrest. I was on bond until they had my trial. They had my trial, and I was given five years probation.

I became a youth director of the Bessemer Voters' League. Very few of my friends and relatives were involved. They were proud, but they were scared. Anybody who got out there, they were supportive, but they weren't going to become involved. They supported us and brought us food down on the picket line. In their own way, they were supportive. They called me crazy because I would do things that others wouldn't dare do. The police even thought I was crazy. So I played it to the hilt. They said, "Don't say nothing to him. Don't bother him. He's crazy."

When the police arrested a black man, they were known for whipping up on them. I told them on an occasion when they arrested me, "I'm not taking no whipping. Now, you can arrest me all you want, but it's up to me to prove in a court of law that I did what you are accusing me of." I told them, "Don't you hit me." I used to see police come in one direction, and I would be going the other, and I would turn around and let them chase me. I didn't realize how dangerous it was.

I didn't believe in the nonviolent philosophy. We didn't know if we could practice the nonviolence. I think maybe some look down on us for that, for not really being people that were nonviolent. I just couldn't handle that. I had to retaliate, whether it meant life or death.

One time we had some white folks that were working with us. I was trying to give them a lesson of the real thing. They passed out leaflets and manned posts during elections. We did have quite a few whites that didn't mind associating with us at that time.

Well, because of Daddy's job, they were accused of violating the Taft-Hartley Act,[2] and 'cause he was so active in this particular area, Communist personnel did visit, 'cause I had two or three visit me. They left me some books and some information. They left, and I got all the material they gave me out of the house as quick as possible. He was charged once with being in the room with a Communist. He beat that charge, but he was not sitting near nor engaged in conversation with this person in any way. By association, he was labeled as a Communist. The judge dismissed him, 'cause there was no evidence that he had ties to the Communist party. I remember one time, it was just something that happened, I had been invited to Chicago to speak for a W. E. B. DuBois club. The papers that they sent me the information on, there was some doodling on the back. They had written W. E. B. DuBois's name on it, and so Daddy managed to see it. Then he gave me some history behind what the doodles meant. So I had to forego that trip, 'cause I didn't want to . . . I was investigated in Detroit for being a Communist, because I attended a meeting, but I didn't know what I was attending. It was very different from what was advertised than what it was. I had to write to the Justice Department my reason for being there. I'm way out in Detroit, and they are coming to me saying I had Communist affiliations. It went way back.[3]

I got involved when I first came back with the postal service, 'cause I needed a job. There was a fellow that worked at the post office as a carrier, and he kept me posted on where and how I stood, as far as they were concerned. So I went and took the test again. Not so much that it was a job that I wanted, but I was insistent that I did not want to be a clerk. I wanted to be up front to sell stamps, 'cause no blacks had been up front. Then they disqualified me and said I lied again, after another five years, on my application. The question was, Have you ever been arrested? I answered it. I said I don't know how many times I've been arrested. I might have missed one check with the Bessemer police department. This is what I said, and they disqualified me. I appealed it, and I finally heard from them. They wanted to know what night I could come in. So after five days I went in, and all the white clerks were there, and all the attention was focused on me. They wanted to know who was this black fellow coming in here at seven o'clock at night. I asked where the postmaster's office was, and so I went from there. I knew then that they were going to get me.

There was one case with a white woman. They had substitutes. I was a sub before I became permanent. They had sent her out to a rural area, Jonesboro, to work at the post office. I went to the postmaster, and I told him, "I'm top sub." At that time I had the next step to being permanent, and I said, "This lady is working in Jonesboro, and I can't tolerate that. I'm going to have to report this. I can't help it." They said, "No, no, she's only going to be there one more day." I said, "I want it, then." So I knew that they were going to get me.

They got me when I was on the board of directors. Locally, I was on the plan. They elected me to represent them at the general meetings of the JCCEO.[4] So JCCEO lent me to the board. There were two blacks, Pinkie Shortridge[5] and myself were elected to the board. Being active on the board, I had to approach the postmaster about returned soap and toothpaste and that sort of thing, because I wanted to give them to people who could not afford to buy it. So he told me, "Yeah, you can have some." So I went and picked up the stuff and carried it out to my car. Returnable things they returned to the post office 'cause they couldn't deliver. So when I asked, he told me what time to pick it up. He had the people there, and you could see them. So I took the stuff to the car, and when I was ready to get going, these men approached me, and they wanted to talk to me about the mail. They said, "We could take your car," because I had put the stuff in the car. They took me to the county jail, and I stayed there one night, and the next day I got out. The paper said that I had turned myself in.

I went to trial, and they found me guilty of theft of mail. They gave me five years; all of that was suspended except six months. So then I had to do my time. When I turned myself in on that Monday, it was all in the newspapers that I went to turn myself in. He said, "You don't have to go on back there. When we get ready for you, we will call you." So on Thursday they called me and told me to come on in. I came in, and I turned myself in to the marshal. They brought me around to where they were sitting, and I was waiting on the handcuffs. I didn't think they were going to arrest me without handcuffs. So they were ready to go to the marshal's room to get the directions on where I was going. That day, reluctantly, when I was waiting around to be handcuffed, they said, "Come on." I went with them, still waiting on the handcuffs. So they had to go over to the county jail to get another person that was going to Atmore. I had on a suit and tie, and one of the marshals went up and talked while they were getting the [other] prisoner. He was brought out with chains and handcuffs. So on our way to Montgomery, we were engaged in conversation. Then I saw that they wanted to talk among themselves. So I turned to the fellow, and I said, "What are you in for?" The man looked at me and said, "I thought you were one of them."

I spent four months, this is when I got the six months. See, on the other one I got five years probation on that time. On this thief thing, I got five years, but all of it was suspended but six months. So actually I only stayed there for four months. My mother came down there, and some of the guards were showing off in front of the white people. I told Mom, I said, "Now look, I'm in jail, but I'm still a man. Now, go on about your business before I get myself in more trouble." So they treated me pretty royally at first, because the grapevine knew that I was coming, and they knew Daddy's activities. They would socialize with me until I put a stop to it. I said, "We are on different sides of the fence. I don't want too much socialization because these other fellows will think I'm giving you information. So, suppose you stay on your side of the fence and go home to your wife and children at the end of the day."

Edited by Horace Huntley. BCRI Oral History Project, vol. 31, sec. 1 (Oct. 29, 1997).

Notes

1. For a summary of the career of Asbury Howard Sr., see Gary M. Fink, ed., *Biographical Dictionary of American Labor* (Westport, Conn.: Greenwood Press, 1974), 303–4.

2. The Labor Management Relations Act of 1947 amended much of the National Labor Relations (Wagner) Act of 1935, and it nullified parts of the Federal Anti-Injunction (Norris-LaGuardia) Act of 1932. It also provided that no union could use the facilities of the National Labor Relations Board unless its officers filed affidavits that they were not Communists. Christopher L. Tomlins, *The State and the Unions: Labor Relations, Law, and the Organized Labor Movement in America, 1880–1960* (New York: Cambridge University Press, 1985), 282–300. Asbury Howard Sr. was one of several officers of Mine Mill charged with conspiracy to falsify affidavits, but the charges against him were eventually dismissed.

3. For a discussion of the Red Scare in Alabama, see Horace Huntley, "The Red Scare and Black Workers in Alabama: The International Union of Mine, Mill, and Smelter Workers, 1945–1953," in *Labor Divided: Race and Ethnicity in United States Labor Struggles, 1835–1960*, ed. Robert Asher and Charles Stephenson (Albany: State University of New York Press, 1990), 129–45.

4. The Jefferson County Commission on Economic Opportunity, established 1965 in connection with the federal War on Poverty. See Robin D. G. Kelley, *Race Rebels: Culture, Politics, and the Black Working Class* (New York: Free Press, 1994), 94–96.

5. A funeral parlor owner and activist in the ACMHR.

Luther McKinstry

Born in 1920 in Aliceville, Pickens County, Alabama. Grew up in Fairfield. Father was a coal miner at TCI. He started work for TCI at age twenty-two as a cleanup man. Would become a hooker for the crane, and eventually filed a suit against U.S. Steel for job discrimination and became a crane operator. *"There were white-men jobs and black-men jobs. A black man could work on any job out there, but you couldn't go up in the crane. But any of the jobs, like millwright helper, you could work them, but you couldn't make one-day or one-minute seniority, you were a helper. The black man was in class five or six, and the skilled jobs were from fourteen through twenty-five, and he couldn't get in there. . . . After I sued the company, then I had to sue the union. It was a class-action suit against the union for equal opportunity. The first job I asked for was crane operator. Since I had worked on and around the crane, why should I be kept from having the opportunity to operate a crane? They said, 'No, no, no, you can't do that.'"*

"After I Sued the Company, Then I Had to Sue the Union"

My parents were living here but were from Pickens County. My mother took me back to her hometown, Aliceville, in Pickens County, to be born. Immediately after I was born she brought me back to Fairfield. I grew up here. My father worked in the mine, in the TCI coal mine, number two mine. My mother just worked at home and worked in white people's home. Both of them just went to elementary school. I had two brothers and one sister, and I am the second child. The oldest child was a boy, then I was born, and the third one was a boy, and the fourth one was a girl.

I never went to school here in Fairfield. After my father passed, my mother's people came here and got us and took us to Aliceville and raised us. And as we grew up and got up in age, then we came back to Birmingham to live. But my schooling was in Aliceville. I went to the fourth grade. After my older brother, James, got up in age, he came back to live in Fairfield. He came down to Pickens County and talked to me about how I could make more money in Birmingham rather than on the farm. So I came with him and got started here. The first work I done, I worked a year with J. B. Owens Construction. Then I went on and went to Fairfield U.S. Steel and got hired out there. I was about twenty-two when I came up here. My brother got me hired at U.S. Steel. To me it was great working there, because I had never worked in a place like that. The first shift I worked was three to eleven. I was a cleanup fellow. I cleaned up there for a while. Then they changed me and put me hooking on a crane. I think I was in class four while I was on the floor.

I was on the ground, and the crane had a big magnet on it, which was hooked up to the electricity. The operator just let the magnet down on a plate and picked it up and drug it wherever he needed to carry it. And then when he had them pans, big buckets of iron or whatever, he just set it down and cut them magnets aloose and put hooks or chains on it and then go and let it down. I would flag them down, carry them over, and then I would hook up some chains on whatever was to be moved. I was directing the crane operator from the ground.

There were white-men jobs and black-men jobs. A black man could work on any job out there, but you couldn't go up in the crane. But any of the jobs, like millwright helper, you could work them, but you couldn't make one-day or one-minute seniority, you were a helper. The black man was in class five or six, and the skilled jobs were from fourteen through twenty-five, and he couldn't get in there.

We could work only as helpers. That's all we could do, be helpers. You could work with a millwright and eventually with the welder, but we had to be helpers. No matter how long you worked there, until I filed that suit, you were a helper. You couldn't get in the line of promotion. They had what they called line of promotion, and it would come up so far, and then they pick up and come over here, and you may work that opening, but you couldn't join the line of promotion. For instance, they had a circle drawn here with the pipe fitters, and other jobs in their own circle. You couldn't leapfrog, that's what they called it, to go over in another circle. The black man could work over in that circle, but he was a helper, and so he didn't make any seniority in there whatsoever. The white boy would be hired in the line of promotion, and if they want to, they hired him over in the circle, but we were still in the pool. So [class] six would probably be the highest that a black man would go, and that white boy could go up to twenty-five.

So as a working man on the floor, I just knew if I got a chance to get up on that crane, I could operate it. Because I had learned every which-a-way and what it is supposed to do. All I had to do is get up there and learn how to work levers. I asked for it, and they said, "You asked for the wrong thing, that's a white man's job. You'll never get that job."

I was a member of the union. But the question of job discrimination never came up in the union meeting. See, that is what is hard to get people to understand. After I sued the company, then I had to sue the union. It was a class-action suit against the union for equal opportunity.[1] The first job I asked for was crane operator. Since I had worked on and around the crane, why should I be kept from having the opportunity to operate a crane? They said, "No, no, no, you can't do that."

I heard about a federal government man was here taking applications and wanting to understand about U.S. Steel. He was at Miles College. His name was Hugh Graham.[2] I went up there one night after I got off work at 11:30, and I asked to speak to him. The black guy out there was guarding the door and wouldn't let me go in. So we got to talking loud, and the man came out and asked what was going on. Somebody said something about U.S. Steel, and he said, "That's what I am here for. I want to hear about that." He said, "Let him alone." So I went on in there and sat down and talked with him. He told me that he had heard a lot about U.S. Steel, and that it was his business to find out about the largest employer in the area. He said, "Come on and tell me." He asked me about my job and about working conditions, and I told him the truth. He said, "Well, give me two days, and I will call for you to come back." He got my phone number, and sure enough, within two days, he called for me to come back up there. He said he would rather work with you at night. I went back up there after I got off work the next two nights. That's when he wrote up the case.

Other workers didn't know I had talked to Graham until he had studied what I told him. He agreed to take the case, and then I told them about it. They were scared and told me, "You gonna get us fired." All backed off except this one guy, Robert James Hubbard.[3] He said, "McKinstry, if you got nerve enough to go ahead, I am going to take a chance with you." I said, "Will you, little buddy? He said, "Yeah." Hubbard took the chance, and he signed the paperwork. I always went to talk with Graham after my three-to-eleven shift. He asked if I could bring Hubbard with me the next night. We went to Graham's office that night after we got off at eleven. I signed, and then Hubbard signed the paper and sued with me. And that was the only person that signed it with me.

Graham did not seem to understand how the company kept black men out of the line of promotion, out of the circles and forever without promotions above six. So I said, "I done talked to you and talked to you until I just don't know what else to tell you." I said, "Why don't you just go out in the plant and look?" He said, "I have to get permission from the head man of U.S. Steel to do that." I said, "Well, you try to get permission, and I will be glad to go out there and walk through with you."

So about two or three weeks later, he got permission and asked me to go with him. I said, "Yes sir, I would be glad to go." He said, "Okay, next Tuesday morning I want you to meet me down here at this motel, and we'll go out there and look." When we met at the motel, he called the company, and they said he could come out and look. But they told him the mill is going to be shut down. You can walk through the mill and look at anything you want to, but no one will be working. I said, "Well, y'all can go out there, but I will not go." He said, "Why?" I said, "I would be defeating myself if I do that. Shutting the plant down and just coming out looking at a machine, you won't know what's going on." I said, "Now Mr. Government Man, they'll let schools, high schools, and college students come out there and walk through while we're working. If they can go through, how come y'all can't come through while they working?" I said, "I'll be defeating myself if I carry you out there and just show you a machine. Let's see the men working."

Graham agreed with me, and then he called and talked to them. They told him ain't no way they gonna let us come through there while they are working. "It's too dangerous." I said, "Well, I won't go. Y'all go, keep my name out of it." I say, "Because I'll be defeating myself. You go out there and look at a machine, you don't know what's going on." Graham agreed again, and he called back to talk with the headman again. He asked Graham to put me on the phone. The TCI boss said, "McKinstry, you want to be a hard damn boiled egg don't you?" I said, "Since you talking to me, and I'm talking to you, I'm a grown man, you a grown man. I can't sass you, and you can't sass me, but we can tell each other what we feel and what we know. I say if I bring them out there, and they look at the machine, they don't know which man works where." I said I wanted them to see the men work. I said, "And since you say I want to be a hard damn boiled egg, I say ain't no feather on me nowhere, but I ain't gon' come out there and kneel down." I say, "If them students can come through and look at it while they working, why they can't do the same?" And so the government man said, "Give me the phone." He said, "Look, I see what McKinstry speaking about, and if we can't come through while the men are at work, we'll federalize it, and bring troops through. And if you shut it down, you gonna pay for it. We are going to have to look at the men on the yard working. We don't know what it's like to look at just the machine there. I see what he means, we want to see the men at work." TCI then said, "We will give you thirty minutes."

When we finally went through, Graham couldn't believe it. He couldn't believe it. The black man had the nastiest, hardest jobs with the cheapest pay. Scrapping of the heavy surplus iron, sometimes three to six inches thick, was routine. The men wore aprons made with splits in 'em that came down to their knees. They would hold the iron, and a machine would come by and cut it. The scrapper would roll the metal to the machine for cutting, lay it out, measure it, and hold the little string. And all the cutter had to do is cut that line. And it has four men on them shears to hold it over there. They called them shearmen, shear helpers. And they would carry it over there and get it on the line. When they get it on the line, then they would pull the lever and cut it. They would push it on around then to the inspectors. They would carry it on down, and they would come down to inspect it. The inspectors were white. The shear helpers were black, the scrappers were black, and the man that pulled the lever to bring it down was black, the shearman, and then you had shear helpers. Okay, and then the inspector was white.

The crane operator was white. I was a hooker. There were two cranes, and each crane had a hooker per shift. I was the only helper who talked about operating the crane, and they told me that I was talking damn crazy: "You are going to get your ass run on away from here. You are not going to take these white folks' job talking about going up into no crane, you ain't gon' never do that. You can forget it." White foremen would tell me that I needed to hush my damn mouth before I get run off, because "you ain't going to get up in that crane." I talked about Title VII consent decree,[4] and they would ask, "What are you talking about?" "I am talking about government rules and regulations and equal rights." And the only thing the foreman looks at here is seniority, physical fitness, and ability. Seniority—if you start to work at seven o'clock that morning, and the head-man's son come to work at three o'clock in the evening, you got eight hours seniority, and you supposed to be offered the job first on account of your seniority. Then physically fit—if you want to go up there in the furnace room or wherever, around all that gas and oil, and you couldn't stand it, that will break you down. And ability—if they going to put you up there, and you want to write up or do something like that, well, if you had enough education to write, to use that book and write it, then regardless to the color of your skin, you gets a chance to do it. That's all I am asking for. "You crazy as hell, no nigger ain't gonna be nothing like that out here." I said, "Well, Title VII consent decree. That's all I am asking, which is a federal government order."

When the Movement [first] came, I attended some of the meetings. I met Martin Luther King, we were over at the City Auditorium. I had never met him or talked with him, and he walks up to me. I was standing out there looking.

And how he picked me out, I can't figure it out today. He walked up to me and picked me out of the whole crew. There were some preachers sitting out there. "Hey Doc," someone said. "Doc, what you want from around here? Do you know where you at? You in Birmingham. Where are your bodyguards? Man, I am sitting down. You got no bodyguards around you period, and you walking around here. You don't know, you are here in Birmingham, and these folks would be glad to pick on you here, man. You need some bodyguards."

He walked up to me and said, "Brother, I don't know you, I never seen you before, but in my heart something telling me to talk to you. Stand right here, don't move, don't go nowhere." I said, "Who is you?" He said, "I am Martin Luther King." I said, "Yeah." He said, "Y'all sitting here talking about bodyguards, walking around here with all that brass and uniforms. It's not like that. I am wrapped and tied and leading the bodyguards. You can't see them, you can't walk up and put your hand on them and talk to them like you do me. God has his angels around me. When time come for something to happen, regardless whether it's Birmingham or any other 'ham, it is no different, it will happen, time and place, but not until the time and place come for it to happen. And you can't walk up and put your hands on them, but I am wrapped and tied, and these are the bodyguards." He said, "Do y'all know these bodyguards here?" McNeil, Costen, different ones sitting there, and they shook their heads and said no. He said, "Well, y'all say you don't know him, that's okay. I am going to have to talk to him." He walked up and put his hands on both of my shoulders and looked up. He said, "I don't know what it is God has placed in your heart to do. You are going to have some hard days and nights, dark, bad-looking, but don't give it up, stick with it. Regardless what happens, how it happens, ain't nothing going to happen unless God allows it to happen. Just stick with it, because God put it in your heart to do it, and he let me see it. Stick with it, and when time come for whatever happens, it's going to happen. If you turn your back and walk away from that, you ain't fit to live for God, neither die. God placed it in your heart to do it. There will come some of everything, money will come, bribery, and some tough times. Keep your heart together and keep praying, stick with it."

He hadn't ever seen me before. And how I happened to be standing out there like that and them preachers sitting all around there, I just don't know. I just let it slip out my mind. Because here is a man, here, picked me out from all the folks there and walked up and talked to me like this, and I was in that mess at the time. How did he do it? God!

[After I brought suit against TCI] some of the men thought it was too dangerous for me to participate in the marches. They protected me from being attacked because of my stance with the lawsuit. They said, "If you get out there and them folks know you, they gonna throw eggs and everything at you." And when they came down through Fairfield they wouldn't let me march out there with them, they put me in a car.[5]

[Representatives of U.S. Steel attempted to bribe me.] I was ordered to meet them at the company's bank. When I got there I counted seven men. I was the only black man there. They were used to black men selling out, so they thought I would, once they offered me something to settle the suit.[6] U.S. Steel sent three men from Pittsburgh to talk me into settling out of court. They tried to scare me with rough talk. Sitting at the table in the company's bank, they talked to me and talked to me. These are some of the things they said. They said, "We going to buy this case from you; you got to do it, because U.S. Steel hadn't ever been carried into court by no one. And it won't be carried in there by you. You can just get ready to sign your name and drop the suit and walk out of here. You never knew nobody lived long enough to carry U.S. Steel into court, and you will not. So sign your name to that check there. Pick that damn check up. You don't have to leave it in this bank, you can put it anywhere you want to." He said, "You know how much that check is? That's a million damn dollars." The other one said, "What you shaking your head for?" He said, "Anything you see anywhere in the world, that man have had put together, it is yours if you want it. Just let us know where it is. We are going to start you off on three damn lots as big as this. Three and a half lots and whatever you see man put together, if you want it, damn it, it's yours. Tell us what address, and we will look at it and will have our architects draw it up, and then we will put it on that lot for you, three and a half lots. All you got to do is sign your damn name. And you see that check laying there. What is it?" I said, "You wrote it, tell me." He said, "That's a million damn dollars. Will you accept it?" The other one said, "I got to make him an offer." He said, "That's a million. I am writing out yours over here. Sign your name and pick up the check. That's three goddamn million dollars." And every time they talked to say something they were cussing, using cuss words. I said, "You says what?" He say, "Have you ever seen one goddamn million dollars and had a chance to touch it?" I said, "No, sir." He said, "Well, that's three damn million, and it's all yours. You can put it here in the bank, or you can carry it anywhere you want it, do anything you want with it. Cash it in, just put it in your savings, or whatever way you want to handle it. It's yours. Sign your damn name and drop that suit, and get your ass out of here." It was three of them, and with their lawyer it was four. I said, "But I am not going to sign that paper." "The hell you say, you going to sign it. Have you ever heard of anybody living long enough to carry U.S. Steel to court for unfair practice?" I said, "I never paid it no attention." "Well, damn it, you better. Ain't nobody ever going to be that lucky, you and nobody else." I said, "Whatever you say, but y'all threatening my life, and I don't like that. I don't like it." "You don't know anybody lived long enough to go to court with U.S. Steel, and you had better think damn quick. You and your damn wife better go ahead on and get your head together." I said, "Look here, don't goddamn my wife. My wife is just as sweet to me as any woman can be. I don't know how you and your wife live, but me and wife live together." I said, "If I say something about yours, you want me to say 'Mrs.' by your last name."

I sat down and talked to Hubbard. I told him, I said, "Buddy, if you want to come out and go and sign it, it's left up to you. I am not going to sign it. I am going to let it stay where it's at, because you know for yourself that they are discriminating out there. The black man is in the pool. The white boy hired in the line of promotion." I said "so-called white." If you get one of those tapes you will hear me on there saying "so-called white." "So now, for me and my part, I am not going to sign this paper and drop this suit." I said, "Whether I live or die, I am going to stick with it." He said, "Whatever you said, I am with you."

They said that the offer stood as long as I wanted it to stand and think about it. But they said, "Ain't nothing to do but to go ahead and sign the paper and take the money." I said, "I am not going to do that," and I didn't do it.

So we went to court, and I had to prove what I was saying, that they were discriminating on the job. I took Adams, Clemon, and Baker [his lawyers], the three government fellows, and the Justice Department, and fifteen students from different schools through the plant and let them walk. Clemon run up on a man, and he told the company, "Here is a job right here, y'all know this too much for one man. That's Mr. Hawkins working there, I know him well. I throwed paper for him out there in Pratt City when I was a little boy," Clemon said. Hawkins showed how scared black workers was when he spoke to Clemon. Most were afraid to lose their jobs. Mr. Hawkins said to Clemon, "Get out of the damn way before you get your damn head knocked off." The boss said to Mr. Hawkins, "Look a here, you don't know who you talking to. McKinstry got the federal government, Justice Department, got them all out here on this job looking at them working, and this man say he knew you when he was a boy. He remember throwing papers for you." Mr. Hawkins said, "I don't know a damn thing about him." Yeah, he kept doing his job. The boss said "look a here" and pulled that switch and stopped the whole damn thing. He said, "You don't know who you talking to out here. These men are out here checking the jobs."

He went ahead and pulled the switch and said "stop." They had shut the whole damn mill down, and we got to listen to these folks. He said, "Mr. Hawkins, I used to throw a paper for you. This job here is too much for one man. We are telling them to put three men on this job. I want three men assigned to the job, so at all times when one go to the bathroom, or wherever, there will be two here." I said, "They had me to work with him, and I worked with him two days." I told him, "Man, they can fire me, put me out the plant, but I didn't want to work with Mr. Hawkins because he cussing every time he says something. He just whooping and hollering at me, and he like to hit me twice." Hawkins said, "Yeah, 'cause you so damn sorry, you too damn slow." The boss said Mr. Hawkins was too bossy. They took him off the job and placed three other men on here.

My suit was this: If the black man couldn't be in the line of promotion, no man could. We are not looking at the color of a skin, we are looking at what the federal government said: Every man is equal, Title VII consent decree.

Opening up the whole line. From the day you hired eight hours, you got first choice to the job. If you could stand to work up here around this furnace room, around this gas, or whatever up here, if you could stand to work there, then you go all the way up to the top. There is no circle here, break that circle out of there. There is no come up here and then leap over here. You start here, you go straight up the line. Physical fit, seniority, and ability put you all the way up to the top. And just like you get up here, and they say your health won't allow you to work up there, around this gas and stuff, but you see that the only something would stop you, your health, won't allow you to work up in there. But if your health can go through, go on through it.

The case changed the whole thing. That mean they can go from the bottom to the top. Freddie Lee White, Omley Crockett, they were there at Ensley, but you see, anywhere the company had three men working anywhere they were under that suit.

It opened up the line of promotion, and I was able to move up, and my choice job was operating a crane, and they put me on a crane. And Kramer was up there, and he was proud in a way. He said, "You ain't taking a white man's job. I am willing to help you anyway. I can show you what to do." I said, "All I got to do is learn how to work these levers here." I said, "I can learn that in a day." He said, "I want you to, because you are a good damn hooker, and you know what to do down there. You know the safety, how to operate a crane, and how to get around, so what the hell difference. The rest of them can learn it, too."

The company tried to move two guys, James Payne and Eli Gambler, ahead of me in operating the crane. This was to get back at me for filing the suit. The judge wouldn't let them do it. You see, a black man could discriminate on another black man according to what the company wanted to do. They could take a black man and put [him] anywhere, and he was used to discriminate against you, just like a white man.

The suit was about ending black jobs and white jobs. You had white jobs and black jobs before the suit. But after the suit, then your age put you up there, your first eight hours, seniority had to be recognized. The man said, "You crazy if you think you gonna take these white folks' jobs and give to no damn niggers, you crazy." And after I sat down on it and when I pushed back that three-million-dollar check, that drove them crazy.

The union and the company was in the bed together, and I had to put a class-action suit against the union. They claimed they had three black men on the union staff, and come to find out they didn't have one. The federal government man, Brimm, said he had searched through and ain't found a black man there on the staff. He said, "I tell you what I want you to do, his name is Jimmy Lee Williams.[7] Have you heard of him?" I said, "Yeah." I said, "We are deacons in the same church." He said, "What?! I want you to put his name on there and ask for him to go on the stand." I said, "Well, you write the letter and type it out, and I will read it, and then I will sign it." He was going to put Jimmie Lee on there first. I said, "Okay, and who else do you think I should put on here?" I said, "Virgie Pearson,[8] what about him?" He said, "Yes, I'll put his name on there." And when he put it on there, I took the letter, and I put "please" by Jimmie Lee Williams's name on the staff [USWA], and that's what he did.

Yes. So I put that there, and in three weeks the letter come back approved. We went up to Miles College where we had our meeting. This guy went to cussing, talking about Jimmie Lee ain't never been to college. I said, "I am not going by that." I said, "I got advisors, and I am working with my advisors." That's why he put Jimmie Lee in there first.

He was the first one. You had men, they claimed they pushed up there, you see, this here Kramer boy was pushed up there, and they kicked their men from up there. But when it came down to the real business part, and the ones that were recognized and considered by the federal government, that was Jimmy Lee. After the man come here and searched the union all the way, and he didn't find a black man on the staff. Searching through the union, he said they were more mechanical. I don't know what it mean by "mechanical brain." But the better brain about the union and understanding and explaining was Jimmie Lee Williams.

They couldn't hand-pick by color. They had to go by the man with the best mechanical brain and understanding of the union. They put me on the wage and policy committee [of the USWA]. Over there at UAB Hospital, you know, they had you go down on them stairs and go down under there.[9] I was the one went to work and filed a case on them.

UAB hospital had a practice of keeping black patients in the basement. I walked through and didn't find a black above the basement. One lady complained about me being there asking questions. She said, "You get your ass out of here. You don't come in here asking no damn questions." I told her that I was on the wage and policy committee, and we could change this. I told them that I will ask that no one that worked for U.S. Steel come to that hospital. And they brought them black folk from down in that basement.

I wanted to work on the crane, and that's where I got, that's where I retired after about twenty-eight years. My older brother also worked in the mill. He told me himself, he said, "Luther, I am not mad at you or jealous at you or nothing like that, but you just don't know what a condition it got me in." He said, "When I would hear that whistle blow for the millwright [meaning something had broken down], I would come out sweating, just half-crazy, just knowing they done something to you. And they blowing for millwright and knew I would come on in and see. They just had me on my tiptoes. I don't never work a day out here satisfied on the account of you." I said, "James, you know what I told you some months ago. I meant that. If you in the bed with these so-called white folk, and you couldn't turn loose and be adjusted as a man, I told you, if you were coming down the railroad track and you were walking with them, and I was on the train, and if you were walking along there with them, I would run over your damn ass just like I would them." He had never heard me say "lie," "hell," "shit," or nothing like that. He said, "What did you say?" I said, "I am telling you, if you was in the bed with them and you wouldn't change out and wanted to stay in there with them, and I am coming down the track and you was on the track with them, I would run over your damn ass just like I would them." He widened his eyes.

After I done that they put [my brother] up as a millwright, not a helper, and put him over some. They had a guy named Jim Davis, lived down in Bessemer, told them that he didn't want to work with no damn black man over him as a boss man. Davis was a black man. The first day they got into it. He told me, "Luther, this is a rough job, but I am going to stick with it." Jim wouldn't do what he told him. They got into it. He got off work at three o'clock that evening, and coming on home, he stopped down there at a lady's house, down there where her son married our sister. He had a heart attack on her steps. They carried him to the hospital, and he never did go back into that plant. He lived about four weeks after that.

He told me this. He said, "I am not against what you are doing, I am proud of it, but I just ain't able to take it or stand up to it. But if God put it in your heart to do it, regardless of what it cost, stick with it. I am not against you as much as you think, but I am just scared to death for you. Anything might happen to you around these here damn white folks out here the way they are acting. And by me working with them, I heard a lot of things that you didn't hear. And I am just scared to death. When they blow that whistle out there, the four longs like that for millwright, I come out there looking." Four long for the millwrights, and three shorts for electricians. If something broke down, you need a millwright to fix it.

You blow that for them, and he know when that whistle blew that something had happened to someone or some of the machines and that we got to go down there and check it out and see what it is. They were coming along there. They had all the cables and the hammers and the long bars, and they be loaded down. The white folks walking in the clear. You was a helper. Get them cables, them bars, and hammer and come on down here. We would come down there, I would start taking them chains aloose and hooking up them cables. I would cut the magnets loose from the crane and get over there to them.

Edited by Horace Huntley. BCRI Oral History Project, not indexed (Feb. 16, 2000).

Notes

1. The ad hoc committee of black steel workers assisted by the NAACP brought suit against TCI in 1966, but the Justice Department did not bring the case to court until 1970, when the union was also charged. See Judith Stein, *Running Steel, Running America: Race, Economic Policy, and the Decline of Liberalism* (Chapel Hill: University of North Carolina Press, 1998), 104–7, 153–55.

2. This was Richard A. Graham of the U.S. Equal Employment Opportunity Commission.

3. Hubbard lived in Smithfield and was a deacon at Sixth Avenue Baptist church.

4. Title VII prohibited discrimination in employment, promotion, and job security. William H. Harris called it "the most important part of the Civil Rights Act of 1964." Harris, *The Harder We Run: Black Workers since the Civil War* (New York: Oxford University of Press, 1982), 157–58. The consent decree for the steel industry was issued by Judge Samuel C. Pointer in 1972 in his judgment on cases that had been brought by McKinstry and others against TCI and the USWA. It was signed by the company, union, and government in 1973 and joined by other steel companies in 1974. Stein, *Running Steel,* 103–7, 153–68; Bruce Nelson, *Divided We Stand: American Workers and the Struggle for Black Equality* (Princeton, N.J.: Princeton University Press, 2001), 279–81.

5. The Fairfield march was in 1966, after McKinstry and others had brought charges against TCI with the support of the NAACP. Stein, *Running Steel,* 106–7.

6. Other black members of the ad hoc committee that brought the suit were offered supervisory positions by U.S. Steel. Ibid., 107.

7. Vice president of the coke plant local of the USWA.

8. Pearson started work at ACIPCO in 1945 and Fairfield Steel in 1948. In 1967 he became a staff member of the USWA. See Stein, *Running Steel,* 54–55, 107.

9. Black patients were confined to the basement of hospitals. These patients were evidently hospitalized under the provisions of the contract between the USWA and U.S. Steel.

Afterword

Odessa Woolfolk

To understand the meaning of the Birmingham Civil Rights Institute (BCRI) and the movement it chronicles, we must first recall the early history of the city. The way of life that the movement challenged was set in place by Birmingham's incorporators and early settlers.

Nestled in a valley at the foothills of the Appalachian Mountains, Birmingham, Alabama, owes its origin to abundant deposits of iron ore, coal, and limestone, the essential ingredients for making iron and steel. Ambitious industrialists and land speculators began developing natural resources immediately after the Civil War, or, as many southerners called it, the "War between the States." A labor force of native white and black Alabamians, white immigrants from Europe, and prison convicts mined the minerals for capital-intensive corporations.

Birmingham was described by social workers of the era as the city hardest hit by the Great Depression, and the black population suffered the most. The social disorder of the 1930s resulted in increased unionization, and with the shift to wartime production the city began to bounce back, as civic leaders diversified the economic base. Yet despite the returning prosperity, blacks, who comprised 40 percent of the total population, received unequal opportunity and substandard municipal services. After fighting for freedom abroad, returning black veterans grew incensed at the dismal living standards in their community.

The owners and managers of Birmingham's businesses were indifferent to entreaties from the black community, and black demands for municipal services were met with hostility and repression. The civic and economic elite

Odessa Woolfolk is the founding president of the Birmingham Civil Rights Institute.

tended to reside outside Birmingham's city limit. Postwar prosperity allowed some workers to move to newly developed suburbs, as well.

After the 1954 Supreme Court ruling in *Brown v. Board of Education,* many white families with school-aged children left the city. Racial hostility and discrimination in Birmingham accelerated following the *Brown* decision. The local governing City Commission and its head of public safety, T. Eugene "Bull" Connor, an unrelenting racist, fomented rather than contained violence. During Connor's reign, Birmingham earned the designation "Bombingham," which referred to the scores of unsolved bombings of houses in predominantly black neighborhoods.

Despite the determined and harsh defense of white supremacy by city officials and white vigilantism, new leadership emerged in the black community. In 1956, when the State of Alabama banned the NAACP from operating in the state, Rev. Fred L. Shuttlesworth organized the ACMHR. The new organization pledged to "'press forward for freedom and Democracy and the removal from our society of any forms of Second Class Citizenship.'"[1]

On April 12, 1960, Harrison Salisbury wrote about Birmingham in the *New York Times.* He observed, "Every channel of communication, every medium of mutual interest, every reasoned approach, every inch of middle ground has been fragmented by the emotional dynamite of racism, reinforced by the whip, the razor, the gun, the bomb, the torch, the club, the knife, the mob, the police, and many branches of the state's apparatus."[2]

In 1962, Reverend Shuttlesworth invited Dr. Martin Luther King Jr., head of the SCLC, to join forces with the ACMHR in their challenge to the city's segregation ordinances. The citizens' revolt, highlighted by the 1963 children's marches, subsequently struck the final blow to de jure racial segregation in Alabama and prompted the federal government to pass legislation prohibiting discrimination. The historian John Hope Franklin described the resulting 1964 Civil Rights Act as "the most far-reaching and comprehensive law in support of racial equality ever enacted by Congress."[3]

Race has always been a fault line in the social environment of Birmingham. It is a weak spot easily aggravated by outsiders' criticism and by the tension between "race rebels" and civic boosters. The Birmingham that provoked nonviolent resistance was a place whose citizens were intimidated by a lawless element. Moderate whites, downtown retailers, and many blacks were intimidated into silent acquiescence to a system that they knew was morally corrupt.

How to portray this past in a healing and nondivisive manner, while portraying the harsh truth, was a challenge to the founders of the BCRI. The idea that the city should build a museum-like facility to memorialize its civil rights history originated with David Vann in 1978 during his term as mayor. A political liberal, Vann was a law clerk to Supreme Court Justice Hugo Black when the landmark *Brown v. Board of Education* decision was handed down.

Returning to Birmingham to practice law, he became a leader in the effort to defeat Birmingham's racist city officials by changing the form of government from a commission to a mayoral council. Years later, on a trip to Israel, he was impressed by the museums of the Holocaust and Jewish Diaspora. His visit convinced him that respectful remembrance of horror could be therapeutic for a community. Perhaps Birmingham could heal itself through recalling its civil rights struggle and celebrating the changes it produced.

His successor, Richard Arrington Jr., Birmingham's first black mayor, committed his energy and public funds to pursuing Vann's vision. He appointed a Civil Rights Museum Study Committee to begin formulating ideas. The group recommended that Birmingham create an official organization with resources to plan a city-sponsored museum. The city acquired property in the area where the 1963 marches and demonstrations originated.

In 1986, more than seven years after Vann's proposition, Arrington appointed a task force with explicit instructions to craft a mission statement and thematic plan and to give guidance to an architectural firm and planning consultants hired by the city. The task force represented a broad range of citizens, including educators, civil rights activists, city government officials, business and community leaders, and local historians. Task-force members envisioned the facility as an institute rather than a museum to imply an action-oriented establishment.

Documenting the past meant hearing the voices of a range of participants in the movement, from the unsung foot soldiers to celebrated leaders. The task force advocated "history from the bottom up," a phrase that the researcher Stephan Therstrom applied to the study of everyday people in social movements.[4] Clearly, the overthrow of racial segregation in Birmingham could not have succeeded in the 1960s without the brilliant leadership of Reverend Shuttlesworth and Dr. King; nor could it have happened without the fervent following of countless ordinary people. Their eyewitness accounts are essential to a valid re-creation and understanding of the past. Their stories and memorabilia document the "stride toward freedom."

Opposition to so prominent a depiction of Birmingham's past emerged well before the groundbreaking for the facility. Birmingham's elected officials had tried to forget the past. Many civic leaders recoiled at the thought of summoning up old images of fire hoses and police dogs. "Why open up old wounds?" some asked. "Such an institute will only alienate whites of goodwill," said others. "Money could be better spent improving neighborhoods," was another common objection. A small number of foot soldiers fretted that their stories would be left out in deference to the better-known leaders.

Further evidence of opposition to the proposed institute was the trouncing of two separate bond issues proposed by the mayor in 1986 and 1988 to finance the project. The bond issues presented to the voters included revenue for schools, recreation, and public works, but funding for a civil rights museum received more "no" votes than any other item. Eventually, the city obtained funds by issuing general revenue bonds that did not require a referendum. In time, however, civic leaders and foot soldiers of the movement financially supported the institute.

"The Healing of a City by Design" is the title of a 1992 cover story in the *Birmingham Business Journal* about the newly revitalized Civil Rights District, regarded as "sacred ground" by supporters of the civil rights movement. The district is home to the historic black business district, including the old Carver Movie Theater; the Kelly Ingram Park, which was used as a gathering place for protest marches; the Sixteenth Street Baptist church, where four little girls died in a hatred-inspired bombing; and the Birmingham Civil Rights Institute.

As summarized in its mission statement, the institute sets out to "focus on what happened in the past, to portray it realistically and interestingly, and to understand it in relationship to the present and future developments of human relations in Birmingham, the United States, and perhaps the world."

From its inception, the institute founders recognized the universality of human conflict. After all, Dr. King had been deeply influenced by the religious and ethnic conflicts in India, parts of Africa, and Eastern Europe earlier in the twentieth century. In time, these and other nations drew positive lessons from the American civil rights movement. Given this broad historical context, the institute perceives human rights as a universal striving. The events that occurred in Birmingham, Alabama, in the mid-twentieth century offer a relevant case study of conflict resolution with potentially global application.

As a learning center, the institute offers richly detailed exhibits, photographs, media clips, timelines, and historical artifacts, with particular emphasis on the American civil rights revolution. As a living institution, it prepares curriculum resources for schools and maintains an archive of primary documents, books, and artifacts. Through a state-of-the-art multimedia resource gallery, it offers access to digitized oral histories and scores of databases. The institute hosts major conferences and workshops that examine civil and human rights violations and policies at the local, national, and international levels.

The BCRI signifies that Birmingham does not hide from its past. It acknowledges that where once the city housed two separate communities, black and white, unknown to one another except through the painful thread of segregation, Birmingham now embraces its past, neither forgetting nor dwelling on it but using it to foster understanding.

The institute recognizes the redemptive importance of memory. It is both a time capsule and a think tank focused on seeking equitable solutions to contemporary problems. In some ways the BCRI functions as a town square where the community gathers to discuss common concerns. It is a place where yesterday's struggles inspire a brighter tomorrow. It is a meeting ground for the makers of everyday history and for those who write about the present.

Notes

1. Alabama Christian Movement for Human Rights, "Declaration of Principles," quoted in Andrew M. Manis, *A Fire You Can't Put Out: The Civil Rights Life of Birmingham's Reverend Fred Shuttlesworth* (Tuscaloosa: University of Alabama Press, 1999), 96.

2. *New York Times,* April 12, 1960, 1.

3. John Hope Franklin, *From Slavery to Freedom: A History of African Americans,* 3d ed. (New York: Alfred A. Knopf), 635.

4. *Harvard Encyclopedia of American Ethnic Groups,* ed. Stephen Therstrom (Cambridge, Mass.: Belknap Press, 1980).

Index

Horace Huntley is the director of the Birmingham Civil Rights Institute Oral History Project and is an assistant professor at the University of Alabama at Birmingham. He is a contributor to the *Encyclopedia of African American Culture and History.*

David Montgomery is a professor emeritus of history at Yale and a series editor for the Working Class in American History series. His books include *Citizen Worker: The Experience of Workers in the United States with Democracy and the Free Market during the Nineteenth Century* and *The Fall of the House of Labor: The Workplace, the State, and American Labor Activism, 1865–1925.*

The Working Class in American History

Worker City, Company Town: Iron and Cotton-Worker Protest in Troy and Cohoes, New York, 1855–84—*Daniel J. Walkowitz*

Life, Work, and Rebellion in the Coal Fields: The Southern West Virginia Miners, 1880–1922—*David Alan Corbin*

Women and American Socialism, 1870–1920—*Mari Jo Buhle*

Lives of Their Own: Blacks, Italians, and Poles in Pittsburgh, 1900–1960 —*John Bodnar, Roger Simon, and Michael P. Weber*

Working-Class America: Essays on Labor, Community, and American Society —*Edited by Michael H. Frisch and Daniel J. Walkowitz*

Eugene V. Debs: Citizen and Socialist—*Nick Salvatore*

American Labor and Immigration History, 1877–1920s: Recent European Research—*Edited by Dirk Hoerder*

Workingmen's Democracy: The Knights of Labor and American Politics —*Leon Fink*

The Electrical Workers: A History of Labor at General Electric and Westinghouse, 1923–60—*Ronald W. Schatz*

The Mechanics of Baltimore: Workers and Politics in the Age of Revolution, 1763–1812—*Charles G. Steffen*

The Practice of Solidarity: American Hat Finishers in the Nineteenth Century —*David Bensman*

The Labor History Reader—*Edited by Daniel J. Leab*

Solidarity and Fragmentation: Working People and Class Consciousness in Detroit, 1875–1900—*Richard Oestreicher*

Counter Cultures: Saleswomen, Managers, and Customers in American Department Stores, 1890–1940—*Susan Porter Benson*

The New England Working Class and the New Labor History—*Edited by Herbert G. Gutman and Donald H. Bell*

Labor Leaders in America—*Edited by Melvyn Dubofsky and Warren Van Tine*

Barons of Labor: The San Francisco Building Trades and Union Power in the Progressive Era—*Michael Kazin*

Gender at Work: The Dynamics of Job Segregation by Sex during World War II —*Ruth Milkman*

Once a Cigar Maker: Men, Women, and Work Culture in American Cigar Factories, 1900–1919—*Patricia A. Cooper*

A Generation of Boomers: The Pattern of Railroad Labor Conflict in Nineteenth-Century America—*Shelton Stromquist*

Work and Community in the Jungle: Chicago's Packinghouse Workers, 1894–1922—*James R. Barrett*

Workers, Managers, and Welfare Capitalism: The Shoeworkers and Tanners of Endicott Johnson, 1890–1950—*Gerald Zahavi*

Men, Women, and Work: Class, Gender, and Protest in the New England Shoe Industry, 1780–1910—*Mary Blewett*

Workers on the Waterfront: Seamen, Longshoremen, and Unionism in the 1930s—*Bruce Nelson*

German Workers in Chicago: A Documentary History of Working-Class Culture from 1850 to World War I—*Edited by Hartmut Keil and John B. Jentz*

On the Line: Essays in the History of Auto Work—*Edited by Nelson Lichtenstein and Stephen Meyer III*

Upheaval in the Quiet Zone: A History of Hospital Workers' Union, Local 1199 —*Leon Fink and Brian Greenberg*

Labor's Flaming Youth: Telephone Operators and Worker Militancy, 1878–1923—*Stephen H. Norwood*

Another Civil War: Labor, Capital, and the State in the Anthracite Regions of Pennsylvania, 1840–68—*Grace Palladino*

Coal, Class, and Color: Blacks in Southern West Virginia, 1915–32 —*Joe William Trotter, Jr.*

For Democracy, Workers, and God: Labor Song-Poems and Labor Protest, 1865–95—*Clark D. Halker*

Dishing It Out: Waitresses and Their Unions in the Twentieth Century —*Dorothy Sue Cobble*

The Spirit of 1848: German Immigrants, Labor Conflict, and the Coming of the Civil War—*Bruce Levine*

Working Women of Collar City: Gender, Class, and Community in Troy, New York, 1864–86—*Carole Turbin*

Southern Labor and Black Civil Rights: Organizing Memphis Workers —*Michael K. Honey*

Radicals of the Worst Sort: Laboring Women in Lawrence, Massachusetts, 1860–1912—*Ardis Cameron*

Producers, Proletarians, and Politicians: Workers and Party Politics in Evansville and New Albany, Indiana, 1850–87—*Lawrence M. Lipin*

The New Left and Labor in the 1960s—*Peter B. Levy*

The Making of Western Labor Radicalism: Denver's Organized Workers, 1878–1905—*David Brundage*

In Search of the Working Class: Essays in American Labor History and Political Culture—*Leon Fink*

Lawyers against Labor: From Individual Rights to Corporate Liberalism —*Daniel R. Ernst*

"We Are All Leaders": The Alternative Unionism of the Early 1930s—*Edited by Staughton Lynd*

The Female Economy: The Millinery and Dressmaking Trades, 1860–1930 —*Wendy Gamber*

"Negro and White, Unite and Fight!": A Social History of Industrial Unionism in Meatpacking, 1930–90—*Roger Horowitz*

Power at Odds: The 1922 National Railroad Shopmen's Strike—*Colin J. Davis*

The Common Ground of Womanhood: Class, Gender, and Working Girls' Clubs, 1884–1928—*Priscilla Murolo*

Marching Together: Women of the Brotherhood of Sleeping Car Porters —*Melinda Chateauvert*

Down on the Killing Floor: Black and White Workers in Chicago's Packinghouses, 1904–54—*Rick Halpern*

Labor and Urban Politics: Class Conflict and the Origins of Modern Liberalism in Chicago, 1864–97—*Richard Schneirov*

All That Glitters: Class, Conflict, and Community in Cripple Creek —*Elizabeth Jameson*

Waterfront Workers: New Perspectives on Race and Class—*Edited by Calvin Winslow*

Labor Histories: Class, Politics, and the Working-Class Experience—*Edited by Eric Arnesen, Julie Greene, and Bruce Laurie*

The Pullman Strike and the Crisis of the 1890s: Essays on Labor and Politics —*Edited by Richard Schneirov, Shelton Stromquist, and Nick Salvatore*

AlabamaNorth: African-American Migrants, Community, and Working-Class Activism in Cleveland, 1914–45—*Kimberley L. Phillips*

Imagining Internationalism in American and British Labor, 1939–49 —*Victor Silverman*

William Z. Foster and the Tragedy of American Radicalism—*James R. Barrett*

Colliers across the Sea: A Comparative Study of Class Formation in Scotland and the American Midwest, 1830–1924—*John H. M. Laslett*

"Rights, Not Roses": Unions and the Rise of Working-Class Feminism, 1945–80—*Dennis A. Deslippe*

Testing the New Deal: The General Textile Strike of 1934 in the American South —*Janet Irons*

Hard Work: The Making of Labor History—*Melvyn Dubofsky*

Southern Workers and the Search for Community: Spartanburg County, South Carolina—*G. C. Waldrep III*

We Shall Be All: A History of the Industrial Workers of the World (abridged edition)—*Melvyn Dubofsky, ed. Joseph A. McCartin*

Race, Class, and Power in the Alabama Coalfields, 1908–21—*Brian Kelly*

Duquesne and the Rise of Steel Unionism—*James D. Rose*

Anaconda: Labor, Community, and Culture in Montana's Smelter City —*Laurie Mercier*

Bridgeport's Socialist New Deal, 1915–36—*Cecelia Bucki*

Indispensable Outcasts: Hobo Workers and Community in the American Midwest, 1880–1930—*Frank Tobias Higbie*
After the Strike: A Century of Labor Struggle at Pullman—*Susan Eleanor Hirsch*
Corruption and Reform in the Teamsters Union—*David Witwer*
Waterfront Revolts: New York and London Dockworkers, 1946–61 —*Colin J. Davis*
Black Workers' Struggle for Equality in Birmingham: The Birmingham Civil Rights Institute's Oral History Project—*Horace Huntley and David Montgomery*

The University of Illinois Press
is a founding member of the
Association of American University Presses.

University of Illinois Press
1325 South Oak Street
Champaign, IL 61820-6903
www.press.uillinois.edu